FOOTBALL CULTURES AN...

D0525636

...t John College

...ntre

Football Cultures and Identities

Edited by

Gary Armstrong
Lecturer in Criminology and Sociology
University of Reading
England

and

Richard Giulianotti
Lecturer in Sociology
University of Aberdeen
Scotland

palgrave

First published 1999 by
MACMILLAN PRESS LTD
Houndmills, Basingstoke, Hampshire RG21 6XS
and London
Companies and representatives
throughout the world

ISBN 0–333–73009–7 hardcover
ISBN 0–333–73010–0 paperback

A catalogue record for this book is available
from the British Library.

This book is printed on paper suitable for recycling and
made from fully managed and sustained forest sources.

Transferred to digital printing 2001

Printed & bound by Antony Rowe Ltd, Eastbourne

Contents

Acknowledgements

As captains of this collection, we take full responsibility for team selection. We thank every one of our squad members for playing a full part in this enthralling encounter. Each player carried out their allotted task, showing initiative, discipline and, as we hope you'll agree, considerable flair on occasion. All players were encouraged to show a combative approach, occasionally resulting in the odd over-the-ball tackle on deserving opponents. No cautions were administered, nor tears shed (to the best of our knowledge). There was no need for flying crockery during intervals when the game plan was not being adhered to. In emulation of the footballing genius Ruud Gullitt, we similarly acknowledge that professionals in this game cannot perform properly if covered in tea. We encourage all our contributors to experiment with new styles of play and to continue scouting for new talent. The captains have yet to see the benefits of vitamin tablets, faith healing and other New Age foibles for improving performance. Hence, we invite all our team-mates to meet at some point for a traditional British post-match tête-à-tête that will include beers and chicken kebabs.

In putting together our squad, we have received invaluable assistance from several talent scouts at home and abroad. We would like to thank Eduardo Archetti, Adam Brown, Ogden Caradovic, Rocco De Biasi and Alessandro Dal Lago, Gerry Finn, Malcolm Hamilton, Rosemary Harris, Kate Longley, Tony Mason, Stephen Parrott and Norman Stockman. Karen Kinnaird and Sallie Scott provided invaluable back-up in tidying up any technical weaknesses in attack and defence. Our thanks are due to Annabelle Buckley for commissioning the collection and to Keith Povey for an excellent job in editing and proof-reading. Finally, as always, many thanks to our two recent but hopefully permanent signings, Hani Darlington and Donna McGilvray.

June 1998   GARY ARMSTRONG
                                                                          RICHARD GIULIANOTTI

Notes on the Contributors

Pablo Alabarces is Lecturer and Researcher in the Faculty of Social Sciences at the University of Buenos Aires. His book *A Ballgame Question: Football, Sport, Society, Culture* was co-written with Maria Graciela Rodríguez and published in 1996. His other research interests include media studies and social theory. He is currently working towards the completion of his doctorate and co-ordinating a sports research network throughout Latin America.

Torbjörn Andersson studied at universities in Stockholm and Lund before working as a researcher in the Department of History at the University of Lund. His research interests are in the social and cultural history of Swedish football. Together with Aage Radmann he wrote the book *From Gentleman to Hooligan?* (1998).

David L. Andrews is Assistant Professor in the Department of Human Movement Sciences and Education at the University of Memphis. He teaches and researches on a variety of topics related to the critical analysis of sport as an aspect of contemporary popular culture.

Gary Armstrong is Lecturer in Criminology and Sociology at the University of Reading, England. He completed his doctorate at the Department of Anthropology, University College, London in 1996. In the field of football, he has written *Football Hooligans: Knowing the Score* (1998), *Blade Runners: Lives in Football* (1998) and has co-edited (with Richard Giulianotti) *Entering the Field: New Perspectives on World Football* (1997).

Alan Bairner is Lecturer in Politics at the University at Ulster at Jordanstown. He has written widely on sport and society in Scotland, Sweden and Ireland. He is a co-author of *Sport, Sectarianism and Society in a Divided Ireland* (1993) and joint editor of *Sport in Divided Societies* (1997).

Iris Bar, a graduate in anthropology, at the University of Haifa, is conducting postgraduate research into football in Israel.

Yoram S. Carmeli undertook his doctorate at the Department of Anthropology, University College, London, then returned to Israel where he took up a position as Lecturer in the Department of Sociology and Anthropology at the University of Haifa. His main research area has been in the anthropology of circuses.

Freek Colombijn is an anthropologist who obtained his PhD from Leiden University with a thesis on the urban development of Padang in the twentieth century. He is presently working on an environmental history of Central Sumatra. He started his football career in club teams at the age of nine as right-back at the Haarlemsche Football Club, and ended it the age of 36 as left-winger at Lugdunum.

Hugh Dauncey is Lecturer and Researcher in French Studies at the University of Newcastle and has published on a variety of aspects of contemporary French societies and culture, including high technology, television and news media.

Richard Giulianotti is Lecturer in Sociology at the University of Aberdeen, Scotland. He was employed as an ESRC Researcher from 1990 to 1995 on projects investigating football fan culture in the UK and Ireland. He has co-edited the books *Football, Violence and Social Identity* (1994) *Game without Frontiers* (1994) and *Entering the Field* (1997). His book on the general social and historical aspects of football will be published in 1999.

Matti Goksøyr is Associate Professor of Sports History at the Norwegian University of Sport and Physical Education, Oslo. Well known for his work on sport and state politics and national identity, he has published extensively both in Norway and in international journals.

Geoff Hare is Senior Lecturer in French Studies at the University of Newcastle. He publishes mainly on the subject of French television and broadcasting. Together with Hugh Dauncey, he is working on a research project centred on the 1998 World Cup in France.

Hans Hognestad is an anthropologist who conducted ethnographic fieldwork among the supporters of Heart of Midlothian FC between 1992 and 1995. He spent three years working at UNESCO in Oslo as a cultural attaché. He is currently working as a researcher at the Norwegian University for Physical Education and Sport in Oslo.

Can Kozanoglu is a sociologist, author and a former journalist. He is the author of *Football in Turkey: We Will Win This Game!* (1990), *The Age of the Varnished Image: Media Stars of Turkey and Social Change in the 1980s* (1992), *The Pop Age Fever* (1995) and *Internet, Full Moon, Community* (1997).

Drazen Lalic studied at the University of Split, where he completed his doctoral study of Croatian football fans, later published in the book *Torcida: an Inside View* (1993). He has also published books entitled *Graffiti and Subculture* (1991) and *Heroin Addicts: Death Histories* (1997). Dr Lalic is a Director of the Youth Information Centre, and a councillor on Split City Council.

José Sergio Leite Lopes is Professor of Anthropology at the Museu Nacional, Universidade Federal do Rio de Janeiro, Brazil, from where he obtained his doctorate in 1986. He has published and researched extensively in the anthropology of industrial societies, working class culture, and sports culture. Recently he has been engaged in research into the political anthropology of pollution in Brazil.

Hiroko Maeda is Assistant Professor in the Department for Interdisciplinary Studies of Lifelong Sport and Physical Exercise, at the National Institute of Fitness and Sports in Kanoya, Japan. She received her master's degree from Kobe University in 1989. Her major areas of study are in the sociology of sport, gender issues and the socialisation of top athletes.

Udo Merkel is Senior Lecturer in the Chelsea School at the University of Brighton, England. His academic and research interests are the sociology of sport and leisure, comparative (European) studies and football. He has published various articles in English and German and co-edited (with W. Tokarski) *Racism and Xenophobia in European Football* (1996).

Jon P. Mitchell is Lecturer in Social Anthropology at the School of Cultural and Community Studies, Sussex University. His doctoral research, conducted in Malta, is oriented around three main themes: politics and the dynamics of the public sphere; history and memory; ritual and religious experience, which are developed in a forthcoming monograph, *Politics in Everything: Ritual, Memory and the Public Sphere in Malta*. Current research interests are on such diverse topics as evil eye and devil beliefs, tour-guides and tourism, and football.

John Nauright is Senior Lecturer in the Department of Human Movement Studies at the University of Queensland, Brisbane, Australia. He has studied at universities in Canada, the US and England, specialising in southern African history. He has written numerous journal articles; he co-edited (with Tim Chandler) the book *Making Men: Rugby and Masculine Identity* (1996) and has published the book *Sport, Cultures and Identities in South Africa* (1998).

Haruo Nogawa is Professor in the Department of Sport Management at Juntendo University, Japan. He was formerly employed at the National Institute of Fitness and Sports in Kanoya. He received his doctorate from Oregon State University in 1983. His major research interests are in the sociology of sport and leisure, tourism, ethnic relations and sport for development.

Aage Radmann studied at universities in Trondheim, Norway, and Lund, Sweden. He is a sociologist, working in the Sport Research Centre at the University of Lund. His research interests are in youth and sport culture in Scandinavia, and he has written articles on Scandinavian youth and football culture. Together with Torbjörn Andersson he is author of *From Gentleman to Hooligan?* (1998).

David Russell is Reader in the History of Popular Culture at the University of Central Lancashire. He is currently Head of the Institute of Football Studies, a joint venture between the university and the Football Museum, Preston, and is the author of *Football and the English* (1997) and numerous essays and articles on the histories of sport and music.

Ramon Sarro was born in Barcelona. He recently completed his PhD in social anthropology at University College London on the subject of Baga identity in the Republic of Guinea, West Africa.

Peter Shirlow is Lecturer in Geography at Queen's University, Belfast, and a director of the Socio-Spatial Analysis Research Unit. He has written on para-militarism, political identity and deprivation. He is the editor of the book *Development Ireland* (1995) and *Who are the People? Unionism, Loyalism and Protestantism in Northern Ireland* (1997).

Srdjan Vrcan was born in 1922, and has retired from his post as Professor of Sociology at the University of Split. His major books are *Social Inequality and Modern Society* (1978) and *Sport and Violence Here and Now* (1991) (both in the Croatian language). He has also published numerous articles in Croatian and Italian journals.

Detlev Zwick has received a bachelor's degree in economics from the University of Hagen, Germany, and a master's degree in sports management from the University of Sport in Cologne, Germany. After studying aspects of sports and leisure commerce at the University of Memphis, he is currently a doctoral candidate in marketing at the University of Rhode Island.

Introduction

Football in the Making
Gary Armstrong and Richard Giulianotti

The game of football has a rich global history. Most cultures and civilisations seem to have played some kind of proto-football, involving the kicking of a ball between various groups of players. The Chinese game of *CuJu* was played during neolithic times. The indigenous peoples of North and Central America played ball games as part of their fertility rites. In medieval Europe, French peasants practised the violent ball game of *soule*; the Florentine Renaissance men performed *calcio*; the Scots and English played various 'folk football' games in towns and villages.

The modern game of association football originated in the English public schools during the middle of the nineteenth century. Various codes of football were created by the schoolmasters, to restore order in these institutions and to develop the young players into 'muscular Christian gentleman'. The Harrovian and Cambridge code of football established its rules in 1863, banning hacking and the handling of the ball. The latter practice was retained by the Rugby Football Union which established its code in 1871.

Socially and culturally, the games of rugby football and association football were soon set on different paths. Rugby remained staunchly amateur and middle class, quickly establishing itself in the civil societies of Britain's colonies and dominions (such as South Africa, Australia and New Zealand). Northern English clubs split from the southern-based authorities and formed their own football code, the '13-man' game of 'rugby league', in 1894.

The Football Associations of England and other home nations of Scotland, Ireland and Wales all favoured the retention of amateur rules for association football. Yet, by the late nineteenth century, the game had established itself as the dominant sport among the urban working classes. Clubs had been formed that reflected a strong sense of local and civic pride; two-team rivalries were profitably situated in the major conurbations; the office-holders at clubs converted their 'leisure associations' into genuine businesses, complete with share-holdings and boards of directors. Inevitably, with the inception of the Football Leagues in Scotland, England and Wales, association football turned professional. The custodians of amateurism, like Corinthians in England and Queens Park in Scotland, became anachronistic symbols of a bygone era.

By the outbreak of the First World War, football had secured its position as the global game for the twentieth century. British sailors, educationalists, traders and workmen brought it to all corners of the world. Primarily, football was a sport that seemed to lack any hegemonic strings. Unlike cricket or rugby union, its introduction to a distant culture did not obviously secure the consent of natives to British political or economic rule. The game was transmitted through trade and educational routes rather than a directly imperial relationship between the 'Mother Country' and its dominions. In Europe, the recreation of British sailors and workers brought football to Iberia and Scandinavia; British teachers taught schoolboys from central Europe how to play the game. In Latin America, sailors were instrumental in spreading football in Chile. The British schools in Argentina, Uruguay and Brazil were at the vanguard of the new sport's popularisation, along with the railway workers then building up the sub-continent's infrastructure. In Africa, football's colonial associations were far stronger, although the game soon became a vehicle for the cultural pride and ethnic solidarity of the indigenous peoples. Although football failed to become the 'national' game in North America and Australasia, it is now well established as a major participatory and spectator sport among many of the large ethnic communities in those nations.

Football's early development might therefore be regarded as a study in one of the earliest forms of cultural globalisation. Most nations highlighted their cultural and economic 'relative autonomy' when developing their specific forms of football association. In Latin America, distinctive national playing styles began to emerge, although the pro-British elites that controlled the national game often preferred to use English as the official medium and opposed the introduction of professionalism until the 1930s. In Europe, distinctive playing styles and technical skills also came to prominence, while respect and admiration for the British game and its historical legacies remained. Administratively, the world game has been overseen since 1904 by the Fédération Internationale de Football Association (FIFA), although full British recognition of its powers (and of Britain's declining international status) did not begin until after the Second World War. The UK's home nations continue to exert a major influence on the world game, most notably through the International Board that presides over changes to the rules of football. Yet from 1974 to 1998, the hegemonic bloc that dominated FIFA was manufactured in the New World rather than the Old, as the president João Havelange garnered his support in the new football nations of Africa and Asia.

At Havelange's final World Cup in 1998, football's global appeal was reflected in the fact that 173 nations had entered the tournament; 120 million players were registered with FIFA, either as amateurs or professionals; eight of the world's top ten 'most watched' sports events had been televised football matches. Indeed Havelange was ready to pass on contracts worth $4 billion to his successor. As football becomes an increasingly prized cultural pastime and an increasingly lucrative business, the politics of access to the global game take centre stage. The fiasco by which tickets were distributed for matches at France '98 comes to be seen as a symptom of a deeper malaise within the 'football industry'.

ABOUT THIS BOOK

As football enters the new millennium, there is heightened public and academic interest in the game's global dimensions. Numerous UK television programmes, on mainstream terrestrial and subscription satellite stations, have examined *football mundiale*. Travel writers and journalists have produced a plethora of books that discuss football culture in different world societies.[1] Academics have turned to explore the social continuities and differences that exist between specific football cultures.[2] This collection seeks to contribute to that emerging *oeuvre*. It contains eighteen studies of eighteen football nations by leading scholars working within the academic disciplines of anthropology, sociology and history.

The first section is entitled 'The Old World Superpowers: Veteran Players'. The authors examine some specific cultural and historical aspects of football's key political and cultural players in the 'Old World', namely England, Scotland, France and Germany. The key moments and social movements which lie behind English football's cultural history are discussed by the historian David Russell in the opening chapter. Russell focuses particularly on the long-term class and gender construction of English football, and its relationship to the regional identities that the game encapsulates, as expressed through the North-South divide. The contemporary condition of English football suggests the export of the game has come full circle. In 1997 the Premiership alone had 133 foreign-born players from 37 different countries. The European Championships one year earlier had been hosted under the nostalgic slogan, 'Football's Coming Home'. Latterly, the English FA and political authorities emphasised the virtues of heritage in their bid to host the 2006 World Cup finals.

Scottish football has been greatly influenced by Scotland's paradoxical relationship with England, in which a cultural and economic dependency on this larger nation is suffused with a deep sense of cultural antagonism and hostility towards the English and English*ness*. Since the late 1970s, the Scots have sought to focus away from battles with England towards more international competition. This England/global duality figures heavily in the cultural identities of Scottish supporter groups, which are discussed in the chapter by Richard Giulianotti. Drawing upon fieldwork research, Giulianotti explores the continuities and differences of two fan cultures: the 'ambassador' supporters known as the 'Tartan Army' who follow Scotland abroad; and the 'soccer casual' hooligan groups which operate at club and, more recently, international level. Both owe their origins to the traditional association of Scottish football with fan violence: while the Tartan Army have sought to distance themselves consciously from this heritage, as a mechanism for defining themselves against the disorderly English fans, the soccer casuals have exploited their cultural links with the 'Auld Enemy' by cultivating this southern hooligan style. Since 1994, the apparently discrete spheres of activity of these two fan groups have collided more frequently at Scotland's international matches.

Although Scotland and England were at the heart of football's legal and cultural foundation, the world game owes its institutional organisation to France. As Hugh Dauncey and Geoff Hare explain in their chapter, the French were instrumental in forming FIFA, introducing the World Cup finals, organising the European governing body UEFA, and starting the European club championship. Yet France's football players and teams have failed to match these administrative leads.

Juste Fontaine and Michel Platini may be among the game's most legendary players, but France's national team has won a solitary European Championship (in 1984, on home soil), while its clubs have only two recent successes to claim in three European competitions. French spectator culture has always failed to match the rooted fandom found elsewhere in Europe (Mignon 1996). Consequently, the lustre of hosting the 1998 World Cup finals has been soiled by the complaints of millions of France's marginalised about the tournament's expense.

Conversely, German football culture resembles that of the UK. The greatest number of successful club sides hail from the industrial Ruhr, while the fan culture is redolent of the terrace culture found two decades earlier on British terraces. However, as Udo Merkel's chapter on the German game demonstrates, there are important and unique dimensions as well. Historically, German clubs have been the subject of relatively strict institutional rules which preclude their share capitalisation on the open financial markets. Moreover, the texture of German football culture has been transformed by the fall of the East European state socialist regimes and the subsequent reunification of Germany. The German *Bundesliga* (First Division) subscribes to this vision of a united Germany, although the western clubs' financial and professional head-start has greatly weakened the eastern clubs' competitiveness. Football therefore comes to dramatise the deep structural inequalities that persist between the two former nations. Some easterners show their alienation through symbolic forms of protest (e.g. neo-Nazism, racist chants) to highlight the limitations of the new German nation-building project, with particular focus on the absence of 'moral integration' (Dumont 1970).

The second section is entitled 'Glory and Innovation: Pre-eminent Players' and focuses on a second category of football cultures from Europe and South America that have competed most effectively at the highest level. It begins with an essay on one Calvinist nation that seems to have few problems in terms of social and cultural integration. The chapter by Torbjörn Andersson and Aage Radmann examines how a 'Swedish model' of football emerged to mirror the political and economic organisation of the nation. Latterly, as that social model has began to fragment, so Swedish football has been required to readapt, leading to further successes on the international stage. A key impetus for these successes was the new training and playing techniques that were introduced during the 1970s by English coaches.

The deepest integration of football and political culture is often assumed to exist in Latin America, most particularly in Argentina and Brazil. During the 1960s and 1970s, populist and military leaders sought to exploit the successes of their national sides for ideological purposes. Argentina's Peron and the subsequent military junta exploited the symbolism of Argentina's World Cup involvement; Brazil's military rulers claimed that their great national sides reflected their vision of a 'powerful, disciplined and technocratic' society (Humphreys 1986: 134). Even on the left, Che Guevara aligned himself with support for the working-class team of his native city, Rosario Central (Scher 1996: 177, 282).

Yet, as the respective chapters by Pablo Alabarces and José Sergio Leite Lopes demonstrate, the football-politics nexus in Argentina and Brazil is far more complex than this picture assumes.

As Alabarces explains, in Argentina's case, the game has been central to the ideological and technological integration of the capital, Buenos Aires, and the vast provincial interior. The 'Argentinian style' was formulated early in the nation's modern history, and subsequently transmitted throughout its territory via the new network of cable television. Public disquiet at military rule was reflected in fan disorder, particularly in confrontations with the State's forces of social control (Archetti and Romero 1994). The new democratic framework has precipitated a New Right political hegemony, of economic privatisation and social austerity. For Alabarces, the fragmentation of the class structure and other aspects of social stratification has precipitated an ideological crisis within Argentina. One symptom is the growth of violence among the *barras bravas*, the militant fan groups that follow each club.

Historically, the deep social and economic inequalities in Brazilian society have been heavily influential in shaping the political dimensions of the national game. Brazil's 'melting pot' international persona masks an obdurate system of ethnic stratification. White elites have always controlled the economy and important cultural structures such as the football industry. Symbolically, this hegemony has been challenged by the irresistable talents of black and 'mixed race' players (Leite Lopes 1997). Friedenreich, Leonidas, Garrincha, Didi, Pelé, Jairzinho, Romario and Ronaldo have fashioned a rich lineage of non-white success, though only relatively recently, particularly by transfer abroad, have their fortunes been economically secured. As social inequalities have hardened, white players have risen in importance, while Brazil's poorest *favelas* have struggled to reproduce the next generation of fit and healthy players or dedicated supporters.

The third section of the book, entitled 'Waiting in the Wings: Marginal Players', discusses three nations whose intense football passions have been consummated by minimal international success. In the first of these chapter, Gary Armstrong and Jon Mitchell examine the case of Malta, perennial losers in European and world competition. The anthropologist Jeremy Boissevain described Malta's cultural identity as imbued by 'amoral familism', specifically the attitude that actions are legitimate so long as they benefit the individual or his own clan. This *mentalité* feeds through into football, most notably through the underlying antagonisms of the Maltese towards their patronising treatment by former colonial masters. The Maltese have turned to foreign players and coaches to raise their national standard, but without any significant effect. Meanwhile, concerns remain that corruption may expand as professionalism and commodification begin to prevail in the domestic league.

The issue of European integration dominates debates on Turkish football and society, as the journalist and sociologist, Can Kozanoglu, demonstrates in the following chapter. The foundations for modern Turkey were laid by the nationalist leader Kamil Ataturk, leading the nation on the path to Westernisation but without introducing the democratic political system that is found in all EU nations. In partial consequence, when Turkish application for EU membership arrived, 'the European establishment reacted as if one of the ugly sisters had asked the prince for a dance' (Pope and Pope 1998). Turkish football culture encapsulates these deeply ambivalent attitudes toward European integration. Football clubs and supporters play in some fear of being humiliated before Europe, while European successes are regarded as intrinsically Turkish triumphs. Football may be an emblem of modernity and Westernisation within Turkish society (Stokes 1995), but it also enables Turks to distinguish themselves culturally from the West.

Similar tensions between East and West, and between democratisation and modernisation, prevail in Indonesia. The huge population of over 200 million, with its vibrant football culture, has failed to deliver to date. As the chapter by anthropologist Freek Colombijn explains, the historical development of football in this peripheral nation was rooted in the Dutch East Indies' early colonial status. Subsequently, the game became a venue for deeper political conflicts to be played out between European, Japanese and nationalist forces before military rule was imposed in 1965. In the post-war period, the democratic and military rulers in turn have sought to promote national and cultural integration through football. However, geographical and cultural divisions between Indonesians continue to undermine this project. In May 1998, Indonesia was rocked by a fortnight of major rioting and revolutionary fervour in opposition to the Suharto regime. The looting and protesting came to a temporary halt, however, when the English FA Cup final was beamed to the Indonesians live on television.

The fourth section of the book, 'Contested Decisions: Disunited Players', looks at four cases of social and nationalist conflict within football. The chapter by the anthropologist Ramon Sarro looks at football among the Baga people of Guinea, West Africa. Football tournaments were introduced by the French in the late 1980s and serve the same unifying functions as the old masquerades and carnivals had performed in the past. The game may be a symbol of modernity, yet the tournaments have become a crucial cultural battleground for the Baga allowing them to express underlying conflicts between young people and their elders. Sarro reports that the elders appear to have gained the upper hand. Football matches are seen as important contests during which the honour of the village is at stake; the rituals surrounding the matches appear to be notably traditionalist, with drumming and dancing, witchcraft and prayers, all taking place. Within this modern sport, the Baga elders are able to revitalise their influence over the village.

In Northern Ireland, as the chapter by Alan Bairner and Peter Shirlow demonstrates, ethnic divisions exist along religious and constitutional lines. The majority group is comprised by Protestants committed to Ulster's current union with mainland Britain; the minority group is comprised of Catholics favouring the North's integration within the Republic of Ireland. This religious and political division of Northern Ireland is reflected further in the spatial divisions of the two communities, and consequently on the football field. Some clubs have emerged quite naturally from deep within communities that have long been associated with Unionism, Loyalism, Nationalism or Republicanism. Other clubs have gradually become associated with the Catholic or Protestant communities due to a movement of 'homes' or a long-term build up of one community near the football ground. In the case of Derry City, a growing association with Catholicism and Republicanism resulted in the club's withdrawal from the North's Irish League in 1971, and then a switch over the border to the South's League of Ireland in 1985.

In Israel, football oppositions have traditionally between constructed within the majority Jewish population. The Israeli football league had been founded in 1932 while Palestine was still under British control with its first competition being won by the British Police team. Since then, Israeli clubs have tended to divide along ideological rather than ethnic lines. Clubs with the prefix Hapoel hail from the sports organisations of the Israeli trade unions; those with the prefix Betar tend to back the right-wing nationalist Likud Party; liberals tend to back clubs with the prefix Maccabi. However, in 1997, this framework was upset by the promotion of Hapoel Taibe to the Premier Division, becoming the first Arab club to compete at this level in sixty-five years. The chapter by anthropologists Yoram Carmeli and Iris Bar explores the footballing fortunes and social experiences of the club and its supporters during its promotion year, against the background of continuing political and territorial struggle between the ruling Israeli majority and the Palestinian minority.

The chapter by Drazen Lalic and Srdjan Vrcan explores the case of the former Yugoslavia, and the role of football in nurturing ethnic hostilities and sparking civil war. After the Second World War, the new Yugoslavian state struggled to contain the tensions and hostilities of its rival peoples. Yugoslavian football teams, especially the national side, did retain a capacity to unite as well as divide the different ethnic communities. The death of the Yugoslav leader, Marshal Tito, in 1980 and the fall of the Eastern Communist bloc nine years later were key historical preconditions for the end of the modern Yugoslav system. But its actual implosion and collapse into civil war was signalled by the resurfacing of ethnic antagonisms, most particularly within the football context. Matters came to a head at the match between the Croat side Dinamo Zagreb and the Serbian team Red Star Belgrade in 1990, which ended in a mass brawl as Serb police and Zagreb fans and players battled on and off the field. Days later, as Lalic and Vrcan put it, the two sides had moved from the stadium to the trenches to face one another, as Yugoslavia slipped from the playground of football to the theatres of war.

The final section, 'New Tactics: Contemporary Players', explores the relatively new football cultures that have come to the fore since the 1980s. It begins with a study of one football nation, South Africa, that links up with the previous section on ethnic conflicts. The chapter by John Nauright examines the long-term historical development of South African football. During the long period of white political domination, football tended to lack the elite support given to other sports like rugby union and cricket. On the other hand, the game became highly popular in black townships as local clubs emerged, often under the aegis of key political leaders. In the post-apartheid era, the rebirth of the nation seemed to have been commemorated by the victory of a multi-ethnic South African side at the 1996 African Nations' Cup. Football has also avoided the charges arraigned against other sports in the new South Africa: that they continue to be a form of political apartheid by proxy, to the exclusion of non-white groups. The possible delivery of the 2006 World Cup finals to South Africa may provide a further important opportunity for football to unify South Africans of all ethnic backgrounds.

A rather different set of structural circumstances lie behind the rise of Norwegian football, as the chapter by Matti Goksøyr and Hans Hognestad explains. Since the early 1990s, top English club sides have purchased a large number of Norwegian players. At international level, these players have secured qualification for the past two World Cup finals by applying the long-ball strategy of Egil Olsen, the Norwegian coach. Nevertheless, Goksøyr and Hognestad demonstrate that Norway's football culture is lengthy one, rooted in a passionate if distant following of the English club game. Indeed, support for English clubs has tended to outstrip the backing given to local sides. In this sense, we might speak of Norway's football culture as an early post-modern one, in which the mass media and a distant 'imagined community' of fellow fans become the key reference points in shaping supporter identities.

In the United States, a similar relationship was long thought to exist between football followers, the mass media and distant sports clubs. Football, was considered by many to be an 'unAmerican' sport, followed only by ethnic minorities that had failed to assimilate and who preferred instead to follow the fortunes of club sides 'back home'. However, that image of 'soccer' has been greatly eroded in the past decade, as the US has hosted the 1990 World Cup finals, founded a major new professional league (MLS) and contributed up to 16 million football players. The chapter by David Andrews and Detlev Zwick highlights how the United States' soccer boom is underpinned by the economic and cultural privileges of the white suburban middle-classes. The game is used at child and youth level as a social vehicle for reproducing the norms and homogeneity of this class. The expense of joining many youth soccer clubs is prohibitive to all but the most well-heeled. In Bourdieu's terms, a certain 'distinction' is attached to soccer club participation. While these class divisions may seem to be an exceptional soccer characteristic of the United States, the general commodification of world football is certainly undeniable. As Andrews and Zwick indicate, to arrive at a fuller understanding of the nexus between leisure and class relationships, more research needs to be undertaken among the privileged social groups in the suburbs.

The final chapter by Hiroko Maeda and Haruo Nogawa examines the situation of soccer in Japan, one of the co-hosts of the 2002 World Cup finals. Like the United States, Japan's new soccer culture leans heavily on the creation of a new professional league; the recruitment of foreign stars to play alongside local players; and the marketing potential that is afforded to football by hosting the World Cup finals. Culturally, the Japanese game has opened up a new leisure space for young people, notably women. Antagonisms between the Japanese and the ethnic Koreans underlie football's organisation (as is the case with other sports in Japan); FIFA's decision to award the 2002 tournament to both nations was a defensive exercise rather than a real attempt to generate a cultural rapprochement. Maeda and Nogawa demonstrate that Japanese football generates strongly expressive and often violent forms of civic and national pride. These outbursts of 'passion' are initially at odds with the Western view of Japan's 'Yamato spirit', of self-control and social harmony, no matter how ideologically artificial these cultural values may be (Dower 1996: 101). Most notably, the Japanese form of 'militant' fandom may result in public violence and damage to property (as found in the West and Latin America). But it may also involve a peculiarly Japanese ritual in which the team coaches and players, who have failed to satisfy the fan collective, are ceremonially humbled in public. In this instance at least, the Japanese follow all other football cultures, by adapting or 'creolizing' football's basic properties to fit with their local circumstances.

June 1998

Notes

1. See, for example, Kuper (1994), Watson (1994), Cresswell and Evans (1997), Taylor (1998).
2. See, for example, Lanfranchi (1992); Giulianotti, Bonney and Hepworth (1994); Giulianotti and Williams (1994); Sugden and Tomlinson (1994); Wagg (1995); Murray (1995); Duke and Crolley (1996); Mangan (1996); Armstrong and Giulianotti (1997); Giulianotti (1999); Finn and Giulianotti (1999).

Part I
The Old World Superpowers:
Veteran Players

1 Associating with Football: Social Identity in England 1863–1998[1]

David Russell

'If your work interferes with your football, give it up' ran a pre-war Lancashire saying. While its exhortation to mass absenteeism should not be taken too literally, it captures effectively the central role that Association Football has played in many people's lives for the past century and a quarter. The English game has passed through several distinct phases and this chapter can only explore some elements of its rich and complex history. At the very least, however, it will demonstrate the essential wisdom underlying that most hackneyed of clichés informing us that football is 'more than a game': it truly has been a major site for the reflection, reinforcement and construction of key social and political identities.

A PEOPLE'S GAME?

Association Football formally originated in a series of meetings held in London in 1863 and in its early years was largely a game for social elites. Its first major trophy, the FA Cup which began in 1871–2, was initially dominated by sides rooted in the public schools and Oxbridge: revealingly, the kick off of the 1873 final was rescheduled to 11.00 a.m to allow the players to watch that afternoon's Boat Race. Being a footballer conferred gentlemanly status. By the late 1870s, however, rising real wages, a significant increase in the number of workers gaining a Saturday half-holiday and a burgeoning interest in the game among the industrial and commercial middle classes, stimulated the emergence of a network of 'gate money' clubs with particularly strong roots in Lancashire and the North and West Midlands. Blackburn Olympic's defeat of the Old Etonians in the 1883 FA Cup final announced the transfer of power on the pitch from the public school old-boys sides to the new, more popularly based clubs, a process made irreversible by the introduction of limited professionalism in 1885 and the establishment of the Football League three years later (Lewis 1997; Mason 1980; Tischler 1981). In 1871, only 50 clubs were affiliated to the Football Association; by 1914 the figure had reached 12,000. Similarly, while total attendances for the (12-club) Football League in its inaugural 1888–9 season reached approximately 600,000, by 1913–14 the (20-club) First Division could attract 8.7 million fans. The game had passed from being a badge of social distinction to a truly popular pastime.

Football has long drawn the majority of its players and supporters from what can broadly be termed the skilled and semi-skilled working class. From the late nineteenth century, football has been something that numerous working men 'did', providing a consciousness of class if not class consciousness (Mason 1980: 222). However, it has been administered and governed largely by the middle and upper-middle classes and this social configuration has generated much speculation both in regard to 'ownership' of the game and its role in the structuring of wider social relationships between dominant and subordinate groups. At one extreme Steven Tischler, writing about the period before 1914, has argued that

> commercial-professional football, like other entertainments controlled and financed by the bourgeoisie, arguably created a safety valve through which pressure generated by industrial capitalism could pass safely, without endangering the basic relationships of society. (1981: 136)

At the opposite pole, others have stressed the popular capacity to deflect ruling-class ideology and to invest the game with proletarian values, arguing that working people 'were not sacrificial lambs to capitalist enterprise and domination ... the Proletariat, in brief, discovered in modern sports possibilities for the culmination and advancement of their own interests' (Jones 1986: 11, 25–6).

Some studies of contemporary fanzine production and other modes of 'independent' fan culture take a similar (although not necessarily class-centred) perspective when describing that culture as a 'highly significant ... [and] at least in part successful contestation of commercial tendencies' (Jary et al. 1991: 591).

It is undeniable that from the late 1870s on, working-class fans have succeeded in stamping their identity, values and culture on the game through forms of active spectatorship featuring noise, spectacle and partisanship. The result, rather more than the game, has become 'the thing'. However, those interpretations which equate such displays with any real popular control of the game, let alone any wider significance, are investing them with too much importance and missing the more substantial point that real control has remained firmly invested in the hands of elite groups. The label of 'the People's Game', often attached to English football but rarely interrogated, describes patterns of consumption and not patterns of control. It is not suggested here that bourgeois control of the game has translated into a wider social and political hegemony or that middle-class authority within the game has gone unchallenged. Fans have often been highly critical of football's governing bodies and caustically aware of the range of self-seeking motives that have guided some boardroom careers. Nevertheless, until the emergence of an 'independent' fan culture from the later 1980s (and even then only to a limited extent and with mixed success), elite leadership has rarely been challenged. Fans are often simply too addicted to the game to threaten the structures that provide it, while many working-class fans have treated it much as they have treated wider social and political structures, as something to be tolerated and manipulated to suit needs, rather than overthrown.

This emphasis on popular/elite relationships should not obscure the fact that football has also served to sharpen and define antagonisms within classes. The battles for the game's soul that reverberated around the issue of professionalism in the late nineteenth and early twentieth centuries, although never reducible to a simple formula, can be viewed as a conflict between privately educated members of the professional middle class who had started the game and the industrial-commercial middle classes that had begun to develop the 'gate-taking' clubs from about 1880. As association football became ever more firmly rooted in the national culture and as sports like rugby union and hockey provided new opportunities for those seeking an untainted sporting culture, such tensions eased without disappearing altogether; the history of the sometimes strained relationship between the Football Association and the Football League could usefully be considered in this context. Interestingly, albeit in a very different climate, contemporary conflict between independent fan groups and the 'football world' (especially professional clubs) can also be represented as a conflict within the middle class.

THIS IS A MAN'S GAME

While debates over football and class will keep academics in conference papers for years to come, there can be no argument that the game has always been a decidedly male preserve and a location for the expression of, and experimentation with, a variety of masculine identities. Many of the emotions and attitudes expressed within football accord closely to a cluster of characteristics often considered to represent 'true masculinity' (Holt 1989: 8). There can be no doubt, for example, that celebration of physical strength, loyalty to 'mates' and to a specific territory have long been a feature of football culture. They have been central to many of the more aggressive terrace cultures and to hooligan groups, and are still often prevalent within the world of the professional footballer (Parker 1995). It has also been suggested that the British style of play emphasising speed, strength and aggression (although followers of the game before the 1920s and many Scots for a long period after that might not recognise this description) is rooted in a particularly British notion of manliness (Critcher 1991: 69–72).

However, the game has also always been the site for the safe and controlled expression of a range of softer emotions which can rarely be expressed in the wider culture. Many male fans will admit to crying at particularly important games, while the tears of Bobby Charlton and Paul Gascoigne in the World Cups of 1966 and 1990 respectively, generally won them affection rather than contempt. Similarly, since the late 1950s, footballers have developed an ever-growing repertoire of histrionic practices – elaborate post-goal scoring celebrations, the feigning or exaggeration of injury – which suggest that football can be a laboratory for masculine style and a place for the display of its 'confusions and contradictions', as well as a location for the reinforcement of its 'traditional' forms (Critcher 1991: 74).

Long-lasting Victorian notions of a 'woman's place' characterising access to commercial leisure pursuits as a 'reward' for the male breadwinner, proscribing certain types of boisterous public behaviour as unsuitable and defining physical exercise as threatening to maternal health, guaranteed women a decidedly secondary place within football culture (McCrone 1988). Women therefore played no role in the senior administration of the game until the 1990s, formed only a small albeit committed and informed minority among spectators and met considerable hostility when they attempted to play.

The women's game blossomed briefly between about 1916 and 1921, with the main impetus provided by young women involved in war work in factories: by 1921, there were at least 150 teams in England (Williamson 1991). However, at a time of concern over the scale of women's political and economic gains since 1914, it was not difficult for those instinctively opposed to the women's game to build a case against it. In December 1921, using largely unsubstantiated claims that monies from women's charity games were being diverted into private hands and adding the revealing rider that 'the game of football is quite unsuitable for females and should not be encouraged', the FA banned it from all grounds under its jurisdiction (Williamson 1991; Russell 1997: 95–8). Although the women's game survived, this conscious act of exclusion weakened it enormously and it was not until the late 1960s that it began once again to assert itself.

This does not necessarily imply that there was a large pent-up demand among women either to play or watch football. Many women had little interest in it (something also true, of course, of many men) and probably welcomed the moments on Saturday afternoons when houses suddenly became emptier. Over the last decade, women have certainly come to play a far larger role – although still very much a minority one – in the football world. Recent surveys would suggest that between 10 and 15 per cent of fans are women, which, even allowing for the lack of hard evidence from earlier periods, is probably an historically high proportion. From the late 1980s and early 1990s, there has been an increase in the number of women playing the game, with a national league being founded in 1991, and a small but growing number have gained access to both the game's administration and to the media that surrounds it (Coddington 1997; Duke and Crolley 1996; Lopez 1997).

Such developments are open to quite varied interpretation. While at one level, much of this can be seen as 'progressive' in the sense of widening women's access to a male domain, it can also be seen as a process reinforcing patriarchal structures. The women's game remains a very low profile one, while 'it is women who are joining the men's game on men's terms ... a footballization of women' is taking place (Duke and Crolley 1996: 144). It is certainly significant that in terms of spectatorship, the football authorities and football clubs have assigned to women a very traditional role as guardians of male morality, with the increased attendance of women believed to be a method of reducing the levels of violence in grounds. More simply, women and the 'family group' are also clearly viewed as a largely untapped source of spectator revenue. As it has sought to move from the crisis of the mid- and late 1980s, football has called up women as a reserve army of leisure. Perhaps most crucially, against the context of fundamental shifts within the social, educational and economic structure of gender relations, many males look with concern at challenges to their territory. The epithets 'women' and 'tart' hurled at male footballers who have just demonstrated some supposed incompetence, remain two of the more frequently deployed and highly charged words in the footballing vocabulary.

KNOWING YOUR PLACE

From its earliest moments, football has proved a potent vehicle for the generation of territorial loyalties. By the late nineteenth century, as towns and cities grew too large to be 'knowable' to their inhabitants, support of the local team provided 'symbolic citizenship': to stand with thousands of other local fans, most of whom were not known to each other, renewed people's sense of being from Bury, Burnley or wherever (Mason 1980: 234; Holt 1989: 159–79). Similarly, in the later twentieth century, as rehousing, individual social mobility and other factors weakened community structures, football stadia, and especially revered locations within them, such as Liverpool's Kop, became important symbolic and practical sites for the re-establishment of local roots (Kelly 1993: 31). Football has also provided a fertile source of empowering local myths, all the more effective when they have gained purchase within the national imagination. Newcastle (and indeed the north-east in general) has enjoyed being seen as blessed with a particularly passionate, knowledgeable and committed football culture; the supposed wit of Liverpool's Kop and the long history of good relations between Liverpool and Everton fans (perhaps declining in the 1990s) has allowed Merseyside soccer to be presented as reflecting a stoic and heroic working-class culture which gave much sustenance during battles with the Tory government in the 1980s and early 1990s.

Interestingly, many such representations depict football as the shared passion of a closely unified community. The reporting conventions adopted by the local press, especially in smaller towns, has played a major role here. This can be seen most clearly in the description of post-FA Cup Final celebrations when journalists used an unchanging set of stylistic devices to suggest an undifferentiated level of enthusiasm throughout the local community. In ideological terms this creation of an 'idealised community ... sought a magical resolution of the many internal tensions and conflicts that in fact beset the communities' (Hill 1996: 106). In this sense, football culture arguably helped cement social stability.

Local allegiances could be intense – from the late nineteenth century, football hooliganism has received at least some of its impetus from rivalries between neighbouring towns – but until relatively recently they could run alongside or be subsumed by wider regional identities. There is plentiful oral testimony suggesting that, until the 1960s, fans could support two (or even more) local sides and/or draw pleasure from the success of any side that came from a particular region. In such cases, a gentle regional or county patriotism mingled with an intelligent appreciation of football as art and thus capable of being enjoyed without excessive emotional commitment.[2] In such cases, football was probably building on existing mentalities but it could also construct new ones. Growing support for Newcastle United among the miners of east Northumberland from around the turn of the century meant that 'for the first time the miners did not look on Newcastle as the arch enemy but rather as carrying the pride and hopes of the north east' (Metcalfe 1996: 30).

Football certainly contributed considerably to the articulation of a perceived 'North-South' divide within English society. Although southern journalists rarely missed an opportunity to portray northern football fans 'oop for the coop' (or whatever fake dialect they chose) as picturesque if somewhat gauche provincials on the loose, it was northerners who drew the greatest imaginative sustenance from the game: the dominant south had only limited need of the cultural capital it offered. From early in the twentieth century northern fans have honed a potent set of oppositions setting their tough, competitive selves against 'soft southerners' who wilt when travelling beyond Hertfordshire (Holt 1989: 175–9). Similarly, northern successes over southern opponents have taken on considerable symbolic importance. This was undoubtedly the case in the 1930s when Arsenal's dominance of English club football was seen by many to mirror a (much simplified) economic situation exemplified by northern hardship and southern prosperity. Writing in 1956, a native of Teesside remembered how Arsenal were disliked for coming from 'the soft south, from London, from the city of government, where, it was imagined, all social evil was directed against places like Teesside' (Read 1964: 231–2).

While this sketch still has some purchase at the end of the century, it perhaps best describes the situation as it existed until about the late 1960s. From that point, new and often apparently contradictory patterns emerge. The media, especially television, and greater ease of personal travel opportunities have combined to foster 'glamour clubs' drawing support from the across the country – Manchester United from the late 1950s were the first and remain the most pronounced example – which have undercut levels of support for smaller town clubs. Interestingly, those fans remaining loyal to local sides show little of the benign tolerance to local rivals noted in the earlier period. From the late 1960s, new styles of fanship placing a far higher emphasis on winning and involving far higher levels of aggression (although not necessarily violence) made it far harder to support or at least show some sympathy for Sunderland and Newcastle, Preston and Blackpool. At the same time, these new styles have increased the antagonism between supporters of, for example, Leeds United and Manchester United and Liverpool and Manchester United, to the point to where any sense of 'northern' identity in the context of football is more likely to flow from a sense of being a member of one specific northern location rather than any wider imagined community.

BEING ENGLISH[3]

In the period to 1930, football carried only a limited burden in relation to the reinforcement and construction of national identity. This partly stemmed from the fact that in an age of powerful local and regional identities, the England team simply did not play regularly enough to establish a firm place in popular affections. An annual match against Scotland was inaugurated in 1872 (a 0–0 draw despite England playing six forwards and Scotland eight) with Wales being added to the fixture list in 1879 and Ireland in 1882. It was not until 1908 that England played a foreign side (Austria), and 1923 that a foreign international side (Belgium) played in England. (An amateur international side was founded in 1906 and played a variety of foreign opponents, winning the gold medal at the Olympic Games in 1908 and 1912.) While such a fixture list could encourage a largely sub-political nationalism within Britain (Moorhouse 1987 and 1995), it carried little wider significance for English nationalism. Perhaps most crucially, however, as a sport largely associated with urban-industrial England, new industrial money and the working class, football lacked many of the characteristics associated with a distinctively configured contemporary notion of 'Englishness' that was shot through with celebrations of the rural, the ancient and the ordered (Dodd and Colls: 1986). Cricket, at all levels from the village green to test matches against imperial opposition, expressed these values far more effectively and on a far wider stage (Holt 1996).

The inter-war period saw significant changes. While many of these relate to the national side and will be discussed below, the game in general took on a more central role within the national culture. The FA Cup Final was of considerable importance here (Hill 1996). Royal patronage from 1914 had been an important milestone, but the game's relocation to the new British Empire Stadium at Wembley in 1923 and its addition to the BBC radio schedule from 1927 and thus a place in the quasi-official calendar of national events, elevated it to a new level. Moreover, as the final enjoyed a higher profile, so the behaviour of those who attended it fell under increasing and, for the most part, benign scrutiny. In 1923, what was generally seen as the orderly behaviour of the crowd when perhaps 200,000 people gained admission to a ground designed for half that number, quietened many fears about popular behaviour. The notion that disaster was averted by the efforts of a few mounted police and the calming effect of the arrival of the King was especially significant in this regard. The essential decency and order-liness of the English working man had been richly demonstrated.

Such notions were enhanced by the addition of community singing, culminating in the rendition of the hymn 'Abide with Me', from 1927. Community singing had a remarkable vogue in Britain in 1926–7 and to some extent can be read as a conscious attempt by a broad coalition of mainly middle-class groupings to reconstruct a sense of national unity after the General Strike and the extended miners' strike of 1926. The *Daily Express*, ideologically and commercially well-attuned to such an undertaking, became an enthusiastic sponsor and added pre-match singing at selected Football League matches to its roster of activities in December 1926. Following an emotional performance of 'Abide with Me' at the 1927 Good Friday fixture between Tottenham and West Ham, it was decided to include the hymn in the forthcoming Cup Final musical programme. Wembley's annual rendition of Britain's most popular hymn rapidly became a powerful symbol of supposed English virtues as 'that typical sport-loving, merry English crowd lifting their hats as one man, [was] transformed by a single thought into one huge congregation' (*Yorkshire Observer*, 23 April 1928). Football had connected with 'Englishness'.

The equating of football with tolerance, decency and public displays of religiosity, a set of ideas with which sections of the left as much as the right could identify, remained a powerful element in representations of the game until the mid-1960s. From that point, however, the game's declining place in the national affection, in which process the perceived distance of star players from the working-class community, the emergence of racism and the rise of hooliganism (real, ritualised and imagined) were significant elements, led to its association with an almost contrary set of characteristics culminating in the almost sepulchral tones of the mid-1980s (Russell 1997: 181–208). The *Sunday Times'* famous comment post-Heysel tragedy that soccer was 'a slum sport, played in slum stadiums, watched by slum people' (2 June 1985) stands as an extreme but instructive counterpoise to the virtuous depictions of an earlier age. It is no coincidence that as the football industry has tried to re-invent itself from the late 1980s, nostalgia for an earlier 'golden age' has grown up among club directors, and indeed many fans. The naming of football grandstands after Tom Finney, Stanley Matthews, Nat Lofthouse and other unproblematic folk heroes from more innocent days, demonstrates not simply commercial astuteness but also a plea for history (or nostalgic versions of it) to remedy contemporary problems.

PLAYING FOR ENGLAND

From about 1930, interconnecting patterns of sporting, cultural and social change saw the England side take on an ever-growing importance. First, England's fixture list expanded significantly: whereas only 52 games had been played in the period 1900–1914, the figure rose to 107 between 1919–39 and then to 186 between 1946–66 as England rejoined FIFA in 1946 and contested the World Cup for the first time in 1950. Furthermore, the quality of continental opposition was now generally far higher, forcing the English (and other British national sides) to reconsider football's international balance of power and its wider ramifications. Admittedly, the national side was not held paramount by everyone in the professional game and the issue of 'club versus country' dogged football, particularly from the 1950s. While the motives that have led clubs to withdraw players from international fixtures have much to do with League points and financial security, it is worth prefacing the following discussion of the national side with the cautionary note that the very existence of a club/country tension, suggests clear limits to the expression of English nationalism through sport, and indeed, to the entire English national project.

England's increased involvement on the world stage took place against the background of fundamental contextual change. At a domestic level, the dramatic growth of a popular press anxious to expand its sports coverage and, from the 1930s, to do so with a more populist, sensationalist style, gave football, including the international game, an increasingly high public profile (Fishwick 1989: 100–7). These twin processes were gradual at first, accelerating noticeably following the launch of the tabloid *Sun* in 1964, and becoming relentless by the 1980s (Wagg 1991). On a wider front, internationals have been played and reported against the background of political and economic challenges to Britain's world position. In the 1930s, the rise of European fascism provided the key element, while after 1945 the Cold War, decolonisation, Britain's relative economic decline, and debates over its role in Europe all helped shape the discourses that surrounded and increasingly politicised international football.

Unsurprisingly, this process was denied by many of the game's key personnel and by many commentators. The notion that English sport, unlike much of its foreign equivalent, was 'above' politics, was deeply ingrained in the national imagination, an idea of great intellectual value for a benign imperial nation. In 1934 the *Manchester Guardian* stated that any impression that the forthcoming England–Italy international was 'associated in any way with the prestige of either country – for such are the impressions to be had from certain foreign papers – are to be regretted' (14 November 1934). The next year, Sir Frederick Wall, recently retired as secretary of the FA, claimed that: 'Abroad, international sport has a political aspect. Football in England is not carried on for the purposes of playing a foreign country and gaining a victory. Football in dear old England is merely a sporting entertainment' (Wall 1935: 223). Such comments were frequently made well into the 1950s and even beyond. By 1973, the politicisation of sport on a world scale was too advanced to be disaffirmed, but Frank Butler of the *News of the World* (21 October) could still portray the history of that process as a tale of English (he meant 'British') good intention defeated by foreign influence:

England took up football as a sport. They then taught the world this friendly pastime. It is became good entertainment, but has been built into a rat-race industry ruined by politics and political tension.

Undoubtedly, English football has not carried the overt political overtones that has marked the game in so many countries since the 1930s (Murray 1994; Mason 1995). Indeed, the studious attempt of the football authorities to eschew 'politics' has at times been a positive hindrance: issues relating to hooliganism from the 1960s and racism from the 1970s might have been addressed much earlier if the football world had not seen itself as somehow socially autonomous and free-floating. Nevertheless, from at least the early 1930s English international football clearly became increasingly politicised and to stand as a mirror for the national condition (Clarke and Critcher 1986; Wagg 1991). At institutional level, the most famous, albeit extreme example, is provided by the FA's acquiescence to Foreign Office demands that England's players give the Nazi salute in Berlin in 1938 (Beck 1982). Less dramatic, but still significant was a relaxation in the 1930s of the ruling that a sending off meant automatic disqualification from the national side (Fishwick 1989: 140). Prestige was beginning to matter and it became increasingly difficult to distinguish between its sporting and its political manifestations. Scattered political statements can be found across the post-war period. In September 1966, for example, the *FA News* used England's World Cup victory in the midst of 'the sombre economic situation which faces the country this summer', to argue that:

> The players who have made it possible worked hard and made many sacrifices. They have set, we suggest, an example of devotion and loyalty to the country which many others would do well to follow.

It has been, though, the popular press that has done most to make the national team a symbol of national virility. The arrival of a talented Austrian side in December 1932 drew forth some of the earliest coverage of this type (Edworthy 1997: 28) and the visit of the Italian world champions in November 1934 added to the stock:

> At Highbury this afternoon, there is at stake not merely the pride of English football, but the prestige of England. If we could beat the Italians by ten goals and on the day deserve such a margin, the stock of England not merely of English football, would jump as it had not jumped for years. (*Daily Mirror*, 14 November 1934)

The *Mirror*'s exhortation was unusually extreme but it pointed up a general trend. From 1945, comment was mainly concerned with establishing links between sporting performance and England's declining status as an international power. 'As Britain declined economically, shed its empire and faced up to a world dominated by two new superpowers, Fleet Street spoke as if a still great nation was being betrayed by the bunglers and shirkers who ran, or were, its football team' (Wagg 1991: 222). Those who ran it were a particular target, almost as if the often anonymous committeemen of the FA were symbolic of the 'faceless bureaucrats' of Whitehall, the local town hall and, later, Brussels, believed in many popular versions of contemporary British history to be responsible for many of the nation's problems.

From 1929 (when, in Madrid, Spain became the first-ever foreign side to beat England) until the early 1950s, concerns over sporting/national prestige were to some extent mollified by a belief that foreign football owed much to the 'industry and ability of British coaches' working abroad (*News of the World*, 5 December 1937). There was an acknowledgement that continental players had made what one leading English player called a 'very remarkable improvement' since 1918 and a willingness in many quarters to acknowledge that Britain could learn from the best European practice. There was even an acceptance of the inevitability of home defeat. After a Stanley Matthews hat-trick had helped England squeeze to a 5–4 victory over Czechoslovakia at Tottenham in 1937, the *News of the World* (5 December) commented that:

> It does not need the wisdom of a Solomon to foresee the day when England must surrender her cherished record of invincibility to an invading continental team. It will happen as surely as night follows day.

While the scale of Hungary's 6–3 victory which ended England's unbeaten home record in 1953 was unexpected, the actual defeat was not, therefore, the profound surprise to the English football establishment and the nation as a whole that has sometimes been claimed. The talking down of prestigious (communist) opponents in some sections of the popular press before the match, should not obscure the wiser counsel that was in plentiful supply.[4]

After further away defeats against Yugoslavia (0–1), Hungary (1–7) and Uruguay (2–4) in the next seven months, that small but significant point of unity began to dissolve, leaving two broad but discernible responses to footballing achievement. These in turn represented two versions of Englishness as it was reshaped in a changing global context. The first and, certainly, the minority position, was typified by a sensibility which balanced a desire for an improvement in the quality of English football with a critical awareness of the achievements of other nations. Within journalism, *The Times* football correspondent Geoffrey Green was a notable contributor to this school of thought as when describing Hungary's 7–1 demolition of England in Budapest in 1954 as 'football one could sit and watch until old age finally overcame one' (*The Times*, 24 May 1954). Magazine journalist Eric Batty was another showing a willingness to make an unpopular comment (which later became received wisdom) in the prelude to the 1966 World Cup:

> I do not want England to win! Not that I am unpatriotic but my feelings stem from the certain knowledge that English football very urgently needs to be

reformed and reorganised at almost every point, and to win the World Cup would set back these reforms. (*Soccer Star*, 8 July 1966)

Crucially, the FA and especially its secretary Stanley Rous were active subscribers to an 'internationalist' position, using its many (although low circulation) publications to alert the insular English to foreign example and, most famously, encouraging Manchester United's involvement in the European Cup in 1956–7 against Football League advice.[5] It is unhelpful to characterise this loose collection of individuals and ideas in terms of any specific political ideology but it is not difficult to hear echoes of those voices in the contemporary political arena favouring decolonisation. An article in the 1952–3 *FA Yearbook* used the telling phrase 'The pupils have caught up with the teacher', and that pupil-teacher metaphor became a key feature of the debate. Just as some found it possible to accept the loss of empire as the inevitable result of the quality of English rule, so the loss of sporting domination could be seen as the price paid for teaching 'our' games so well. Such a view lost some of its power in the post-colonial period but a more global vision has lived on in the work of some journalists, coaches and administrators and has shown signs of becoming more deeply rooted in the closing years of the century.

Against this position, there has emerged a collection of more aggressively nationalistic responses to footballing failure and national decline. These arguments have found their most potent expression in the popular and tabloid press, although they doubtless articulated a popular mood as much as they constructed it. They have been characterised by a reluctance to acknowledge and learn from foreign achievement and this clearly impacted on discussion of the reform of coaching and tactics. At one level, the popular press instinctively preached the need for major rethinking after any significant disappointment: clarion calls for the 'getting down to fundamentals' began as early as 1932 after England's narrow 4–3 defeat of Austria (*News of the World*, 11 December 1932). Yet suggestions that the national squad spend long periods together or that intensive coaching might be required, were often rejected almost on the ground that they were 'foreign'. Certainly, anything that smacked of centralised planning was unpopular.

After reporting that communist Hungary spent £10 million each year on sport and that the team had been together for three years, the *News of the World* argued: 'As we don't have a Minister of Sport – and don't need one either – we can't adopt such drastic methods in order to win a game of football' (29 November 1953). For much of the period it was believed that innate national characteristics would allow English sides to overcome those with superior techniques allied to more brittle temperaments (Clarke and Critcher 1986; Critcher 1994). As *Soccer Star* noted in 1966, 'whatever the team lacked in skill it more than made up for it with the type of display that owed more to the British character than any special football prowess' (12 August 1966). Such sentiments still find echoes in the press, in popular discussion and within a professional game that, in marked contrast to continental Europe, allows its leading sides to be run by individuals without coaching qualifications.

At worst, this insularity evolved into a xenophobic nationalism. Britain's former enemy Germany, a ubiquitous footballing rival and, after the UK joined the European Union in 1973, an unpopular partner, has been a particular target. This reached a climax immediately before and during the 1996 European Championships when, even allowing for the knowingness and self-parody embodied in the structures of tabloid journalism, new levels of disparagement were reached (Kelly 1998; Moore 1997: 106–23). Again it is not helpful to tie these ideas too closely to specific political philosophies or social groupings. There is no doubt, however, that at the extreme margin they fed and spilled into the often violent, openly racist, specifically English (not British) nationalism that began to emerge first around club sides and then the international team from the middle and late 1970s (Williams et al. 1989).

Certainly, this rather negative picture ignores too easily football's potential to provide moments which truly bind the nation in celebration and shared pleasures: the triumphs of 1966 and highspots of Italia '90 and Euro '96 certainly showed such things to be possible. The popular press played a cheerful and willing role here, even if that sometimes necessitated argumentative shifts and contradictions of quite remarkable proportion, with yesterday's 'plonkers' becoming today's 'heroes' within the space of ninety minutes (Wagg 1991: 225–37).[6] However, English international football has long been set in a context in which national insecurity and uncertainties have often led to players being expected to fight the nation's battles while being denied the support mechanisms that they require. Playing for England has never been easy.

NEW FOOTBALL, NEW LOYALTIES?

At the end of the twentieth century, English professional football is experiencing its most fundamental upheaval since the emergence of the professional game in the 1880s (Conn 1997; Horton 1997; Redhead 1997). Cash-rich from satellite television, played in (generally) much improved stadia, and almost frighteningly fashionable, at one level it appears as though a new game is crystallising and bringing with it the potential to generate new identities and loyalties. 'New football' appears to be rather more democratic in the sense that it is drawing on or at least showing an increased awareness of, the previously neglected supporter constituencies and especially women and minority ethnic communities; many fans are now also more attuned to the European and world games. Perhaps from these new forces, may emerge a football culture that transcends its traditional social, sexual and geographical basis. Yet fashion is a fickle creature and football's search for new roots and its attempt to remove some aspects of its historical burden is potentially hazardous. Football may one day have to make renewed overtures to the many working-class fans priced out of the major stadia and displaced to other areas of the game, or to the public house satellite screen and the radio set. All that is certain is that the game will provide a rich source of pleasure. For whom and with what consequences, is far less clear.

Notes

1. I am grateful to Tony Mason and Gary Armstrong for helpful criticism of an earlier draft.
2. Gavin Mellor's doctoral work in progress on football fans in the north-west since 1945, at the Institute of Football Studies, University of Central Lancashire, is shedding valuable light on these issues.
3. I gained much initial stimulus for this section from 'Football and the crisis of national identity', an unpublished paper by Jeffrey Richards of Lancaster University. There is inevitably some slippage between the words 'England'/'English' and 'Britain'/'British' in what follows. Hopefully, British has only been used when referring to issues relating to the whole of the UK.
4. England's 2–0 defeat by Ireland at Goodison Park in September 1949 has never been acknowledged as a defeat by a 'foreign' side, largely because most of the Irish players were regulars in the Football League and thus representative of the 'British' game.
5. Interestingly, however, the FA did not take part in the first European Nations Cup in 1958 claiming that it might mean giving up more important games for championship fixtures and that 'too many championships and competitions with their associated intense partisanship may not be for the good of the game' (*FA News*, August 1957).
6. See the *Daily Mirror*'s wonderfully knowing 'apology' to Paul Gascoigne, 17 June 1996.

2 Hooligans and Carnival Fans: Scottish Football Supporter Cultures

Richard Giulianotti

Scotland's contribution to the historical development and cultural richness of world football cannot be denied. Scottish players taught the world the benefits of the 'passing game' at the turn of the century, and became the first to defeat England regularly home and away (Walvin 1994). Scottish players and managers have been vital to the success of British clubs in domestic and European competition, while Scottish coaches and administrators continue to play a leading role in world football's affairs. However, Scotland's influence in the playing and administration of football has been in some decline in recent years. It may even be said to have been outshone by the Scottish supporters, whose international significance has long been noteworthy.

This chapter discusses the major social properties of two key fan subcultures within Scottish football culture: the 'Tartan Army' who follow the Scottish national team abroad, and the 'soccer casuals' who represent the hooligan wing within the supporters of Scottish football clubs. The discussion draws heavily upon the findings of a full-time research project, undertaken between 1990 and 1994 with these two fan groups, and upon subsequent fieldwork (cf. Giulianotti 1996a).[1] This chapter begins with a brief genealogy of Scottish fan violence, and the attempts of the authorities to eradicate 'hooliganism', then examines, in fuller detail, the culture of the soccer casuals and the Tartan Army respectively.

SCOTTISH FANS: THE HISTORICAL BACKGROUND TO THE SOCCER CASUALS AND THE TARTAN ARMY

Traditionally, the Scots regard themselves as the most passionate of football followers. The old aphorism is often trotted out, that Scottish football attracts more spectators per capita than any other European nation apart from Albania. This national obsession is underscored by the failure of any other team sport to rival football with a significant professional base or large spectating tradition.

Scottish supporter cultures have been equally vigorous, in backing their favoured sides and showing hostility towards their opponents. Soon after their formation, Scotland's 'Old Firm' (Rangers and Celtic) were being followed home and away by raucous supporters' clubs (the 'Brake Clubs') (Murray 1984).

Violent confrontations involving these and other supporter groups were not unknown prior to the First World War (Tranter 1995). A 'sectarian' edge was added to the Old Firm rivalry, driven particularly by the deep intolerance of many Protestant Rangers fans and officials towards the Catholic Irish traditions of Celtic (Finn 1991a, 1991b, 1994). By the outbreak of the Second World War, the two sides had generated their own supporter subcultures, most notoriously Rangers' 'Bridgeton Billy Boys' (Murray 1984: 144–5). Ernie Walker, the former Chief Executive of the Scottish Football Association, referred to this legacy in declaring solemnly that football hooliganism was one of the 'gifts' that Scotland had bestowed upon the world game.

During the 1960s, other Scottish clubs began to produce their own supporter subcultures, while Rangers fans frequently caught the media's attention for violence in Scotland, England and abroad. The more notorious incidents involving Rangers fans occurred at Newcastle (1969), Barcelona (1972) and Birmingham (1976), while in Scotland a pitch invasion at Motherwell effectively won Rangers the 1978 league title. A 2–0 deficit was soon converted into a 3–2 win after the disorder, earning Rangers the two points that would later be the margin between them as champions and Aberdeen as runners-up. In 1980 the peak in Old Firm violence occurred when the two sets of fans invaded the pitch and fought one another. Mounted police charged with batons drawn as millions of viewers in the UK and overseas watched on television.

At about this time, the culture of support for the national team was also changing. The 'Tartan Army' had always harboured a popular strain of anti-Englishness, although this was diluted rather than inflamed by the carnival culture of 'Wembley Weekends'. A sharper edge was added during the 1970s, as more liberal dress codes and behavioural norms, less financial preparation and more haphazard accommodation, began to predominate. Significantly, an amorphous political nationalism came into play. The 1970s were marked by the rise of the Scottish Nationalist Party, the Devolution debate, and the discovery of North Sea oil. The relative successes of the national football team also seemed to symbolise how the Scots could leave a decrepit England behind (at least until the 1978 World Cup finals). When the Scots won 2–1 at Wembley in 1977, the celebrating Tartan hordes invaded the pitch, tore up the grass and broke down the goal-posts. The English press roundly condemned such 'hooliganism', while the Scottish media reported the celebrations with some amusement.

In response, the recommendations of the 1978 McElhone Report on Scottish football were enacted through the Criminal Justice (Scotland) Act 1980. The legislation identified alcohol consumption as the major factor in Scottish fan disorder; it banned alcohol from inside grounds, and prohibited the admission of any fan under the influence of drink. Its measures were later introduced in England and in matches overseen by UEFA and FIFA. Though the football and political authorities claimed that the Act was an immediate success, it did not eradicate the male supporter traditions of heavy drinking before and after matches. But it did coincide with a bifurcation in the identity of Scotland's most militant football supporters. On the one hand, the 'Tartan Army' that follows the Scotland national team to matches abroad, began to become known for boisterous, gregarious, heavily intoxicated, yet strictly non-violent behaviour.

Meanwhile, at club level, Scottish domestic football saw the emergence of the 'soccer casuals', a new generation of football hooligans. The Tartan Army took the wearing of Scottish colours and symbols to new lengths (for example, with kilts, tartan suits and even 'fancy dress'). The casuals reflected a more conscious interest in youth cultural style, by exchanging their football motifs for expensive sportswear and designer menswear (with brand names like Lacoste, Diadora, Tacchini, Armani and Chevignon). The casuals also represented a clear empirical challenge to the Scottish authorities' official line, that 'normal' hooliganism had been 'solved' (Home Affairs Committee 1990). This position was also undermined by the violence that overshadowed England–Scotland matches throughout the 1980s, and in which the casuals figured with increasing prominence. In 1989, after around 250 arrests at one match in Glasgow, the oldest international fixture was suspended indefinitely, and has yet to be reactivated in full (Giulianotti 1994a).

BATTLING INTO THE 1990s: THE SCOTTISH CASUALS

The Scottish casuals originated in Aberdeen and Motherwell in 1980–81, and soon appeared in Edinburgh, Dundee and Glasgow. Historically, the major casual groups have followed Aberdeen, Hibernian, Dundee and Dundee United, and Glasgow Rangers. Comparative research into the Scottish casuals was principally undertaken with the rival groups following Aberdeen and Hibernian (Giulianotti 1995a). These casual formations clearly operate along subcultural lines. Classically, each casual formation possesses a particular name or acronym, such as the Hibs casuals' Capital City Service (CCS) or the Aberdeen Soccer Casuals (ASC). In terms of dress, the Scottish casuals are also tied into the wider youth cultural 'casual' style that originated in England in the late 1970s (Redhead and McLaughlin 1985). The main objective of each casual group is to enhance its status vis-à-vis its rivals, and to support its claim to be the 'Number One' casual 'mob' in Scotland. Status is most obviously secured during confrontations, when each side seeks to 'do' the other, by 'standing' and attacking the opposition, 'decking' them, forcing them to back off, or chasing them. Various degrees of prestige and respect are gained by casuals who have stood and fought 'gamely' while still coming off the worst. Those who have turned and run from a confrontation are considered to have been humiliated.

Additionally, shared codes of action exist between the rivals in discriminating between 'legitimate' and 'illegitimate' targets. No prestige (but plenty of ridicule and disdain) is gained from attacking ordinary supporters. However, there are occasions when this principle is regarded by some casuals as optional. First, some of the oldest Aberdeen and Hibs casuals have explained that they appeared in reaction to the random hooliganism of Old Firm fans during the 1970s and 1980s. These old antagonisms are important parts in the 'collective memory' of the casuals, and frequently render most male Old Firm fans as 'fair game' in the eyes of many casuals. Secondly, there may be moments when other rival fan groups 'get out of order' in their actions towards the casuals, resulting in further opportunities for 'legitimate' conflict. Similarly, the casuals themselves may perceive that they will get some 'back up' from the more raucous elements of their club's general support. Nevertheless, long-standing 'ordinary supporters' frequently stated that they did not fear being caught up in football hooliganism because the casuals usually 'fight among themselves'.

During their strongest periods in the mid-1980s, each casual formation was able to attract between 250 and 500 lads for the biggest matches. However, the numbers of Scottish casuals declined sharply during the latter half of the 1980s by 50 to 80 per cent. Currently, peak numbers for the leading groups range from 50 to 100, depending upon the significance of the match and recent history of rivalry between the two sides. Research in Aberdeen and Edinburgh indicates that, within each group, there are different degrees of participation: the leading casual groups tend to have a core of 15 to 20 lads. Hibs and, to a lesser extent, Dundee casuals have previously been augmented by formations of younger casuals ('baby crews'), though these are no longer present. In the last couple of years, Aberdeen casuals have also benefited numerically from the arrival of some younger lads. Nevertheless, each casual formation tends to have a relatively slow turnovers. It is relatively rare for new casuals to appear within the group; instead, the vast majority of casuals tend to have been part of the group for several years. Whereas in the mid- to late 1980s the average age of each group would be in the late teens or early twenties, today the majority of casuals are in their late twenties or early thirties.

The research found relatively little evidence for the argument that football hooligans hail from lower-working-class locales. Aberdeen, Hibs and Dundee casuals shared broader, local perceptions of which localities were the 'roughest', and very few of them were brought up in these estates. The Scottish evidence emphasised the social and economic *incorporation* of the casuals within mainstream society, rather than their structural exclusion. In the limited lexicon of leisure that one finds in conventional class analysis, the casuals would seem to conform more with the economic and cultural attributes of the upper working class rather than the lower working class. The casual 'habitus' requires the individual to possess economic and cultural capital, the essential attributes of which are money, an information network, and knowledge (at local and subcultural levels). Money is important for socialising in pubs, clubs, football grounds and so on; for travelling to matches in the UK or abroad; for purchasing menswear or other commodities.

Individual casuals will also be tied into a large network of football or non-football local relationships, and be well informed on latest news. In this sense, local knowledge can be a resource for future recreation, employment or basic conversation. Consumption of goods also requires a subcultural savoir-faire; casuals exercise a distinctive 'taste' in buying and consuming particular menswear or other leisure products. This has two unanticipated consequences. First, the lack of such knowledge among plainclothes police officers means that they have tended to stand out very visibly when seeking to mingle within casual mobs. Secondly, in terms of masculine style, the casuals quickly eclipsed those supporters that they disparage as 'shirts' or 'Christmas trees' – 'tastelessly' coated in club colours. The casuals have been influential here: the wearing of scarves and club colours among mainstream fans has since declined, while the wearing of 'smart but casual' menswear has increased. In this sense, the casuals have acted as 'cultural intermediaries', through introducing a new style into the football ground, which has been incorporated by many ordinary supporters (cf. Giulianotti 1993a).

The decline in numbers and rise in the average age of the casuals reflect the informal and voluntary social nature of each formation. The casual groups are not organised along the lines of military bureaucracy, into 'Generals', 'Lieutenants', 'Armourers', 'Foot-Soldiers' as the police and media tend to presume. Instead, each formation carries 'top boys', whose status is secured in classically masculine terms, by their regular attendance and 'gameness' in confrontations. 'Top boys' usually make up the 'front-line' in confrontations and represent the most prized targets for opposing casuals. The group's informality is further reflected through the casuals' argot, when they refer to the 'mobs' that each one can muster. More generally, each formation may otherwise be described as a network of small groups of friends. These friendships may owe their origin to long-term involvement within the casual group (especially the case among the 'top boys'). They may also reflect long-term friendships outwith the football scene, such as in work, in school or further education, in the family, or in a particular leisure space (e.g. pub or night-club). This voluntary association of friends allows for two kinds of non-violent activity within the group.

First, there are friends of the casuals who may have no interest in football, but who socialize with the group on a regular basis. Secondly, the 'top boys' know that not all casuals will participate with equal vigour in confrontations. This problematic scenario might be explained in the cost-benefit terms of rational choice theory. In joining the group, each individual obtains some personal reward (socialising with friends, the 'buzz' experienced on match-day, being part of a group with a lot of subcultural prestige). However, they may also be 'free riders', who do not really contribute towards the main goal of the group (securing prestige through violence). If there are many 'free riders', then the entire group is threatened. It may lose status in the eyes of others and become known for 'running'; the group will then fragment as individuals explore other, more personally rewarding leisure activities. Hence, when discussing confrontations, the 'game' lads spend some considerable time evaluating the merits of their peers, directly questioning their commitment, or critically reflecting on the actual fighting power of their mob. Significantly, some of the oldest casuals argue that there have been side benefits to their numerical decline over the years. They suggest that the non-fighting 'free riders' have gradually disappeared, leaving a 'hard core' residue that will always try to 'stand' in battles.

The settings for the casuals' violence have gradually changed in the past fifteen years, usually as the casuals attempt to avoid police measures against them. The casuals themselves emerged after the segregation of rival fans inside football grounds had been established in Scotland. For a relatively short period, so long as the police were generally unaware of the casual style, groups of casuals were able to circumvent this obstacle and find entry into the rival fans' ends. Some casuals then began to 'dress down', wearing cheap and out-dated clothing styles. The new dress code represented a temporary exploration of the 'post-casual' youth style. It also helped to avoid police monitoring, given that officers were now being dispatched to find 'smartly dressed hooligans'. However, by the mid-1980s, the best opportunities for fighting rival fans were clearly to be found outside the ground.

The most important venues were in the streets near to the stadium or, increasingly, at major transport points (such as train or bus stations) and city centre areas (such as pubs or shopping thoroughfares). By the late 1980s, confrontations between rival casuals were on the decline, primarily because of more organised police measures. Casuals travelling to away matches by train usually attracted police escorts which would continue throughout their time in the destination city. During the early 1990s, road travel (by bus or car) tended to be preferred, as this allowed the casuals more freedom of movement, in deciding when and where to arrive in the destination city. However, as the links between the various regional forces became more regular and effective, police escorts became more frequent. Occasionally, the new Criminal Justice Act has been invoked by Scottish police to detain large travelling groups.

Since 1994, the 'national question' has greatly preoccupied the Scottish casuals. When UEFA awarded the 1996 European Championship Finals to England, the Scottish casuals began to form an internal alliance to tackle the large English mobs at the tournament (Finn and Giulianotti 1998). In May 1994, a 120-strong Scottish 'firm' of Hibs, Aberdeen and Dundee casuals travelled to Utrecht for a Holland–Scotland friendly match. Although 47 were arrested and the atmosphere between some of the rival casuals had been tense throughout, the general consensus was that future alliances of Scottish casuals had been helped rather than hindered. At Euro '96, Scotland were drawn to play two matches in Birmingham and one in London (against England). Police initiatives aimed at preventing disorder reached new heights. The English and Scottish forces established a regular liaison; money and other inducements were offered to known casuals to 'spill the beans' on their preparations. Top boys from Edinburgh, Dundee and Aberdeen met prior to the tournament to discuss possible strategies.

Meanwhile, the 1995–96 season passed with few significant incidents, so as to minimise police actions against the casuals. At Euro '96, the main disorder involving the casuals occurred on the day of the match against England. Around 250 travelled south, composed of Aberdeen, Dundee, Rangers, Hibs, Falkirk, and smaller groups of Airdrie, Kilmarnock and Celtic. Before the game, the main action took place in the vicinity of Trafalgar Square and Leicester Square as Scottish casuals attacked a bar full of English lads. After the match, a ring of police at Trafalgar Square struggled to contain the inner group of Scots and the outer group of local hooligans from mixing and fighting. Again, the Scottish alliance was characterised by internal tensions; two of its major constituents had long-standing ties with particular groups of English hooligans, and so had some conflicting loyalties on the day.

Since the tournament, groups within the Hibs and Rangers casuals have been prime movers in forming a more long-standing 'national firm'. A significant number of lads within one of these groups remains opposed to the alliance, while the failure of Aberdeen casuals to join in has also placed them at odds with the new formation.[2] The alliance tends to contravene the 'traditional' casual philosophy, that each team should have its own specific mob which fights rivals at domestic games without recruiting others to 'do their fighting'. Proponents of the alliance would argue that the domestic scene is already too heavily policed, and that a more numerous and settled formation is essential if a Scottish mob is to make an impression in England and abroad (where the action is thought to be).

AMBASSADORS FOR SCOTLAND? THE TARTAN ARMY

Research was undertaken with the Scottish international fans (the 'Tartan Army') at several home and away fixtures, and in particular at three tournaments: the 1990 World Cup finals in Italy, and the 1992 and 1996 European Championship finals in Sweden and England respectively. Two formal surveys were carried out with the Tartan Army at matches in Romania (low prestige) and Sweden (high prestige) (Giulianotti 1994b).[3] The key research findings were that:

1. The Tartan Army is drawn from throughout Scotland, proportionate to population, but with an additional emphasis upon the cities of Glasgow and Edinburgh; a sizeable minority (15–20 per cent) live outside Scotland.
2. 'Old Firm' fans are under-represented, particularly at 'low prestige' matches; but there is an over-representation of supporters of 'intermediate' and small Scottish clubs (such as Clydebank, Ayr United, Partick Thistle, Dunfermline, Meadowbank Thistle/Livingston).
3. The long-standing, 'hard core' support is drawn disproportionately from the 'blue collar elite' (foremen, skilled workers, self-employed tradesmen). By contrast, the bigger tournaments attract greater proportions of younger,

white-collar workers and students. It seems that this process reflects a gradual 'turnover' of supporters within the 'Tartan Army'. It will continue for two
principal reasons: the high price and relative scarcity of tickets for subsequent tournaments (especially France '98 and England '96); and the decom-
position of the 'traditional' working class in Scotland, concomitant with the
rise in service sector employment.

4. Where possible, the supporters, especially the hard core ones, prefer to con-
    trol their own travel and accommodation arrangements. This has given rise to
    one 'hard core' fan setting up his own travel outfit, which is popular with his
    friends and colleagues.

5. Overall, there appears to be no major socio-economic difference between
    Scotland fans and those who follow England, Ireland or Denmark (cf.
    Eichberg 1992; Giulianotti 1996b, 1996c; Williams et al. 1989). It would
    appear, therefore, that a cultural rather than socio-economic explanation
    should be found for the fundamental differences in the identity of 'friendly'
    Scotland fans and 'hooligan' English supporters.

In the last decade, Scotland's international fans have become renowned overseas for their friendly, gregarious and raucous good-humour. This reputation has
been largely derived from their behaviour at major international tournaments, during which they have established a positive and peaceful rapport with their hosts,
opposing fans, police and media. At the 1990 World Cup, the Scots were roundly
praised by their Italian hosts, particularly in their 'base' in Genoa (Giulianotti
1991). At the 1992 European Championships, UEFA awarded the Tartan Army its
'Fair Play' accolade for the best behaved supporters (Giulianotti 1993b, 1995b).

Much of this positive identity is premised upon the 'performance management'
of supporters and the particular interactional rituals that they employ to present
themselves as 'non-violent' or 'anti-hooligan' fans. Internally, the club-based rivalries of Scotland fans are suppressed when they congregate as the 'Tartan Army'.
The Tartan Army's social code decrees that club colours should not be worn, to
avoid reactivating domestic antagonisms. Externally, at matches overseas, a vital
part of the Tartan Army's social repertoire involves establishing their national
identity through a differentiation from England and 'Englishness'. By presenting
themselves as 'anti-English', the Scots play upon the international stereotype that
'English fans are hooligans'; hence, the Scottish fans are also 'anti-hooligan'. The
Scottish authorities have sought to influence the behaviour and reputation of the
Tartan Army. In 1981, the SFA set up the 'Scotland Travel Club' (STC) to distrib-
ute match tickets among its members; any member convicted of football-related
offences is ejected from the STC.

At the major tournaments, the Tartan Army are also accompanied by a
'Scottish Liaison Unit' (consisting of police officers, civil servants and SFA officials), which issues the occasional newsletter among fans, encouraging them to
'keep up the good name of Scotland'. However, the more voluntary and informal

techniques of policing among the fans are far more effective in establishing this friendly reputation. Many of the 'hard core' fans trace the origin of this 'ambassador' identity to a friendly in Israel in 1981, when their behaviour was praised by the local media, in a form of 'labelling' which the Scots found to their liking. Subsequently, techniques of 'self-policing' have emerged to help keep in order unruly or excessively boisterous fans. Meanwhile, the Tartan Army have become adept at winning over local media, posing for photographs or giving interviews that thank them for their hospitality, etc. The Scottish press have tended to mark out their national identity vis-à-vis English-based competitors, by contrasting the friendliness of their compatriots (Scots fans) with the hooliganism of others (the English). Diachronically, this media presentation helps to reproduce the Tartan Army's dominant identity as new members become well aware of the behaviour expected from them.

However, there are variations on the extent to which any or all of these methods of collective presentation are performed or attempted. For example, lower prestige overseas fixtures tend to see some groups of fans attired in their club colours, though those of the Old Firm (especially Rangers) tend to be particularly disparaged by fellow fans. A positive rapport with home fans is not always favoured by locals (e.g. in Portugal and Greece) and can lead to tense stand-offs or isolated incidents of violence (e.g. the throwing of missiles, the mugging of individual Scots). Moreover, self-policing is an imprecise science. There are occasions when Scottish fans have been picked up by police for aggressive behaviour, violent exchanges or damage to property. In such cases, police later release fans 'without charge' or upon reimbursements, allowing the Scottish media and authorities to continue with the 'official' line that Scottish fans do not get arrested.

Scottish newspaper columnists also occasionally question, in a light-hearted style, the extent to which the 'average' Scotland fan provides a positive impression of the nation. Reference is made to his physical blemishes, intoxicated demeanour and incoherent conversation; his unsubtle strategies for seducing local women; and his conviction that in football the Scot has no equal ('Wha's like us?'). Finally, the most searching question concerns the centrality of anti-Englishness in shaping the Scots' national identity. On the one hand, the recent empathy of the English press and politicians towards their fans serves to undermine the Scots' assertion that their southern neighbours are uniformly violent. On the other hand, if Scotland is to be a serious partner in the European Union of the twenty-first century, its sense of national identity will have to be far more forward-thinking than the current mantras about 'anti-Englishness' can ever allow.

This latter criticism draws on a deeper meta-narrative concerning the relationship of football to Scotland's civil society and political identity. For over twenty years, Scottish political and cultural commentators have mused on the nationalist 'false consciousness' of football; where the quest for political self-determination and a truer sense of national identity has come to founder. The kilt and associated tartanry are put forward as invented symbols of this neurotic '90-minute nationalism'.

They may seem to represent something that is uniquely Scottish, and be very popular among the Tartan Army and young Scots generally. But historically, the critics point out, these kitsch items owe their modern presence to patronage by English monarchs and consumption by foreign tourists (Nairn 1981; McIlvanney 1991; McCrone 1992). Meanwhile, the Tartan Army and the Scottish casuals would seem to extend the 'schizophrenic' Scottish character into the football arena, through two extreme, Jekyll-and-Hyde forms of national identity.

This dark critique continues the misguided search for some kind of political nationalism within Scottish fan culture. It would be fairer to accept that Scottish football culture, like any other sport, is not a passive mirror of the wider society's structural patterns and conflicts. The game has 'its own tempo, its own evolutionary laws, its crises, in short, its specific chronology' (Bourdieu 1991a: 358). Consequently, the investigation of football's relationship to political conflict or ideological control is better served by focusing these issues upon the sport itself. In the case of the Tartan Army, there is little doubt that their activities have the capacity to upset the form of social order which the Scottish football authorities, and their fellow institutions, would prefer. The activities of the Tartan Army overseas represent an extension of traditional, Scottish working-class public festivals (e.g. Hogmanay, the Glasgow Fair which witnesses thousands of workers holidaying *en masse* in Blackpool). As a form of male carnival, the supporters engage in prodigious carousing, talking, reminiscing, socialising with new and old acquaintances, heavy drinking and sexual adventure.

The carnival culture certainly involves the collapsing of internal class distinctions. Additionally, it is relatively open to the involvement of ethnic minorities, though some significant differences may exist between the traditional licence of the Tartan Army and the generally abstemious lifestyle of Scotland's large Asian community. More radically, the carnival culture also includes symbolic and discursive challenges to the Scottish authorities. The STC's rules of membership require that Scotland fans adorn themselves only in 'moderate' colours while drink should be avoided; both restrictions are observed by fans only in their breach. The carnival culture occasionally involves abusing and mocking Scottish football officials and other authority figures. These moments of 'excess' tend to be interpreted with little humour by their targets: sports journalists who are criticised write poisoned condemnations of the Tartan Army; officials who are abused send out petty warnings to fans about the possible consequences of tarnishing their good reputation.

Initially, the major threat to the reputation of the Tartan Army would appear to come from any matches against England. However, at Euro '96, there were few signs that the mainstream Tartan Army was interested in fighting English hooligans. Most took advantage of the heavy police presence in Birmingham, in the city centre or at camp-sites, to drink peacefully into the small hours. Even at the fixture against England in London, the Scottish fans congregated in their hotel bars or known 'Scottish' pubs without any real molestation. The only threat from

England hooligans came (predictably) at Trafalgar Square or outside the major train stations. Future disorder at England–Scotland fixtures will almost certainly be precipitated by English hooligans rather than the mainstream Tartan Army. The violent anti-Englishness of the Scots appears to have dissipated into a ritual form of nationalist rhetoric. However, their previous excesses in London remain long in the 'collective memory' of English fans, in the same way the Hibs or Aberdeen casuals recall the disorder of Old Firm fans during the 1970s and 1980s. Hence, it would appear that, for English hooligans not just the Scottish casuals, but most members of the Tartan Army, remain a legitimate target on match-day.

Consequently, the major internal challenge to the Scots' positive reputation would appear to come from the alliances of Scottish casuals. Relations between the Scottish casuals and Tartan Army are rather complex. When they gather as distinct social collectives, the two sides exhibit a frosty antagonism towards one another. At the individual and small group level, however, the two sides tend to mix relatively freely, swapping drinks, stories, jokes and banter. Some of the Tartan Army's fans are also, at domestic level, part of casual formations. They juggle the two identities of ambassador and hooligan without much trouble, so long as the presence and intent of the Scottish casuals are not particularly large or violent.

To date, an important asset to the Tartan Army has been its positive portrayal by the Scottish and overseas media. However, there are signs that the Scottish media are beginning to hedge their bets. In the early 1990s, Hibs casuals were the subject of a short 'moral panic' within the Edinburgh media, which briefly challenged the official line that Scotland did not have a 'hooliganism problem' (Giulianotti 1994c). Since then, important changes within the Scottish media have underpinned the 'rediscovery' of football hooliganism. Most 'British' newspapers have intensified their battle for markets by creating 'Scottish editions' with more space devoted to Scottish-based stories. Meanwhile, local and regional newspapers in Scotland have adopted the tabloid format, with more down-market and sensationalist stories. A new generation of young 'news reporters' has been recruited who have been able to establish contacts with, or garner information about, the Scottish casuals with greater ease than their older colleagues. In this new context, it seems inevitable that some sections of the Scottish media will also cover more negative news about the Tartan Army should the occasion arise.

Collectively, the Tartan Army and the Scottish casuals represent the latest points in the long genealogy of Scottish fan culture. In its 'traditional' phase, the disorderly aspects of the supporter groups seems to have been associated with informal supporter clubs. More historical research in this area is necessary for firmer conclusions to be drawn (cf. Tranter 1998: 46–8). The 'early modernity' of football hooliganism begins with the emergence of specific, violent subcultures within the general body of club supporters, initially with the Old Firm, and subsequently at most other clubs. In typically modernist fashion, the police and political authorities intervene to 'fix' the problem through legislation in 1980, but by then Scotland's fan subcultures have already moved on, into 'late modernity'.

The reflexivity of Scottish fans becomes apparent, as the casuals and the Tartan Army explore different identity options relating to violence. The casual formations demarcate themselves from earlier hooligan styles, and become engaged in a relatively exclusive battle to secure domestic supremacy. The Tartan Army emerges with a conscious code of non-violent conduct, its aim being to promote Scottish identity abroad by differentiating its members from English 'hooligans'.

Latterly, the condition of these two fan groups would appear to have entered the 'post-modern' phase. For the casuals, the question of alliances has transformed the domestic scene; hooliganism has been 'rediscovered' through fragmentary discourses within the Scottish media and authorities. For the Tartan Army there is a deeper paradox. On one hand, the English authorities are questioning the idea that their national fans are predominantly hooligan. On the other, when Scotland play England, the 'friendly' Tartan Army is unable to defend itself (in word or deed) from attack by this hooligan 'minority'. Perhaps a future post-modern solution will involve the Tartan Army accommodating the Scottish casuals as a defensive unit for tackling any violent opponents.

Notes

1. The research was funded by the UK Economic and Social Research Council.
2. At one Dundee v. Aberdeen fixture in Edinburgh in late 1997, Aberdeen fans were attacked first by a mob of Dundee boys, and then by an alliance of some Hibs and Rangers casuals.
3. 250 Scotland fans travelled to the match in Romania in October 1991; 82 were interviewed. Around 5,000 travelled to the tournament in Sweden in June 1992; 440 were interviewed (Giulianotti 1994b).

3 The Coming of Age: The World Cup of France '98

Geoff Hare and Hugh Dauncey

France is not commonly regarded as a major footballing nation, yet football is the most popular sport in terms of players and spectators. Football and other modern sports were imported into France in the late nineteenth century from England. The first football club was founded in Le Havre in 1872. Since 1894 and the first amateur 'national' championship between six Parisian clubs, the game has become a national sport, professionalised in 1931, but still retaining nearly two million registered amateur players and 23,000 clubs, far ahead of any other sport, including rugby. Football's early development in France, as in Britain, has much in common with the creation of a shared sense of place in the emerging urban working-class communities. But the French game differs from Britain organisationally. Its regulatory system and its governing bodies and clubs have been shaped by the French state's concept of public service, of republican and democratic values, and of centralist interventionism, as opposed to laissez-faire individualism (Miège 1993). French administrators, following in the footsteps of the founder of the Olympic movement, de Coubertin, have helped move football beyond the national context, at a time when its English inventors were turning their backs on Europe and the rest of the world.

Hosting the 1998 World Cup Finals reflects France's long commitment to the world game, despite limited success at both club and international levels. Over the years, nonetheless, Frenchmen have promoted the international dimension of football. Despite opposition, the world governing body, FIFA, was created in 1904 on the initiative of French and Dutch representatives, and the President of the French Football Federation, Jules Rimet, was elected as FIFA President in 1920. The World Cup competition was created by Henri Delaunay, secretary of the French Football Federation, and Jules Rimet, whose name was borne by the original trophy. The idea of a European Club competition came from Gabriel Hanot, editor of the famous French daily sports paper *L'Equipe*. After the English champions Wolverhampton Wanderers had beaten Moscow Spartak and the Hungarian champions Honved in 1954, the *Daily Mail* claimed that they were world club champions. The editor of *L'Equipe* was sceptical and proposed a more structured way of deciding Europe's top club. UEFA had only just come into existence and refused to take responsibility for organising a competition. Eventually *L'Equipe* contacted the relevant clubs, rules were agreed, and FIFA authorised the competition, before UEFA finally agreed to organise it from September 1955 onwards, with the final in Paris (Thomas et al. 1991: 96–8). The European

Nations Championships are attributed to Henri Delaunay, who died before the finals took place, again in France, in 1960. Both in its organisational structures and its international competitions, then, football as a world game owes much to France.

SPORT AND NATIONAL DIVISIONS: CATHOLIC AND SECULAR FOOTBALL

Initially, before the First World War, football in France was played by a social elite, with an estimated 2,000 players by 1900 (Bourg 1986). British workers played in the Channel ports and Paris before the French joined in. French students who had studied in Britain imported the game, particularly to Paris. Football, however, had difficulty getting wider recognition; the widely read sports paper *L'Auto* generally devoted its front page to rugby, despite the fact that football had over twice as many registered teams as rugby. By 1911 there were about 2,000 football clubs (Thomas et al. 1991: 108–12; Wahl 1990a: 126–9).

The French took on further footballing ideas from Britain. The anglophile Henri Delaunay attended the F.A. Cup Final at Crystal Palace in 1902 and was inspired to establish an equivalent in France, partly for its own sake, but also to unify his country's four football federations. The competition had political overtones because, in its early history, football was not immune from the major ideological split in French society, between the secularising republican Left and the Catholic traditionalist Right.[1]

The French Catholic clergy reacted to the secular educational reforms of the 1880s by creating local recreational facilities for young people under a national co-ordinating body. With the support of the Parisian middle classes, the 'Patronages' chose soccer rather than rugby as a team sport and helped spread the game throughout the country. (Augustin 1990: 101). National service was compulsory for young men and football was a common recreation, with inter-regimental and inter-regional games, thereby contributing to the game's popularity. However, in the course of the interminable Dreyfus Affair at the turn of the century, attitudes to the role of the army – torn between the traditionalist ideology of its officer class and its republican duties to the state – were sharply divided.

A simple incident is illustrative of the effect on soccer of these various rifts. A dispute between the different football federations led to the resignation from FIFA of the lay omnisports federation USFSA, the only one recognised by the French Army. In February 1912, a French international team included a national serviceman named Triboulet. He asked for a 36-hour pass, and while the army gave him leave, they forbade him to play, since the national team were not playing under the banner of the USFSA. Triboulet took the train to Saint-Ouen, with the intention of sitting in the stand, however, some players did not arrive and no replacements had been arranged, leaving France with only ten players. Triboulet was persuaded to play, and turned out to be the star of the match, scoring the second goal and making two others in France's 4–1 victory over Switzerland. The next day a proud comrade sent a newspaper cutting to Triboulet's commanding officer; the national hero found himself serving a week in an army gaol for disobeying orders (Thibert and Rethacker 1991: 32–3).

In the face of these divisions, Delaunay, a former player who became secretary governor of the Church's Catholic Sport Co-Federation – the Féderationé Gymnastique et Sportive des Patronages de France (FGSPF), was instrumental in founding an umbrella football body (Comité Français Interfédéral – CFI). However, it took until 1918 to organise a national knock-out Cup competition open to all clubs irrespective of their governing body. The success of the French Cup both increased football's popularity and its organisational unity, leading to the transformation of the CFI into a single French Football Federation in 1919 (Thibert and Rethacker 1991: 40). Social and ideological conflicts continued to structure relations until after the Second World War. Yet, the unification of 1919 is a tribute to football's unifying power which was becoming the nation's mass sport with specialist press such as the magazine *Football* founded in 1910, and *France Football* founded in 1923 (Wahl 1989: 352).

MULTICULTURALISM AND RACISM

Just as football's integrative force was stronger than this Franco-French quarrel in bringing the Federations and Leagues together, so football has reflected other social conflict since the 1970s, particularly the issues of multiculturalism and racism. Among the great French players figure members of the different epochs of immigration: Polish, Italian, Spanish, Black African, North African. Football remains a special road to social mobility in French society, taken by ethnic minority players like Kopa(szewski) (Poland), Djorkaeff (Armenia), Platini (Italy), Fernandez (Spain), and non-white players from Francophone Africa (Tigana), the Maghreb (Zidane), French West Indies (Trésor), and New Caledonia (Karembeu) (Beaud and Noiriel 1990). Despite the terracing self-publicity of small neo-fascist groups, tolerance and integration have been fostered through the fans' idolisation of ethnic players (Beaud and Noiriel 1990: 93). Current concerns about multi-culturalism and 'traditional' French values, however, mean that multi-ethnic clubs and the national team are a focus of debate and the target of criticism from the extreme right.

During the 1996 European Championships in England, a furore arose when Jean-Marie Le Pen, the leader of the Front National (FN), questioned whether the multi-ethnic team could properly represent France, or even sing the Marseillaise. Le Pen's xenophobia was unanimously condemned by other politicians, partly in honest adherence to France's policies on immigrant integration and partly in tune with the surge in patriotic feeling inspired by the French team.[2]

French club football has occasionally been tainted by racist behaviour, especially in the south-east coast and parts of Marseille which have been a fertile breeding ground for FN support. In 1989 when the FN was getting 15 per cent of the vote in Marseille, racist taunts were directed towards visiting black players (Broussard 1990: 192), reflecting of underlying tensions in French society. In the late 1980s, some skinheads following Paris-Saint-Germain seemed to be using football as a far-right recruiting ground, but overall, the fact that the much-admired Youri Djorkaeff is the son of a previous French national team captain of Armenian origin reflects the generally good integration of ethnic players into French football.

NATIONAL CONSCIOUSNESS AND FOOTBALL MYTH

When football acquires national popularity, it can contribute significantly to the formation of narratives of collective national identity. But to what extent did the nation's interest become focused on French football as a purveyor of stories, images, symbols and rituals of national significance? A major event was the national team's first victory over England in 1921 – on the anniversary of Napoleon's death. The growing number of international matches, and the hosting of the 1938 World Cup helped create a shared sense of national identity in supporting the country, especially since the different Federations had settled their differences. The problem was that France was not notably successful in internationals.

The symbiosis of football and politics was recognised early when the French Cup Final became an annual national ritual, with the President of the Republic meeting the teams and presenting the Cup. The other symbiosis, between football and the press, led to the creation of a pre-war star system to exploit interest in the game. Although this began in earnest in the 1950s with the growth of radio and photo-magazines (Wahl 1989: 287), there were significant early stars. One hero of the 1920s was perhaps the only famous goalkeeper in French history, Pierre Chayrigue, a player for Red Star with a huge personality to match his frame. He was reputed to claim enormous expenses and medical bills in the days of shamateurism. On at least one occasion he arrived at FFF headquarters on crutches, and left with a large cheque in his pocket ... without his crutches (Thibert and Rethacker 1991: 65). Despite his size, this picture of Chayrigue fits the common national stereotype from Maupassant to Astérix of the wily little French individualist putting one over on those in authority.

EUROPEAN SUCCESS AND SWEDEN 1958: TELEVISED MEMORIES

Before live pictures, stories such as these formed the shared folk memory of the game. The main successes of French teams coincided with the rise of national television. During the 1950s, European club competitions and France's unexpectedly good performance in the World Cup aroused national interest in football as a vector of national values. In the first season of the European Cup (1955–6) the French public became increasingly supportive of Stade de Reims, playing all their home matches in Paris to allow bigger gates (Wahl 1989: 315). Reims dominated French football in the 1950s, winning six French championships in twelve years from 1949. With their star forward Raymond Kopa, they lost 4–3 in the European Cup final in Paris to Real Madrid. The national team capitalised on the interest in Reims. France finished third in the 1958 World Cup with striker Just Fontaine scoring a record 13 goals in six matches. Radio coverage by Europe No. 1 (Bourg 1986: 128) provided the live link with the French public; the commentator underlined the importance of the event by celebrating France's two semi-final goals with a chauvinistic '*Vive la France*'.

Later, the national imagination was caught by Saint-Etienne 'les Verts', during the 1970s. Dominating French football for well over a decade,[3] they found themselves in European competition every season bar three from 1967 to 1983. The Saint-Etienne team had bravura and charismatic players, their European matches had suspense, and were televised live. Developing more slowly than in Britain, French television could, by the end of the sixties, reach the entire nation (Bureau 1986: 97–8). 1975 saw the Greens defeated in the European Cup semi-final by Beckenbauer's Bayern Munich. But the match that remains in the memory of the watching public is a quarter-final fixture against Dynamo Kiev in 1976. Having lost the first leg 2–0, Saint-Etienne snatched victory in extra time in the home leg. Defeat in the final against Bayern Munich (again) at Hampden Park, Glasgow, by a single goal confirmed, for Wahl (1989: 315) 'the national public's attachment to losing heroes courageously resisting inhuman adversaries'.

LOSING HEROES: FRANCE v. GERMANY 1982 (... 1870, 1914, 1940)

Wahl's analysis applies to the next major trauma in French football: Seville 1982. Thirty million French television viewers (65 per cent of the national audience) sat entranced. In reaching the semi-finals of the World Cup, the French national team displayed an attacking panache which won worldwide support. As the French captain, Platini, and his team prepared to meet West Germany, however, the French people needed little reminding that France versus Germany had a history beyond football.

The tricolours with their multi-coloured team were representing France from Dunkirk to Tamanrasset, playing football as beautiful as a fireworks display. The game was seen figuratively as the Technicolor of France versus the black-and-white of Germany (Bureau 1986: 120–5). The most powerful images that remain are of the infamous turning point: in the fiftieth minute, at 1–1, the German goalkeeper Schumacher rushed out of his penalty area and crashed into Battiston, as he chased a through ball. Then came the shocked concern of Platini as he held his unconscious team-mate. The Dutch referee neither awarded a penalty, nor sent off the goalkeeper. The French attacked relentlessly, Rocheteau had a goal disallowed, Amoros hit the bar in the ninetieth minute; Trésor, then Giresse put France 3–1 ahead in the first ten minutes of extra time. A tiring French team conceded a goal before the turn-round and then an equaliser in the 108th minute. In the penalty shoot-out, each side scored four out of the first five penalties. In sudden death Bossis missed, Hrubesch scored. The French team manager, Hidalgo, remained generous and dignified in defeat.

The long intensity of the match plunged a nation into a state of shock, drained by the perceived injustice of it all (Bureau 1986: 97–8). For the TV sports journalist, Georges de Caune, the Battiston–Schumacher incident revived emotions felt during the Second World War (Lecoq 1997: 132). A whole nation experienced the catharsis of shared disappointment for their tragic national heroes. Manager and players immediately entered the pantheon of valiant French sporting losers, like so many Racinian heroes unable to sustain the unequal struggle against the inevitable course of destiny. When a few days later Germany lost to Italy in the final, *France Football* headlined: '*Justice est faite*' (Justice has been done).

Television constantly replayed the first French victory in the major tournament at the European Nation's Cup in the Parc des Princes in 1984. Fans celebrated deliriously in the streets, temporarily diverted from worry over unemployment and socialist economic policy. Hidalgo was proclaimed a national hero; '*Platinix le goalois*', the tournament's top scorer with nine goals, was depicted as a national treasure, a legend in France and a legend in Italy, where he had already won numerous accolades. Losing in the semi-final to Germany in the next World Cup in 1986, and finally finishing third, seems in comparison with the previous events an anti-climax, but nicely fits the Wahl thesis of inevitable and courageous defeats for '*les petits Français*'.

When Marseille dominated the French championship the nation identified with them perceiving them as carrying national values in their European matches. The first European success mobilised national support for Marseille, French league champions five years in succession, 1989–93. After two European semi-finals, they were denied on penalties a European Cup win in 1991 by a negative Red Star Belgrade. The same old story prevailed, gallant losers for the French public. Strengthened by imports Boksic and Voeller, Marscille finally beat Milan in Munich in 1993 by a single goal. Not to be outdone, Paris-Saint-Germain won the European Cup Winners Cup in 1996, and then finished runners up to Barcelona the following year, making it five successive European semi-finals, a feat equalled only by Real Madrid and Ajax Amsterdam.

Subsequent club and national teams have woven a thread of shared experiences, whether mediated by press, radio or television, that Wahl has seen as constituting narratives of collective national identity: pride and elation at French style, artistry and courage often dissolving into heroic disappointment and a feeling that the fates are more often than not against France. The detail of Wahl's analysis may no longer hold true since the recent European victories. Indeed current

French football guides recognise that French success in football has been increasing: their international players are much in demand by richer foreign clubs, while those remaining in France managed to ensure that an unprecedented ten clubs qualified for the three major European club competitions in 1997–8. '*Une France qui gagne*' is the up-beat title of a review of France in Europe over the last decade, putting France third behind Italy and Germany (Rocheteau and Chaumier 1997: 950).

THE NATIONAL TEAM AND FRENCH POLITICAL STYLES

One of the myths commonly mediated through football relates to national styles of play. Beaud and Noiriel (1990: 93–4) see judgements on national style as a construction, a discourse that maintains chauvinism and xenophobia. Nationalism commonly emerges from commentaries and rituals that surround the game (national anthems, flags, exchange of pennants, red-white-and-blue strips). Commentators and journalists have frequently described France's style of play as more intelligent and adventurous and less physical or defensive than that of their northern neighbours. Nussle (1986: 24–5) for example describes French teams of the Platini era as playing 'champagne football' characterised by improvisation, vivacity, a sparkling passing game, but one that was also vulnerable and fragile.

One of the best histories of French football (Thibert and Rethacker 1991: 57) picks out the lasting impact of the Uruguayans at the 1924 Olympic Games in Paris. The Uruguayans were the revelation of the tournament, bringing a new type of football to France. Beating France 5–1 in the quarter-finals in front of 45,000 home spectators, they inspired admiration in giving the French a lesson. Their style has been variously described as combining artistry, entertainment, virtuosity, and professionalism. Their influence in establishing a French style of play (or perhaps in establishing a conceptual framework through which to talk about football and style) was maintained by continued success: Olympic champions again in 1928 and the first World Cup winners in 1930.

The Uruguayan dialectic emerges in descriptions of the French national style by national team managers over the years. Albert Batteux, coach of the successful Reims teams, and successful national manager in 1958, and Michel Hidalgo, manager of the Platini teams of the 1980s, promoted an open, attacking style giving full scope to individual brilliance. Georges Boulogne, national team manager in the 1970s was a partisan of '*football labeur*' (football as hard work). Both approaches have the same basic conception of French national character as undisciplined and individualistic, one seeing it positively, the other negatively. Boulogne's response was to exercise total authority over players to instil solidarity and team-work in players who are naturally individualistic because of competition for places (Wahl 1989: 297–9).

During the May '68 events, Boulogne was attacked by players occupying the FFF offices. As the Federation's coaching director in the late sixties, he had been developing ideas on what he called 'modern football'. For France to succeed, he claimed football had to stop being an enjoyable game (*'une activité ludique'*) and to become rigorous and disciplined. In 1969, after Gaullist hegemony was re-established, Boulogne took over the national team. He saw France's failure to qualify for the 1970 and 1974 World Cups as proof that his country was not a sporting nation. He was rewarded by becoming national technical director in 1972 and was thenceforth able to impose his views (Wahl 1989: 318; Wahl 1990b: 80–2). By contrast, Michel Hidalgo, former head of the players' union, took over as national team manager in 1976. A firm follower of Batteux's attacking style, and of *'le plaisir de jouer'*, he instructed players to go out and enjoy themselves (Wahl 1989: 321). Victory at all costs was not the main object; style became as important as success. The French and Italian publics seemed to agree. Agnelli, president of Juventus, described how Platini brought glamour and adventure to the traditionally Teutonic style of Juventus, adding that his greatest pleasure in life had been watching him play (Leclair 1997: 74–5).

Style of play and political dogma are, in the eyes of some analysts, intertwined. Wahl sees Boulogne's critics in 1968 as harping back nostalgically to a less restrictive past, rejecting notions of industry and performance, just as students and workers were rejecting the consumer society (Wahl 1990: 81–2). Equally the authoritarianism of Boulogne may be seen as reflecting the dominant Gaullist ideology, and while possibly in tune with the way industrial society was developing, was arguably out of step with a post-May 1968 society. De Gaulle reputedly worried about how to govern a country that produced 365 different cheeses and found part of the solution in a voluntarist state. The Gaullist presidential regime sought to give the state and its elected leaders the authority to take decisions in the national interest and cut across the myriad of individual interests represented in parliament's multi-party system. Post-Gaullist France has sought to dismantle some of the authoritarian institutional and mental structures of an earlier age. Hidalgo was more in tune with Mitterrand's France of the 1980s which culminated in both Mitterrand's presidential re-election campaign of 1988 and the Bicentenary of 1989 led by the fashion designer Jean-Paul Goude, both manifesting the triumph of style over substance. As co-director of the World Cup Organising Committee, Platini's desire to turn France 1998 into thirty-three days of *'fête'* is in direct line of descent from Batteux, Hidalgo and May '68. But of course it hides the reality behind events on the pitch: the biggest commercial sporting exposition ever.

Professional football, still reliant on municipal subsidies, has become a key tool in local politics, used, sometimes corruptly, by ambitious local mayors to further their local and national political careers. This aspect of the 'French exception' has come into conflict with European developments and France's national ambitions to create 'a strong France in an independent Europe'. French clubs are essentially non-profit-making organisations, operating within the context of high taxation and exceptionally high social costs on business. They have had to come to terms with the European Single Market and the commercial realities of the Bosman ruling (Miège 1996). The result has been an exodus of the 1996 national squad to English, Italian and Spanish clubs. French clubs, with their low attendances cannot compete with player earnings abroad (Rocheteau and Chaumier 1997: 555). Paris-Saint-Germain was the only French club to sign a top foreign star (Marco Simone of Milan) in 1997–8.

An event that somehow symbolised the decline of French football's reputation was the Furiani Stadium disaster – France's Hillsborough. The ground is home of the Corsican club Bastia, who had defied all comers in 1977–8 to reach the final of the UEFA Cup. Cramped between sea, railway lines and hills, with surrounding barbed wire giving a fortress-like impression, the ground was described in the 1980s as the oldest and most dilapidated stadium in Division 1. The passionate fans saw the club as signifying Corsican nationalism against French oppression, and stood only a metre from the pitch. Their hostility destroyed opposition spirit as Bastia acquired an invincible reputation at home (Urbini 1986: 99–100). At a Cup semi-final against Marseille in 1992, temporary scaffolding that had been erected to increase the ground's 8,500 capacity collapsed killing eleven spectators and injuring 700. The French authorities, out of respect for the dead, had the sense to cancel the whole competition and not play the Final. In the season following Furiani, football was at a low ebb, with blood on its hands, and the shameful smell of bribery and corruption emerging from the Marseille-Valenciennes-Tapie affair. The malaise was furthered by a pitiful elimination from the World Cup after shock results against Bulgaria and Israel, and internal conflict between the clubs and the Federation.

NOUVEAU REGIMES

French national identity owes much to football. From the fifties to the eighties, a recurrent national self-image, 'the Astérix complex', has been purveyed through football (Duhamel 1985). More recently, expectation of inevitable but honourable defeat for '*les petits Français*' has given way to a greater national self-confidence. Footballing successes in the late 1980s and the 1990s, especially the victory of Marseille in the European Cup, have confirmed a sense of France as a nation coming of age. A major soccer guide expresses this as '*Enfin, la France perd sa virginité!*' ('At last France has lost her virginity') (Rocheteau and Chaumier 1997: 953).

Footballing success confirms that France can now play with the big boys, just as the world's fourth economic power now expects to lead in European politics. The 1998 World Cup is one more expression of this new-found national self-confidence. Football has acted as a vector for these national values via its mediation. Not only has the written press, especially the sports daily *L'Equipe*, promoted football, but broadcasting and football have promoted each other's growth and popularity. The early popularisation of television was significantly aided by the coverage of the French Cup Final from 1950 onwards, and then the Saint-Etienne European matches (Lecoq 1997: 133). Now, the biggest sponsor of football is commercial television, and the owner of the biggest club in France, Paris-Saint-Germain, is the highly profitable subscription television channel Canal Plus. The future of French digital television, which has come on stream in France before any other European country, is tied to the selling of pay-per-view subscriptions to French football (Dutheil 1996: 2–3; Bonnot et al. 1997: 9). In parallel to this commercialisation of the game are moves to persuade the government to allow French clubs to be quoted on the stock exchange as ordinary limited companies (De Gasquet et al. 1997: 58). The risks are high and football will either take off in France after 1998 or enter another phase of serious financial difficulty and possible decline.

France's formation as a modern nation state occurred during the nineteenth century, too early for football to have a major initial impact.[4] However, national consciousness and identity are not acquired once and for all in a society. As Schlesinger (1991), Hall (1992), Barker (1997) and others have argued, after Anderson (1983: 15–16), the nation is an 'imagined community'; national cultural identity is constructed and reproduced by narratives of the nation by which stories, images, symbols and rituals represent shared meanings of nationhood. Hence, collective identity is always provisional and has to be continually reinforced, and it is via the media that people are encouraged to imagine the meaning of nationhood. The routine of daily life is only occasionally interrupted by shared consciousness of events of national importance (Giddens 1985), the key collective rituals that impinge on national cultural identity are important political events, such as Presidential elections, serious disasters, national commemorations, state funerals ... or major sporting events.

Notes

1. This ideological divide is sometimes still visible, as for example in the market town of Auxerre, where alongside the First Division club, AJ Auxerroise, is Le Stade Auxerrois, still in the regional leagues that its neighbour emerged from in the 1960s. Le Stade was founded as a secular sports club, whereas AJ was the Church sports club. Some older supporters of Le Stade still refuse to set foot in the AJ stadium across the way (Sowden 1997: 10–11).

2. In January 1998, a scandal broke out over the views allegedly expressed by Christian Karembeu, a French internationalist who stated that he felt as much Kanak (indigenous New Caledonian) as French and was using his selection for the national team to publicise the problems of his birthplace.

3. Saint-Etienne were champions nine times between 1964 and 1981; and Cup winners five times between 1968 and 1977.

4. This was achieved, in the face of major ideological conflict throughout the nineteenth century, through strengthening the ancien régimés already centralised administration, the imposition by Napoleon of a Civil Code, and the spread of the standard French language, replacing provincial dialects, a process completed by the innovation in the 1880s of a free, universal and secular primary school system promoting republican values. The growing transport infrastructure following the building of a national rail network in the nineteenth century, followed by three military invasions (1870, 1914, 1940), helped unite the country behind nationalistic values.

4 Football Identity and Youth Culture in Germany
Udo Merkel

Germany has a remarkable record in World Cup tournaments, having finished as champions on three occasions (1954 in Switzerland, 1974 in Germany and 1990 in Italy). Germany has also won the European Championships three times, most recently in 1996. German football, at the domestic level, is equally global in its horizons, the *Bundesliga* (first division) currently has about 100 foreign players, not only from the 'traditional' football nations, e.g. Brazil and Argentina, but also from the United States and Iran. The match commentators at any *Bundesliga* match require specialist linguistic skills (to pronounce names like Akpoborie, Kovacevic, Rydlewicz, Tyskiewicz and Raducioiu) and a detailed understanding of world geography, to explain the origins of players like Duisburg's Bachirou Salou, who hails from Togo.

Many foreigners are elevated by German fans to the status of local heroes, for example Bulgaria's Krassimir Balakov (Stuttgart), the Brazilian Giovanni Elber (Bayern Munich) and the Portuguese Paolo Sousa (Borussia Dortmund). In addition, foreign managers coach top teams, for example, the Italians Trappatoni at Munich and Nevio Scala at Dortmund, while Huub Stevens from the Netherlands manages Schalke 04. Less cosmopolitan and international however is the German fan culture. By focusing on young supporters, their behaviour and their relationship with the game, two themes will be explored in this chapter: first, the construction, reconstruction and celebration of various personal identities, and secondly, the cultural and social conflicts within the world of football, which both mirror and shape wider social developments.

THE BEGINNINGS: CONFLICTS AND TENSIONS

The Europeanisation of soccer is well documented and certain common patterns are clearly identifiable (Mason 1986). However, there are some major differences concerning the mode and speed of assimilation of soccer into the various national cultures; the (changing) class base of football; the degree of resistance towards the game; and the process of professionalisation. Football was first played in Germany in the last quarter of the nineteenth century not only in the coastal areas, but also in the regions close to the fashionable spas as well as in the nation's trade and industrial centres. Initially the players were drawn from the young male members of the growing middle class, then after the First World War from the ranks of the working class, particularly in the industrial heartland of Germany. This region, the Ruhr, began playing the game and has since remained a dominant geographical stronghold of football. Today about one third of *Bundesliga* teams come from here; famous Ruhr clubs are Schalke 04 based in Gelsenkirchen, the most legendary working-class club in Germany, who won the UEFA Cup in the 1996/97 season, and Borussia Dortmund who won the European Champions League in the same year.

Football's breakthrough in Germany was less a result of private middle-class initiative than of the emergence of workers' sports clubs and associations (Eisenberg 1990: 265). Following the introduction of the eight-hour working day in 1919, football became the sport of the German industrial working class. However, football's arrival and diffusion was not unproblematic, as the powerful *Turnbewegung* gymnastics movement did not appreciate English competitive team sports and actively tried to prevent their spread (Merkel 1998). In some areas, such as Bavaria, football was actually banned until 1913 (Murray 1994). Although, in Germany, football is traditionally considered a working-class sport, the middle-class contribution particularly during football's infancy, should not be neglected. The speed of football's growth in the Ruhr clearly indicates support among the industrial middle class.

Influential elements of local industrial and commercial capital recognised the potential benefits of supporting and promoting sport, in particular football, as an alternative to the state's policies of suppression. They allied themselves with working-class demands for exciting leisure activities against rigorous state control of the German proletariat (Gehrmann 1988). When a group of middle-class soccer clubs founded the German Football Association (the DFB) in 1900, one of its first tasks was to identify 'appropriate' member organisations. Working class clubs were identified as 'wild' and therefore excluded. However, the DFB soon realised it could not ignore the strength and number of working-class football teams and came to accept that conciliation was better than conflict. Consequently, the DFB forced these clubs to establish a constitution and a board of mainly middle-class directors who also functioned as creditors. This arrangement guaranteed the DFB access to the clubs and permitted them a degree of control.

The official history of the DFB suggests a peaceful coexistence between middle- and working-class clubs. However, a number of incidents show that there were limits to the flexibility of the dominant groups. Since the number of football clubs was constantly growing the DFB organised them into several regional divisions, with promotion and relegation. When it became apparent that working-class teams were going to dominate German football, the DFB decided in 1923 to abandon promotion or relegation for at least two years. Officially, the objective was to fight the rise in unfair play which was apparently caused by over-competitiveness and sparked incidents of hooliganism among the fans (Gehrmann 1988: 95). In reality, the DFB was deliberately denying the best working-class teams promotion to the highest divisions (cf. Teske 1977: 59).

Some years later, 'amateurism' was employed to discriminate against working-class players. The issue of professionalism had been controversial since the DFB was founded and reached a climax in the 1920s after its legalisation in Hungary, Austria and Czechoslovakia. At this time, football in Germany was still a predominantly amateur game. Only compensation for lost working hours and expenses was paid officially to players. Professionals were strictly prohibited from DFB competitions. In 1930, the most successful working-class club, Schalke 04, was disqualified as players were given ten Marks instead of five as expenses: 'This practice of giving players more money than allowed was certainly no exception but rather the rule' (Lindner 1983: 56). Such examples clearly show that the relationship between middle- and working-class football enthusiasts was far from harmonious. They also demonstrate that the general development of this relationship followed a similar pattern to England where the middle class pursued a missionary aim of 'conciliation and disciplining of the lower orders into conformity with bourgeois norms of respectability' (Hargreaves 1986: 59).

CONTEMPORARY GERMAN *BUNDESLIGA* FOOTBALL

Only one week after the World Cup draw in Marseilles, in December 1997, the last matches of the preliminary, qualifying round of the Champions League were played. German dominance of European football was confirmed as three teams reached the quarter-finals: Bayern Munich, Borussia Dortmund and Bayer Leverkusen. Each of these three clubs is unique and reflects the diverse composition of the *Bundesliga* as well as some significant characteristics of professional football in Germany. Borussia Dortmund appears to be the most traditional of the three but is actually the youngest, having been founded in 1909 (the other clubs were both founded in 1904). Dortmund is most closely associated with the industrial Ruhr area, whilst Bayern Munich has always had a wealthy parvenu image. Its local, smaller rival, 1860 Munich, attracts the working-class interest in this very affluent Bavarian city. Bayern Munich's past successes, its wealth and arrogance, numerous scandals, boardroom policies of hire-and-fire as well as its geographical base in Bavaria has divided the football nation: people either hate or adore the club.

Conversely, Borussia Dortmund is the darling of the football nation for a number of reasons. It is the only team on a par with Munich; despite its wealth, the management policies appear modest and considerate; the club continuously celebrates its working class traditions and emphasises its obligations to the local community. Anecdotal evidence suggests directors even consulted some fan organisations about lavish spending plans on top-class players, like Andreas Möller. Local community support was particularly important during the early 1970s when the team went through a serious crisis and spent years in the second division. Nowadays, matches are usually sold out weeks in advance, the ground having a capacity of 54,000 with more than 30,000 season ticket holders.

While attendances in Munich depend on the attractiveness of opponents and team form, the crowd in Dortmund are acknowledged as 'true' and faithful supporters. However, a 'true' Dortmund supporter does not necessarily have working-class origins. Dortmund's *Westfalenstadium* has become a melting pot of poor and rich, where the North of Dortmund, the traditional working-class milieu, meets the South comprising the middle class and University students (Schulze-Marmeling and Steffen 1994). Even the South Stand, traditionally dominated by young male working-class fans, has become mixed. Despite Dortmund's successes in the 1990s, the club has remained in touch with supporters who use their right to influence management and policies. Registered members can even participate in various official board meetings. Dr Gerd Niebaum, a well-known Dortmund lawyer, was confirmed in 1986 as club president, a position he still holds. Michael Meier, an accountant and innovative marketing expert, manages the club's business affairs and receives a salary, unlike Niebaum. Both have proved to be highly successful businessmen with a good understanding of football. In Munich, by contrast, both the current president, Franz Beckenbauer, and the general manager, Uli Hoeneß, are very successful ex-footballers.

The full name of the third team, Bayer 04 Leverkusen, is both revealing and confusing. Although the club was founded in 1904 there appears to be a lack of tradition and association with any specific social groups or classes. However, the name also reveals that the team is owned by a large multi-national pharmaceutical company, Bayer AG. It is therefore no surprise that the logo on the players' jerseys advertises 'Aspirin', one of the best known company products. The supporters are as colourless and shapeless as the town of Leverkusen, a few miles north of Cologne. The vast majority of the fans as well as all the players are employed by Bayer AG. The team's achievements are very limited, as it has only ever won the UEFA Cup (1988) and the German FA Cup (1993). However, as football in Leverkusen has long been considered a vital part of the company's business and, in particular, marketing strategy, it is the only *Bundesliga* team to have the owner's name integrated in the team's. Unsurprisingly, the football ground in Leverkusen is one of the few in Germany with hospitality boxes. This can partly be explained by the ownership structure of sport facilities in Germany: most stadia are owned by local authorities and clubs rent them for matches. In Leverkusen this is different, as the football ground is part of a larger sporting complex owned by Bayer AG. Dortmund also owns its ground but has no hospitality boxes. The clubs in Munich and Schalke are currently considering whether to purchase their own stadiums.

However, these three clubs, like all *Bundesliga* teams, have an increasing discrepancy between income and expenditure. The former has risen by about 180 per cent throughout the 1990s, the latter has increased by about 280 per cent. According to a recent interview with Wolfgang Holzhäuser, the secretary of the DFB, professional clubs have a collective debt of around £200 million (*Der Spiegel*, 22 December 1997: 112). Gate money contributes a tiny proportion of their overall budget; the sale of television rights and other economic activities is more important financially. The teams in Munich and Leverkusen have had the largest budgets over the last 15 years. While the latter is obviously promoting Bayer products, the former has been sponsored by Opel, the German version of Vauxhall, which also employs such famous German sports personalities as Steffi Graf and Michael Stich to raise their product profile. Traditionally, Opel cars were considered unimaginative, boring but reliable; the association with Bayern Munich and these outstanding tennis players is meant to generate an image of a dynamic, innovative, and successful car producer.

FOOTBALL FANS: CARNIVAL RATHER THAN FIGHTING?

The British commentator, Steve Redhead, claims that *'in parts of Continental Europe much of the activity surrounding travel to, and attendance at, football matches in the mid-late 1980s and early 1990s constituted an almost satirically accurate impression, or caricature, of British football hooligan styles of the 1970s'* (Redhead 1991: 145). However, there are some significant differences as the following analysis of the style and cultural practices of German football fans will illustrate. Style was initially developed as a concept for the cultural analysis of fashion. Mike Brake introduced the concept into the examination of the sociology of youth cultures. He defined subcultural style as consisting of three main elements: 'image', i.e. appearance, composed of dress and, accessories, such as hair style, jewellery and artefacts; 'demeanour', made up of expression, gait and posture; and 'argot', consisting of a special vocabulary and its delivery (Brake 1980: 12). Since style is the most definitive feature of a subculture (cf. Hebdige 1988), its description and hermeneutic interpretation needs to be presented in detail, because as Brake argues:

> It indicates which symbolic group one belongs to, it demarcates that group from the mainstream, and it makes an appeal to an identity outside that of a class-ascribed one. It is learned in social interaction with significant subcultural others, and its performance requires what theatre actors call 'presence', the ability to wear costume, and to use voice to project an image with sincerity. (13–14)

(i) The Image

The fans' outfit consists of T-shirts, kits, jumpers, coats, scarves and hats in the team colours, often bearing the club emblem. Alternatively, the emblem appears on badges or small flags. More recently, body adornment has supplemented these garments. Colouring the hair and face has become popular; tattoos are worn by others, but these are fairly rare. Less obvious are cigarette lighters and bracelets in the team colours. This form of identification has been prevalent since the 1960s when increasing commercialisation and professionalisation distanced players and supporters. Via these symbols, fans demonstrate not only their team allegiance but also attempt to bridge this distance in an imaginary way – garments and artefacts give the illusion of proximity.

The uniform's outward appearance also contributes to the 'increased longing for group, for like-minded peers, for community' (Pramann 1983: 47). It is an end in itself, helping young people to cope with the transitional problems of their life stage. The voluntary uniformity of these fans contributes significantly to their solidarity and to strong peer pressures that often lead to forms of collective behaviour. A constantly growing number of fans wear personalised football shirts with the name and number of a specific player. These polyester symbols of belonging have grown most dramatically in popularity during the 1990s, which clearly demonstrate that for many, identification with individual players is at the heart of football fandom.

Other images are available for the manifestation of 'true' fandom, particularly for those perceived to be less involved. Many fans wear stickers or badges of the left-wing terrorist organisation the Red Army Faction, sometimes next to fascist symbols such as the swastika. Flags are also waved when on the terraces, primarily to gain the attention of television crews which, in turn, gives fans the opportunity to experience themselves through the televisual media. Given their marginal status, such exposure is likely to produce a significant sense of satisfaction and power.

The wide variety of objects used outside football include everyday articles such as bath towels, bed linen, blankets, glasses, cups and posters. The composition of such a synthetic environment at home can be interpreted as both an extension of childhood and a symbolic transformation of the football ground environment into the domestic arena (cf. Hicketier 1980: 101–2).

(ii) Demeanour

Many fans orchestrate their appearance in such a way that 'signals a body perception whose dominant principles are physical strength and aggressive masculinity' (Becker 1982: 80). Football supporters are historically drawn from the working class which has led to the incorporation of masculine norms and values, such as power and strength, into subcultural practices around football. Crucial to this ethos is the importance of bodily strength via industrial production, but this romanticising view needs to be corrected in two aspects. First, technological changes have undermined the centrality and relevance of muscular strength to industrial production. Secondly, the boom in body building and the increasing interest of the middle class, particularly in 'body shaping' and 'body styling', illustrates that physicality and strength can have an artificial dimension independent of social background. Therefore the value of muscular masculinity can no longer be incorporated in arguments about a homogeneous social milieu.

(iii) Argot

For newcomers to football grounds the most striking feature is the constant level
of noise, in the form of chants and songs. Such chants begin among fans on their
way to the grounds, and among the variety of themes available they will
inevitably display a confidence in their team:

> *Keiner wird es wagen, unsere ... zu schlagen.*
> (Nobody will dare to beat ...)

> *Aber eins, aber eins, das bleibt bestehen;*
> *... wird niemals untergehen*
> (But one thing will exist for ever;
> ... will never go under)

The arrival of opposing supporters at the railway station or in the ground provokes a variety of insults and defamations:

> *Oh, tun mir die Augen weh,*
> *wenn ich nur ... seh'*
> (My eyes really do hurt, when I see ...)

Additionally, the home supporters state their position as such:

> *Hier regiert ...*
> (Here reigns ...)

During the official announcement of the opposing team line-up each name is followed by a loud:

> *Na und!?*
> (So what?)

When opposing players appear on the pitch they are welcomed in the following
manner:

> *Zick, zack, Zigeunerpack*
> (Zick, zack, bunch of gypsies)

The actual course of events on the pitch also provides various opportunities for
comments. To support their team, players are regularly encouraged to 'fight'

(*Kämpfen!*). Once a goal has been scored fans shout for the obligatory 'encore' (*Zugabe*). Dangerous moments in front of their own goal tend to be played down:

> *Eins, zwei, drei, wieder mal vorbei*
> (One, two, three, once again off the goal line)

The referee, police-officers and in particular the opposition goalkeeper are very popular targets for insults:

> *Oh hängt sie auf, oh hängt sie auf;*
> *oh hängt sie auf, die schwarze Sau.*
> (Hang him, the black bastard)

> *Alle Bullen sind schwul, von München bis nach Liverpool.*
> (All cops are gay, from Munich to Liverpool)

Victories initiate dreams:

> *Deutscher Meister werden wir;*
> *Du mit mir, ich mit Dir.*
> (We will be the German champions,
> you and I, I and you.)

> *Oh, Du wunderschöner ...,*
> *Du sollst ewig Deutscher Meister sein.*
> (you most beautiful ...,
> you shall always be German champions.)

On the other hand, defeats have to be coped with:

> *Diese Niederlage tut uns nicht weh,*
> *Meister wird ...*
> (This defeat doesn't hurt,
> Champions will be ...)

Many songs demonstrate a close or even symbiotic relationship between supporters and team. Many chants about the identity of fans show an omnipotent self-perception. Since opponents are a potential threat to this identity and the fragile illusion of closeness, their marginal status as well as inferiority has to be stressed explicitly. To provoke or insult the other fans, comparisons to social and/or ethnic minorities are very often drawn, particularly to those with a stigma, such as gypsies and homosexuals, who do not conform with working-class norms and values and the characteristics of aggressive masculinity. Some chants also contain explicit, violent threats. The public evaluation of events on the pitch shows clearly a one-sided interpretation. There is no recognition of the opponents' abilities, tactics or achievements (cf. Becker 1982).

COMMITMENT, ACTION AND CONSUMPTION

An interesting and systematic study of football fans (Heitmeyer and Peter 1988: 56–63) discovered that, despite a common subcultural style, three different groups of youth spectators can be distinguished according to motivation; those who are attracted by the sport, those who come because of the potential for action in the ground, and those who purely enjoy the football match as a leisure activity. Football-oriented fans consider attendance at all the home fixtures a 'must'. For them, football is not one of many leisure activities but the one with the highest personal priority. It is so important that it even affects many fans' everyday lives and goes beyond the football weekend. The sporting event is only one important element which determines weekly attendance. Planning and organisation of leisure, holidays and financial budgets occur around the *Bundesliga* fixtures. Personal biographies are constructed and experienced in terms of football events.

Action-oriented fans see the game as a means to have an exciting experience. It is not the match and its fascination but rather the opportunity to have a good time which predominantly determines their more or less regular attendance. This group of fans will not avoid violence with other supporters. While they generally attend all home fixtures, away matches are chosen according to the expected excitement and the likelihood of confrontations with rival fans. Consumption-oriented fans consider football matches as one of many interesting leisure activities and as a commercial product. For them, football is primarily a casual hobby and match attendance is clearly dependent on the form of 'their' team or the opponents, the weather, and the availability of alternative leisure. These categories are not static, as the spectator scene is constantly changing. Conflicts with other fans, new experiences with the police and players, or changes in personal situations can obviously generate modifications of attitude, cultural practice and behaviour.

In general however, carnival rather than fighting is fashionable at *Bundesliga* matches and, particularly since the beginning of the 1990s, spectator behaviour in and around German soccer stadia has been closer to the behaviour of fans commonly found in Southern European grounds. Nevertheless, a new quality of deviant fan behaviour also exists. This is shown by the emergence of explicitly racist chants and abuse at *Bundesliga* matches, and by the continued existence of nationalist and chauvinist displays at international matches often combined with hooligan behaviour, particularly in foreign countries. Serious hooligan incidents at international level involving German fans include recent matches against

France, the Netherlands, Belgium and Poland (cf. Merkel et al. 1996). This new style of international football violence even led to the match against England in 1994, originally scheduled for 20 April, Adolf Hitler's birthday, being cancelled.

The German national side, especially when playing matches abroad, has been viewed by right wingers as the most appropriate forum for the expression of heightened nationalism and xenophobia. Media coverage of swastika-wearing fans giving Nazi salutes raised emotional public debates in which even the Conservative Chancellor Helmut Kohl participated. Although the recruitment activities of right-wing political organisations have remained generally unsuccessful, racist chants have been a routine feature in many German football grounds since the early 1990s. More importantly, East Germany has proved a useful recruiting ground for the far right and illegal concerts by skinhead bands can attract audiences of up to 1,500. Eastern teenagers currently appear to want simple answers to highly complex situations; they want to be part of a popular national community governed by 'German virtues'.

The public celebration of *Volk und Vaterland* (people and fatherland) by politicians of all major parties, and the nationalistic excess inspired by German World Cup success in 1990, meant that the distinction between 'us' and 'them' has become more explicit in fan behaviour. Nationally, this is reflected in racist and xenophobic abuse which draws on traditional conventions of 'race' (Merkel et al. 1996). Internationally, this is mirrored in the celebration of the national community, combined with aggressive and often violent expressions of masculinity.

FOOTBALL, NATIONAL IDENTITY AND RE-UNIFICATION IN THE 1990s

Critcher argues with reference to English national identity that 'it is difficult to specify anything, other than war and royalty, which articulates national identity quite so powerfully as the England team competing in the latter stages of a World Cup competition' (Critcher 1991: 81). As the Germans do not have a monarchy or proud war records, soccer success appears to be the most powerful idiom and symbol for the production and reproduction of a sense of nationhood. The impact of Germany's World Cup success story, and the nature of German soccer as a vital source of cultural expression and national identity in general, have been discussed in more detail elsewhere (Merkel 1994). This section sets out to look at the impact of re-unification on soccer and vice versa.

The re-unification of Germany has again raised the vital question of who the Germans are. The German constitution recognises 'German-ness' in those with German parents or those who can prove German origins. The definition of German nationality, based on blood and heritage, has remained unchanged since 1913. After many violent racist disturbances in 1991, voices were raised in Germany calling for a change in citizenship laws, so that the world would see the new German state define itself through its democratic values. But Chancellor Helmut Kohl and his Conservative Party turned a deaf ear. Re-unification has made it even more difficult to define the typical German, or the mythical German as imagined abroad. Two totally different types developed on either side of the Iron Curtain during 40 years of partition and even football 'the people's game', almost became a victim of East-West rivalries in the course of re-unification.

As Wagg noted (1995: 19): '*When the GDR's league, FA and national side were disbanded in 1990, only two East German clubs were invited to join the unified Bundesliga*'. There are at least three reasons for this: immediately after the fall of the Wall many sportsmen and women migrated to the West for higher salaries. Ulf Kirsten (Bayer Leverkusen) and Mathias Sammer (Borussia Dortmund) were among the first signed by Western clubs. Both also made it into the unified national side and are among the most popular players in Germany. After his outstanding performances during Euro '96 Sammer was voted 'Footballer of the Year' by the vast majority of German sport journalists. Second, although football was popular in the GDR the quality of play hardly ever reached the level of West German clubs or the national side. Third, the organisational and financial structure of professional football in the unified Germany is based on capitalist principles and requires both capital and revenue funding – something which hardly any of the Eastern clubs had or could acquire during the quick transformation process. Switching from traditional socialist sponsorship to more commercial forms of support and operating in a free market economy was not easy. In addition, East Germans were simply not interested in sport during this period as they had to solve more pressing problems. Those who could afford an interest in sport focused on the West which had now become accessible.

However, since the mid-1990s, many East Germans have acknowledged the many benefits of their old socialist system, including the free provision of physical recreation and the chance to watch top-level sport. Sports clubs now appear to have overcome the spectator crisis which set in immediately after the Wall came down. Sport, in general, and football in particular, appears to provide excitement in times of stagnating economic depression; the newly emerging middle-class has in football a forum to express itself, particularly during nostalgic moods. For many others, particularly the disadvantaged, football enables the public display of a (re-)emerging self-confidence, based on the celebration of East–West divisions. In some football grounds the old GDR flag has become part of the standard equipment of fans. Chants at football matches, such as 'We don't want any Western swine,' refer to Western opponents, players, supporters and even the referee. This is frequently accompanied by the request to 'Put up the Wall again.' There is no doubt that the terraces of football grounds have become meeting places for both winners and losers in re-unification. They share the desire to publicly express their sentiments.

Although many clubs and teams have changed their names and colours, their fans have started to use the old (i.e. pre-1989) names and colour combinations again. When they refer to Berlin, many add 'East' to demonstrate their distinctive sense of belonging. On several occasions, particularly when top West German sides play East German underdogs, chants referring to the 1974 World Cup match between East and West Germany in Hamburg, which the Western team unexpectedly lost 1–0, could be heard.

These unexpected developments have, in turn, attracted mass media attention (despite the weak performances of many East German teams) and subsequently the attention of sponsors whose money has predominantly been used to buy in new players from all over the world. Only a tiny minority of football, handball or ice-hockey players in East Germany are native East Germans. As fans can hardly afford to regularly buy new kits with the name of new stars on the back, many have started to wear kits emblazoned with 'Ossi', a derogatory term for East Germans used by many West German fans to insult opposing players or referees. Additionally, there are the East German skinheads who use football matches to scream their hatred of the world, brandishing swastikas and reviving memories of the pogroms. The former communist East, which had institutionalised 'Anti-Fascism', played a major role in some of the most disturbing racist attacks on migrants and members of minority ethnic groups in the former GDR. Such sentiments are rooted in hatred of foreigners and intolerance of anything different, but lack any precise ideological outlook.

There is no doubt that playing and watching football is an important cultural practice in Germany which needs to be socially contextualised. Football does not simply reflect society but is part of how social groups symbolise their central themes and express their social and cultural experiences. Given the subcultural style of the predominantly young male fans, it is apparent that their key themes relate to local and regional identities, which can be expanded to include national identities under certain circumstances. Also important are the team's achievement, masculine forms of pride, and other values which are deeply rooted in traditional working-class culture. Although these themes show a high degree of continuity over the last three decades they are also subject to the pressures of change, due to the growing number of female and middle class supporters as well as the shifting economies of the game. There is no doubt that sport events, in general, nowadays offer a significant frame of reference for East Germans, replacing many of the traditional socialist organisations which did not survive the changes. Football matches, in particular, have increasingly become a forum for the construction, reconstruction and celebration of new and old cultural practices, contributing significantly to the re-definition of social and regional identities in the new Germany.

Part II
Glory and Innovation:
Pre-eminent Players

5 Everything in Moderation: The Swedish Model

Torbjörn Andersson and Aage Radmann

The development of Swedish society during the 1900s was strongly influenced by forty years of Social Democratic rule (1932–76). The socio-political process commonly referred to as the 'Swedish Model' emerged during this period, characterised by a substantial degree of co-operation and compromise between employers and workers, industrialists and state officials. Less famously, sport developed a parallel Swedish Model that combined amateurism and professionalism. Via this model a rational amateur system was sought, which could concomitantly be supported by all social groups, provide a respectable recreation for young males, and enable the nation to enjoy substantial international success. The amateur system proved to be outstandingly successful in football. The national team won the Olympic gold medal in 1948, the World Cup bronze in 1950 and a silver medal at the 1958 World Cup finals held in Sweden. Such success was remarkable: the game had permeated every corner of Sweden; and a country which in 1950 still had less than 7 million inhabitants had achieved world wide footballing recognition.

The Swedish societal model has substantially been eroded over the past twenty years, and this deterioration has naturally affected sport. The amateur rules were changed in 1967, enabling Malmö FF to become the first wholly professional football club over 20 years later in 1989. The commercialisation of domestic club football has meant that the game in Sweden has in many ways displayed increasing similarities to the state of the game elsewhere in Europe. Consequent to this development, Swedish club football for the first time achieved an international breakthrough when Malmö FF, became European Cup Finalists in 1979, and IFK Gothenburg UEFA Cup winners in 1982 and 1987. In addition, the national team enjoyed a new golden age in the 1990s, taking third place at the 1994 World Cup finals.

Paradoxically such triumphs have been explained by reference to the Swedish Model. The model has now come to characterise the Swedish *playing* system, which is thought to reflect a Swedish mentality that begets organisation, team spirit and humility. Although the traditional Swedish Model has to a great extent been demolished in sport and in society, the rational approach embodied in it continues to permeate Swedish football.

THE CREATION OF RATIONAL AMATEURISM, 1900–1920

A unique aspect of Swedish development was the centralisation of all sports under one organisation, The Swedish Sports Confederation (*Riksidrottsförbundet*), founded in 1902 (Lindroth 1974) was an absolutely fundamental prerequisite for the emergence of a Swedish sporting model. Participants in various sports were forced to learn to co-operate and internal conflicts were contained and mediated within the Confederation. This mentality has been particularly prominent in the relationship between the Swedish Football Association, *Svenska Fotbollsförbundet*, and the Swedish Sports Confederation. Although the Football Association was the most powerful member of the Sports Confederation, it never broke away, despite occasional threats to do so.

Modern sports encountered some opposition during their infancy. Representatives of the Ling national gymnastics movement were forceful ideological opponents of imported sports (Lindroth 1974). Many influential popular movements – the Free Church, the temperance movement and working-class political organisations – were also alarmed about the rapid expansion of football. It fell to football's ideologues, primarily middle-class men who ruled the national and local football associations, to steer the game's development in the right direction. Quite naturally, English amateur football represented the ideal template. Professional football was resolutely dismissed as a model for Sweden, with the help of some arguments from English amateurs themselves.

In essence, the English ideal of 'fair play' was rooted in the notion of 'the gentleman'; the implication was that anybody could aspire to this identity whatever their social position. Consequently, early football reports abound with authoritative advice and indignant criticism. The tone was exceptionally critical, contained within a strict vertical monologue of talking downwards to those perceived to be of lower status. The educative elements of the game were consistently emphasised; if the game was to be encouraged among young people, those promoting it needed to impress upon them the paramount importance of respectable collective values and concomitant behaviour. Football was thus to be regarded as a respectable activity in the service of society. This kind of respectability was necessary if football's patrons and the authorities were to provide economic support. A great deal of money was needed to construct the football grounds.

These solid amateur foundations did not mean that all forms of professionalism were rejected. From the very beginning the Swedes shared an ambition to be highly skilled and successful. Achieving success while maintaining strict amateur principles was not an unproblematic task. The Swedes commonly assumed that the influence of money on sport would lead automatically to an increase in ungentlemanly behaviour. This meant in turn that British professional teams could not be invited to Sweden because of the potentially adverse effect on players and spectators. Consequently, the first British teams to visit Sweden were all amateurs (Persson 1992). Despite this, Swedish football's authorities remained dissatisfied; the amateur policy was revoked in 1909 and British professional teams were allowed to play in Sweden.

Matches against professionals were necessary to raise the standard of domestic play. The fact that Sweden had begun to play international matches the year before naturally made this decision easier. This shift in values was essential if the Swedes were to emulate the professionals' scientific playing styles. Hence, one could claim that Swedish football was, from an early stage, oriented towards a kind of professional amateurism. English football could, conversely, be interpreted as non-rational or amateur professionalism. The Swedish attitude here was pragmatic; football horizons were extended, while positive elements were discovered in the rational attitudes of professionals. Swedish newspapers discussed the 'respectable' lifestyle of the professionals; their training meant that their physicality was given priority over possible indulgence in alcohol and tobacco.[1]

The determination to beat the neighbouring Danes took Swedish football into ever more rational and controversial directions. Danish football culture was more firmly anchored in the middle class and amateur ideal. The Danes were indignant at their first defeat by Sweden in 1916: they considered that the Swedish training camps introduced prior to the match had overstepped the line between amateurism and 'immoral' professionalism. The training methods copied those of the American national side, which had visited Sweden a couple of months earlier. After this success, Swedish football was permeated by an emphasis on organisation and training, with the focus firmly on creating a successful national side. During the 1920s and 1930s probably no nation played more international games than Sweden.

THE CREATION OF THE SWEDISH MODEL, 1920–50

In hindsight we can see that the pursuit of a respectable image for football was, to a large extent, successful. Football sought and received local government support, particularly during the crisis period in the 1920s and 1930s, when many municipal sport grounds were built during the struggle against unemployment. Economic support became substantial after the state took control of the gambling industry in 1934; large profits from this were ploughed into the sports movement. At the same time, football was spreading throughout Swedish society (Johansson 1953; Lindroth 1974), and as the Swedish Model became fully established during the Second World War, football acquired an elevated social status. When Sweden beat Germany in 1941 and 1942 the national morale received a welcome boost. From then on, practically everybody considered football to be a worthwhile activity for young men, especially in large cities where the increasingly hedonistic lifestyles of the young gave cause for concern. It was then entirely logical that the Football Association should form a special committee on youth football in 1948, and it became increasingly important for the behaviour of players to be beyond reproach.

Even if city-based teams have always more or less dominated club football, the most conspicuous feature of Swedish football has been the many successful teams from very small industrial towns in the countryside (Bengtsson 1975). These generally patriarchal societies served as models for the wider society through the dominant position of the three large popular movements – the Free Church, and the temperance and working-class movements. Up to one third of Swedes belonged to at least one of these movements in 1920, ensuring that the rational and respectable ways of life they all advocated actually had a great impact (Lundkvist 1977; Ambjörnsson 1988; Larsson 1994).

The Swedish Model was epitomised in these small industrial districts, and football was no exception. Towns like Sandviken, Degerfors and Åtvidaberg became synonymous with an exceptionally high standard of football. The latter, a community with 9,000 inhabitants, even managed to win the league championship twice as late as 1972 and 1973. The football culture of these communities was commonly viewed as exemplary and as such idealised. Their model was a study in serious and rational amateurism: not too commercial, but not short of ambition. A clear yet paradoxical expression of this ambition was the fact that their successes were greatly indebted to the clubs' cosmopolitan trainers, especially Central European Jews who were active during the inter-war period. These trainers introduced more rational and systematic training methods, and demanded a new level of player discipline.

Many tensions obviously arose within the Swedish amateur system. This was most clearly seen when a player changed clubs, and accusations of illicit deals were made in the press (Nilsson 1978). The first such controversy dates as far back as 1911 (Persson 1990). Swedish football's entire history has, on the whole, included constant insinuations and charges in the press about the violation of amateur regulations. The most persistent accusations were that clubs tried to recruit players by promising good jobs in the local community. Such inducements were obviously tempting to many unemployed players. Significantly, there were more jobs in small industrial communities than in larger cities. Therefore many first-class players left top clubs in cities like Gothenburg to join small rural teams.

It is difficult to ascertain the extent to which the amateur rules were actually followed. At least since the 1920s, illicit payments to players were documented in the minutes of several clubs. The most famous violation occurred in 1934 when players at Malmö FF were banned for receiving professional payments. The difficulties of maintaining strict amateurism were reflected in the constant liberalisation of the definition of 'amateur', especially after the Second War World. Once again the Swedish system was pragmatic. A specific problem arose after the 1948 Olympic victory when Italian clubs recruited a string of Swedish players. The amateur attitude was gradually liberalised, and these professionals, after being banned from the national team, were allowed to take part in the 1958 World Cup.

The logical end to this long and complex history was reached in 1967, when the amateur rules were finally abolished. Commercialism had undermined amateurism from within; the Swedish sporting model was therefore at an end. Still, it is fair to say that market forces never got the upper hand in Sweden. In reality rational amateurism was replaced by a system that might be termed rational semi-amateurism, or, to put it another way, rational semi-professionalism.

THE CREATION OF SEMI-PROFESSIONALISM

Sport experienced an enormous growth during the first half of the twentieth century. Membership of the Sports Confederation grew from 60,000 in 1910 to 800,000 in 1950 (Lindroth 1987). The abolition of amateurism did not mean that professionalism was now a reality. In fact the first completely professional club in Sweden did not emerge for a further 22 years. It was certainly no coincidence that it was Malmö FF, a big club close to continental Europe, that was the first to take this step. The route to professionalism had gone through several stages: summer professionals, youth professionals, the creation of the Football University and then in 1989, a fully professional first team.

However, sporting successes did not follow automatically. Financially, pure professionalism was not so remarkable. The cost of player salaries increased from 4.7 million kröner in 1988 to 7.1 million in 1989. Then the Malmö FF innovation to professional status was strongly criticised by large sections of the Swedish sports movement and media. Criticism centred on financial issues, as the club was seen as too small to support a professional effort. The club had to regularly sell its best players in order to survive. It was also essential for sporting successes to continue unabated, otherwise sponsors and supporters would turn their backs. The economic situation of the players was also a source of concern. Many believed they earned too little to save for a life after football, while at the same time some thought they earned too much for kicking a ball about for a few hours each day! The professional program of Malmö FF lasted only five years. At the start of the 1994–5 season, and together with several other clubs in the *Allsvenskan* (First Division), the club reverted to semi-professionalism.

As an economic model, semi-professionalism predominates within Swedish football. Interestingly, this has not been dictated solely by the strict requirements of financial liquidity. Some clubs could sustain professionalism economically but choose to help players with civil employment or vocational education on a part-time basis. Hence, the players are equipped to face the world when their football careers end. It is as if full-time professionalism is not really accepted within the sporting culture of Sweden. It is a paradox that, as soon as a player moves abroad, a fully professional career immediately becomes legitimate and meaningful, even when playing at the bottom of the Swiss league.

There is a third kind of professionalism in the *Allsvenskan*, which can be called 'part-time professionalism' (Billing et al. 1994). Under this process the players are in full-time employment outside of football, while the club compensates them for loss of earnings when playing matches. In the semi-professional ethos players do not work full time. The advantage is that there are powerful non-profit-making forces that support all parts of the club structure and which therefore render the club less sensitive to economic forces. Halmstad BK is a good example of the sporting successes that can be achieved by such a model. In 1995 they rocked one of the world's best clubs, Parma of Italy, by beating them 3–0 at home, only to lose 4–0 away. Two years later, they won the league title. Looking towards the year 2000, it seems that the 'semi-professional' model will be chosen by the majority of top Swedish clubs and indeed by the rest of Scandinavia.

THE SWINGLISH MODEL

The Swedish football model had a turbulent time between the mid-70s and the mid-80s. It involved a classic struggle between different schools, or *fields* (Bourdieu 1991b). In this context, a social field is defined as a system of relationships between positions occupied by specialised agents and institutions, which are engaged in an internal struggle for a common value (Broady 1990). Whereas previously the football movement had put all its energies into the arguments for and against professionalism, now the main agenda became concentrated on attempts to define *good* and *bad* football. This is by no means a unique debate, but what made it extraordinary for Sweden was the climax to the discussion resulting in a decree from the Swedish Football Association as to how football should be played in Sweden.

The whole discussion originated with the 1974 World Cup, at which Sweden finished in fifth place. Swedish football was considered to be on the march, the national team was ranked among the best eight in the world. At club level, a young English trainer called Bob Houghton joined Malmö FF. Together with his countryman Roy Hodgson, who had started his career at Halmstad BK, Houghton revolutionised Swedish club football. Their clubs topped the *Allsvenskan* in 1974, 1975 and 1979 (MFF), and 1976 and 1977 (HBK). In 1984 Hodgson joined Malmö FF, where there was an exceptional assembly of young talents in Stefan Schwartz, Martin Dahlin, Jonas Thern and others. Together they won five straight league championships between 1985 and 1989.

The Englishmen contributed to the formation of an occupational identity for Swedish football players. This identity expressed itself not only on the playing field, but also in terms of materials, services, pitches, training and health care (Peterson 1993). Their football system differed from the Swedish model by placing a far greater emphasis on planning and organisation. This gelled with the desired Swedish characteristics of team spirit, judicial thinking, loyalty and a capacity to follow orders to the letter. This expression of the Swedish *habitus* (Bourdieu 1986) fitted hand in glove with the Englishmen's football philosophy. The new football was more effective and more rational, and it had a stronger theoretical foundation than that which it replaced.

Criticism was not slow in coming; the epithet 'robot football' was soon on everybody's lips. It was argued that this style of football was dull and uninspiring to watch, leaving little or no space for individuals, technical finesse or football joy. This extreme version of 'systematic football', which was so successful in making MFF and HBK into the top club teams in Sweden, stirred up a debate as to how an effective i.e. successful, national team could be moulded out of players from such diverse systems. The bitter feud between proponents of 'joyful football' and 'systematic football' culminated in the Swedish Football Association, together with its national trainer Lars Arnesson, issuing a document entitled 'The Swedish Model'. The document was to be the programmatic basis for the work of the Football Association with the national team, and all its other educational activities. Thus the efforts that began in 1973–4, to improve the international standard of Swedish football, ended up in 1980 as the only officially correct and approved way of playing the game in Sweden (Peterson 1993).

One can say that the period of Houghton and Hodgson transformed the Swedish football-field. When they arrived in Sweden, they were, to borrow the terminology of Bourdieu, lacking in symbolic capital (that which is accepted by social groups as valuable, or which is given a value). They provoked suspicion among many of the football public, but because football ultimately always acknowledges results, their reputation increased with each victory, and earned legitimacy when other Swedish trainers appropriated this way of thinking. One of the most successful, in fusing together the opposing football philosophies was Sven-Göran Eriksson, the trainer behind the successful IFK Gothenburg team and later club trainer in Italy with Sampdoria.

THE SWEDISH MODEL AND WOMEN'S FOOTBALL

Whether measured by the number of active participants or by the number of spectators, football is Sweden's most popular sport. Over a third of boys play as part of their leisure activities. Football is also the biggest participatory sport among women, with a quarter of girls aged 13–15 playing club football. In fact there are nearly as many active players in football alone as in all other sports put together. And it is certainly not a coincidence that women are so well represented in football, as in politics, because Sweden is a country in which equal rights between the sexes has come a long way.

In 1970 women's football was placed on the Football Association agenda for the first time; albeit 16 July 1918 is considered the official date on which the first match was played in Sweden between two teams consisting of women. In 1970, 728 women were licensed players. By 1989 this number had grown to 35,000, out of a total number of 181,000 licensed players. The football-playing population of Sweden stands at around 450,000–500,000.

In many ways women's football has followed the men's game with better organisation and a more professional approach to both club and national teams. Research, however, shows that in several areas Swedish women's football has not kept pace with its male counterpart. Women's sporting careers are hindered rather than helped by outside employment. Unlike young men, girls prioritise social relationships (especially romances) over sporting ones. Gender differences also exist in attitudes towards the organisation of sport; whereas men feel they can influence organisations, women feel they have little power over events (Dahlgren 1990). Nevertheless, the spectator figures for the Women's World Cup illustrate that women's football is gaining popularity.

Significantly, sporting organisations and the Swedish government continue to pursue equal rights. The 1989 General Assembly of the Swedish Sports Confederation adopted an ambitious project catchingly entitled 'The Sexual Equality Plan in Sport for the Nineties'. This document aimed to break the power of the (male) moguls in sport, but six years later results have been less than impressive. There are only 25 per cent of women on the boards of the 40 biggest women's sporting organisations (*Dagens Nyheter*, 24 September 1995). The difference between theory and practice was epitomised before the Women's World Soccer Championships in 1995. The Swedish women's team was represented by among others Pia Sundhage, Sweden's top female player. When fans sought autographs there were no publicity photographs of her or any other player to sign. As a makeshift solution, Pia Sundhage had to sign pictures of the Swedish male star, Tomas Brolin; which was not a good example for a country which claims world leadership in 'equal opportunities'.

THE RISE AND FALL OF THE SWEDISH MODEL?

Sweden saw successful years in football during the early 1990s. From an organisational point of view, the country can look back on two successful tournaments, the European Championship of 1992 and the Women's World Cup in 1995. In sporting terms, third place at the 1994 World Cup speaks for itself. The team and its manager, Tommy Svensson, received a euphoric ovation from the Swedish people upon returning home. There was no backlash in Sweden after eventually losing to Brazil, as Kenneth Andersson, one of the team stated: 'Would the world football community ever have forgiven us if we had knocked out the best team in the world?' This hypothetical question brings us to a common expression used to describe the Swedish soul. The word *lagom* can roughly be translated as 'adequate', or mean, more accurately, 'everything in moderation'. History, in the form of losing to Brazil in the 1958 World Cup final, repeats itself. Instead of mourning defeat, everyone was delighted at having advanced further than expected.

Virtually a Swedish motto, *Lagom* is closely connected to a deeply realistic and rational attitude to life (Bairner 1994; Linde-Laursen and Nilsson 1991). One can illustrate how the national character expresses itself in football, by selecting a representative of Swedish football officialdom, Lennart Johansson. Advancing from the workshop floor to the chairmanship of Stockholm club AIK, Johansson then became Vice President of the Swedish Football Association and finally rose to the position of President of UEFA. It has been written that Johansson has not forgotten 'his childhood under simple circumstances, the little sports club and the shop floor. He may eat goose liver pâté and oysters with Havelange, (FIFA President until 1998) but he would rather be eating Baltic herring and mashed potatoes at home with his Lola' (*Sydsvenska Dagbladet*, December 1995).

In 1994 Sweden were one of the best teams in the world, and in Tomas Brolin had one of the world's top ten players, picked to play for a FIFA world team. Brolin symbolises some of the Swedish Model's recent difficulties. After the World Championship Brolin was characterised as the ultimate team player who gave his all for the team when most required. He personified the Swedish sporting ideal. His image was *lagom*, but his performances were world class. When Brolin and Stoichkov, the best player in Europe in 1994, travelled with Parma to play Halmstad in Sweden, Stoichov avoided meeting journalists. Brolin supported his team-mate, declaring that Stoichov was a pleasant fellow, and 'just like the rest of us'. In Swedish eyes, Brolin was a *lagom* professional whereas Stoichov was a *diva* professional. But all is not well. After the 1994 World Cup, Swedish football suffered a serious crisis. The Swedish football team failed to qualify for the 1996 European Championships in England and the 1998 World Championships in France.

Now, in 1998, the situation is completely different. Brolin's performances are *lagom* but his image is 'sensational'. It would be a great insult to Leeds United to call Tomas Brolin the ultimate team player and buddy.[2] But Brolin is not the only individual to have damaged the Swedish Model. A national change of character has seen both sporting identity and self-esteem undergo severe changes. From being the 'big brother' among the Nordic countries, in economic and sporting development, the Swedes have watched Norway and Denmark surpass them. When Denmark, at the start of the 1998 Winter Olympics, was ahead of Sweden in the medals table, the country experienced a major crisis in its national sporting identity.

From this, it would seem that the semi-professionalism of the past has had difficulties adjusting to the commercialisation of football. But questions remain as to whether these conditions are totally new. In the football world there is a strong tendency to contrast the present with a glorious past. This often ignores the fact that the history of football is to a surprisingly large extent dominated by continuity. As early as the 1920s much of the innocence of football culture had vanished. Voices were heard proclaiming that it had been better in the old days, before money and serious attitudes had gained the upper hand. Neither is the growing internationalisation of football as modern and unique as it seems. The case of Degerfors is illustrative. The football played in this small industrial community is profoundly symbolic of the Swedish football culture of the welfare state. Immense changes seem to have occurred when the successes of the Degerfors team during the 1990s were considered as largely due to its imported Yugoslavian players. But as mentioned earlier the football of the industrial communities acquired much of its character from Central European trainers. The industrial community was from its beginnings a relatively cosmopolitan environment for football.

The biggest change for Swedish football today is that money permeates the game more profoundly than before. Following the Bosman ruling the best young players are quick to leave; the quality of the domestic game is thereby diminished. The danger is that spectator interest will fall accordingly. The fan subcultures may have changed from the hooliganism of the 1980s and early 1990s into something more positive, such as fanzines, and a better atmosphere is evident in the stands. Yet it remains a fact that Sweden, like the whole of Scandinavia, is being emptied by football agents keen to sell talent. In January 1998 the number of organised supporters in Sweden was under 20,000, whereas Manchester United's Norwegian supporters' club numbered 30,000 members. Despite the recent failures of the national teams (both men and women), and the economic and social crises in Swedish society, two fundamental ideas remain rooted in the Swedish model: 'everything in moderation' and the spirit of compromise. Or, to express it the Swedish way, *lagom* is best.

Notes

1. Alcohol was a serious problem in the early days of Swedish football. Post-match visits to restaurants became a way of compensating amateur players for their efforts, economic rewards being prohibited by amateur regulations.
2. In 1995 Leeds United paid Parma £4.5m for Brolin. Playing only 19 games he was eventually paid a six-figure fee by the club to leave them. A series of trials at various clubs of lower status than Leeds saw him sign for English Premier club Crystal Palace and to become joint manager in 1998, only to be dismissed a few months later after relegation.

6 Post-Modern Times: Identities and Violence in Argentine Football

Pablo Alabarces

The development of football in Argentina is inseparable from the country's wider social and political context. Argentine football, from its origins in the late nineteenth century, was organised to reproduce the centralist structure of the country, with a centre (Buenos Aires) that retained hegemony over an extensive but pauperised interior. Only two other cities, Rosario and Córdoba, developed economic and industrial (and ultimately football) strength. The opposition of Interior vs Buenos Aires replaces in Argentina the habitual axes of opposition between different cities or regions in other countries. While that is a historical fact, what is contemporary and significant is how, like the rest of Latin America, Argentina has entered the last decade witnessing a rapid modernisation of its economic structure. This modernisation has been founded upon many years of neo-conservative hegemony, and reflected in the restructuring of the economy to fit the global market. The globalisation of economic and communication systems has produced swingeing changes within the social and cultural organisation of the nation. Traditionally a privileged space for understanding the complexity of Argentine society, football has similarly undergone major transformations that allude to these deeper structural changes without routinely reproducing them. The changes within football indicate deeper tensions that are difficult to resolve. This chapter attempts to map out these developments.

POST-MODERN FOOTBALL

Integrated within the development of Western capitalist societies, Argentina has been subject to changes similar to those in other countries. Despite its outlying position and weakness as a producer and exporter of industrial goods, economic reorganisation has followed from the Peronist governments led by Carlos Menem (from 1989 until the present time), which had in turn continued the first wave of political and economic neo-conservatism during the early 1980s. This has involved the reduction of the state's role, a disappearance of the precarious welfare state built during the first period of Peronism (1945–55), and a liberalisation of internal and external markets. Argentina has also suffered much of the adverse consequences of laissez-faire political philosophy. It has failed to confront external competition, especially an exponential growth of unemployment (particular within the old public sector), and a crisis in industry. Official explanations point to globalization as the main cause of these problems. However, globalisation appears, fundamentally, as a product of the mass media. If, at the beginning of the 1990s, CNN became an icon of world information, today Argentine society perceives its inclusion within a global environment through its exposure to such global mediascapes. The expansion of cable television services into half of all Argentine households (including low income ones) allows simultaneous access to global information and entertainment.

Within this process, football has worked historically as a catalyst for technological and cultural change. Colour television began in Argentina in 1979, following technological changes to enable the colour transmission of the 1978 World Cup. Moreover, the expansion of cable services was basically instigated by the inhabitants of Argentina's interior, who wanted to watch a better quality of football transmission from Buenos Aires than was then available to them. In the same way, football's capacity to transform its cultural materials into highly valued commodities inspired, in the early 1990s, the installation and sale of encrypted television services (pay per view). The air waves are thus now invaded by local football; the cable screen by the whole world of football. As in most Western societies, Argentine football has suffered commodification and is now controlled by new mass media monopolies which are organised, fundamentally, around the purchase of transmission rights, thereby enabling large injections of capital into the game (Alabarces 1998). Thus, from its early role in producing and articulating social and cultural identities, to its permanent function as an expressive arena (Archetti 1994), Argentine football has allowed the mass media to transform the game into an exceptional economic product.

This new state of affairs, that we could call 'post-modern football', involves a multiplicity of influences. In a young society, the State's role in the construction of national representations is very strong. But the new economic orientation of Argentina is signalled by the State's retreat from its traditional duties. Even though Argentina failed to achieve full industrialisation, the cartography of social class has been redrawn with post-industrial features, and the most disadvantaged suffer intense social exclusion.

CLASSICAL IDENTITIES: THE MYTHS OF ORIGIN

The rapid expansion of football in Argentina at the beginning of this century followed a similar process to other nations. Beyond its apparent ephemera, football provided a dramatic space for constituting strong identities. In the Argentine case, the foundation of football coincided with a crisis of identity, due largely to the relative youth of the nation-state and the influx of immigrants. The resulting process of identity construction, analysed extensively by Archetti (1994, 1995), gave football a privileged position. The Argentine situation is therefore similar to Brazil where, as Leite Lopes (1997) notes, football built an 'imagined community' that integrated blacks and mestizos, Argentina's football integrated immigrants and their urban neighbourhoods. In its narrative, in journalism, in its system of representation, football possessed an over-representation of the working classes. It was, consequently, a space for the expression of male identity and belonging, particularly via Peronism (see Archetti 1985). Football was seen by intellectuals as a vehicle for manipulating the less gifted cultural sectors (Brohm 1982; Vinnai 1974; Sebreli 1981). The game facilitated the construction of new identities that replaced the original ties of nationality, through support for neighbourhood clubs (Archetti 1994, 1995; Alabarces and Rodríguez 1998; Frydenberg 1997). As football was taking this centre stage, the Peronist populism of the 1940s was incorporating the lower classes into the political limelight (Alabarces and Rodríguez 1998).

Given these processes, the issue of Argentine playing style acquires great significance. As Bromberger (1993b) points out, style is a mythical construction, more narrated that lived, but in the Argentine case the idea of style has revealed a strong capacity for structuring discursive and corporeal practices. On the one hand, style has an ideological component, particularly in journalistic discussions; on the other, it is used as a way of educating the public aesthetically. Sports journalists talk simultaneously of the Argentine style and these styles of particular clubs, commonly explaining the differences according to the presumed characteristics of supporters: Boca Juniors show great fight and courage; River Plate embody a more elegant metropolitan style; the clubs of Argentina's interior display the provincial slowness of 'football peasants'.

The correlation of identity and style shaped local and national reference points. Then came Argentina's catastrophic defeat at the 1958 World Cup in Sweden, which coincided with a moment of massive national uncertainty – the fall of Peronism in 1955. At the time of economic *desarrollismo* (re-assessment), some political groups argued for the imitation of modern European football styles. *Desarrollismo* represented a series of political, social and economic programmes in fashion between the '50s and '60s throughout Latin America, beginning with the conception of CEPAL (Economic Council for Latin America), an institution controlled by the United Nations. CEPAL defended the modernisation of Latin American societies through the introduction of foreign capital (ultimately North American); and the change in forms of sociability, communication and consumption, as a means of overcoming the structural under-development of these societies. Despite some indications of change (for example, the quiet introduction of the Italian *catenaccio* system), the powerful survival of the original style was epitomised in the successful career of Cesar Menotti, who coached the national team (1974–82), winning the World Cup in 1978 and the youth World Championship in 1979. Menotti built a discourse anchored in the original story of Argentine style. Turner has pointed out that this coincides, ideologically, with the moment in which the Argentine military dictatorship defended 'the traditional Argentine style of life' against the 'communist threat' (Turner 1998). However, paradoxically, Menotti's discourse has been considered leftist by certain 'slightly progressive' journalists.

THE CRISIS OF FOOTBALL IDENTITIES

Any application of the term *post-modern* into Argentine football encounters a problem. Primarily, Argentine football is not a popular culture as it traverses all classes, although with a slight prevalence towards the middle and lower middle classes. As noted earlier, the new Argentine class structure is similar to other Western societies, but the new structure makes it increasingly difficult to designate a working class in the strict sense. Similarly, the growth of a so-called *mediatic culture* (Kellner 1995), from the 1970s, indicates the fragmentation of the cultural classification of class. The communications explosion over the last decade substituted the *national-popular* cultures (which were central to classical Latin American analysis) for *international-popular* cultures (Ortiz 1991). In this expansion, football, a fundamental commodity of the cultural industry, also tends to extend its parameters. However, the dynamics of social exclusion also came into play; neo-conservative regimes weaken traditional class boundaries, and intensify social exclusion through working-class unemployment and middle-class impoverishment. Consequently, football contains basic economic divisions: the cost of admission to the stadiums (or to the services of cable television) exclude the 'traditional' public, in what could be called a Darwinian process that was unimaginable a decade earlier. Recent data, especially referring to violent incidents, seem to indicate that the poorest sectors take refuge in minor league football for economic reasons: the tickets are cheaper and transport costs lower.

In Argentina, social exclusion affects football's practice at professional and amateur levels. Professionally, playing at the highest level demands a nutrition in childhood that the lower classes cannot provide; hence, today, the best players tend to come from the middle classes. At amateur level, recreational practice is restricted increasingly to social groups with the time and money that is unavailable to working-class people. To add to this crisis of exclusion, Argentine football practices a symbolic and material imperialism. The clearest sign of this imperial expansion is the *footballisation* of television: the hundreds of hours on cable or satellite television of sport programmes, and the fact that the ten most watched programmes on Argentine television in 1997 were sport transmissions (*Clarín*, 28 December 1997). To this can be added the constant exchange of players, from the small to big teams, and from these into European football or the 'new markets' (especially Mexico and Japan). The traditional continuity of a player, in the same team for an extended period of time, has disappeared. Soon after his appearance, the player is sold to a buyer, thus assuring benefits to all parties except the fans.

In the traditional period of Argentine football, the axes of the team's identity were its colours and its symbolic players, in addition to the team's space (the stadium). Today, because of constant changes in jersey sponsorship and the incessant sale of players, these markers of identity are weakened. Players are the new partners of the local *jet-set,* they dominate television and advertising; they became erotic symbols, their sex lives are exposed. The distance from the common supporter has never been greater.

In response supporters now perceive themselves as the custodians of club identity. Fans are faithful to 'the colours', ahead of 'traitor' players, of managers guided by personal interest, of television controllers busy maximising gain, of corrupt journalists involved in transfers. Supporters develop, in consequence, an excessive self-perception, which produces militant obligations. Their 'assistance' at the stadium is not only the execution of a weekly rite, but a double play, both pragmatic and symbolic. On one hand, there is their participation in the match, which they believe influences the performance and hence the score. On the other hand, the continuity of identity depends, exclusively, on the incessant return to the temple of worship where the symbolic contract is renewed. Meanwhile, the Argentine playing style declines into one dominated by tactical pragmatism in the pursuit of hollow victories. An ethos of hyper-professionalism prevails, displacing the original style (with its emphasis on deception and invention) in favour of order, discipline, training, planning, and even the regulation of attire and hairstyle.

TRIBAL FOOTBALL

These fan processes do not confine themselves to traditional football identities. Instead, their actions confirm a post-modern fragmentation in a process of tribalisation (Maffesoli 1990), which works two ways: first, in constructing the inner nature of the supporters' self-identity; and secondly in their radically negative depiction of various opponents, the *others.* Consequently, local football rivalries are stretched out to the point that they shape primary, almost essentialised identities. Moreover, the national team is affected by them and accused of representing factions. The mythical unity of Argentina is now regarded as subject to tribal logic, with the patrician and bourgeois River Plate of Buenos Aires seen as dominating the national team. Fans are convinced that whatever success the national select may have is subordinate to the success of the club team. Support for the national side is now partial and fragmentary; the previous unity is absent.

Supporter groups have emerged from diverse origins, with their own names, internal functions and duties, and identifying flags and paraphernalia. In the case of Racing Club, one of the fan groups is called Racing Stones, because of their predilection for the Rolling Stones. Another is called *The 95,* simply because, coming from the north of Buenos Aires, they travel to home matches on the number 95 bus. This internal segmentation fragments identities which, in some cases, become irreconcilable. The growing presence of young female fans adds further complexity to the picture. The expansive imperialism of football culture seems to capture the whole symbolic order, today young women attend the stadium in growing numbers, adopting strong and inclusive forms of football militancy. Female fans speak the male language, they are incorporated into its codes without the prospect of creating autonomous space because of the strength of Argentine male traditions and the weakness of feminist ones.

A MASS MEDIA CARNIVAL

The idea of carnival is central to thinking through the practices of Argentine fans, and to determine the extent to which those practices deviate from hegemonic ones. It is easy to register deviations and transgressions in this carnivalization of football. The stadium seems to become the place for inverting hierarchies, for realising the democratic illusion of modernity, and for verifying the point that equality and meritocracy are pure republican fantasy. But sport rituals accept divergent readings. On one hand, the orthodox Bakhtinian position of Arno Vogel interprets the celebration of the Brazilian World Cup win in 1970 as a classical carnival which inverted hierarchies (Vogel 1982); Bromberger (1993a: 99) makes a similar analysis of the Neapolitan party of 1987 (after winning the Italian championship). Archetti (1992) describes the Argentine football ritual as a mixture of the tragic and comic, an oscillation between the violent and the carnivalesque (cf. Bahktin 1968). Archetti's hypothesis is that comic elements prevailed in the classical time of Argentine football, but were progressively displaced by tragic elements in the last three decades (Archetti 1992: 266).

But we also have the possibility that Eagleton (1981) proposes: carnival as a controlled rupture of hegemony, a popular but circumscribed explosion of the tensions between law and liberation, power and desire.

Considering this, one could suggest that football's hyper-spectacularisation favours the rule of law over any deviation. The stadium does not appear as a transgressive place; instead the carnivalesque of Argentine fans has been integrated by the mass media. Today, dressed-up fans parade in front of the cameras to be incorporated into the television narrative, they display their practices like elements of a show. A relatively novel phenomenon is the public screening of football matches on televisions in public bars, described by fans as a new ritual of support (Grimson and Varela 1998; Varela 1998). Carnival, from that perspective, figures as an element in the rhetoric of football television discourse. It becomes merely an image on the opening titles. Such imagery then becomes a new lie in democratic polyphony: a sound without a voice. But ritual remains, hidden in discourse, in order for it to be transgressed.

DISTINCTION: A RITUAL OF VIOLENCE

Like every ritual, football involves a suspension of the social order. Between the use of that suspension and consent to its limits there are several possibilities. One of them is violence, which is on the increase in the Argentine game. Football violence allows us to understand the historical stigmatisation of the lower 'dangerous' classes of the industrial revolution during the nineteenth century, and their reappearance in the same sense during the information revolution (Portelli 1993: 78). The revolts in the stadium entail, from this perspective, a certain kind of distinction: violence is aimed against private property and the body, and it escapes the state's monopoly. The violence could be thought of as a strong form of social expression (Mignon 1992), to be located within the crisis of participation and legitimacy of neo-conservative societies. The crisis occurs in various ways; in the 'status' of the middle classes, the critical social exclusion of lower social classes. All of this leads to the search for new forms of social visibility: violent behaviour against others, or in the political extremism of the right, as Mignon notes in the French case. The stadium provides a sense of communal ownership for those who feel excluded. But that stadium is also a stage for the mass media, a place where behaviour is amplified for millions of receivers.

Portelli has proposed the metaphorical rather than literal use of Oscar Lewis's 'culture of poverty' thesis. Central to these are the following traits: 'lack of actual participation and integration in the institutions of society at large, a sense of crowding and promiscuity, a strong internalised sense of being marginalised, powerless, dependent and inferior' (Portelli 1993: 78). In the football universe, the axis of the hegemonic-subordinate opposition (or 'workers versus capitalist') is displaced by 'rich versus poor', and in the space of representation that this generates, 'the occasional victory of the weak over the strong has a powerful mythic appeal, going back to cosmological mythologies' (ibid: 85).

Also, chance and cheating, while not strangers to the culture of capitalism, are central to the culture of poverty; the game is ruled by imponderable factors rather than by business. In this design, the fan tries to influence the logic of the game with his intervention, in order to re-establish justice. But the violence of these supporters, whether it be symbolic or real, is not an exercise in challenging power:

> Any revolt on the terraces is doomed to failure because it is couched in terms
> of feudal class relations rather than capitalist ones. It represents an eternal
> circle of fate in which submission follows revolt, and social injustice is blamed
> on a crippling sense of supernatural destiny. (O'Connor 1993: 105)

Football violence has received little attention in Argentina, if we understand *attention* as a specialised gaze which helps to construct a strong statute of knowledge. That said, such violence has been framed within a mass of journalistic and political discourses. In this view, the violent are young and 'unadapted', they operate under the influence of drugs and alcohol, and they must be socially excluded – from the stadium and society. These sentiments illustrate the mediocrity of public debate. But at the same time, they reflect the perspective of *other* fans, who themselves read the violent actors as *others*, in terms of class and culture. Before, fellow countrymen of the stadium and the team were all 'victims' of police repression; today, there is a greater tendency for stigmatisation to occur towards violent fans, basically because of their actions.

Argentine football violence reflects wider practices in politics and in the economy. But it has more complex and fewer recognisable forms than that seen during the repression of the last military dictatorship (1976–83). Fundamentally, the persistence and worsening of social violence involves exclusion, unemployment and inadmission to the consumer's market, notably via the privatisation of health and education. In that frame, football violence points in many directions simultaneously. It indicates the persistence of paramilitary groups, today converted into the *barras bravas* on the terraces, with the complicity of a good proportion of the game's leadership. It indicates the racism and discrimination of journalistic discourses, that fail to provide answers to current events. And it indicates the desperation of important nuclei within the young working classes, who find in violence the only practice that grants them visibility, harvesting as it does press and television coverage. The importance of football to the mass media guarantees them an appearance; but it is a contradictory one, where in the same moment that they emerge, they obtain only condemnations.

The observation of contemporary violence, and the study of its historical antecedents, allows us to classify its different properties, assigning causations and meanings. This classification demands new data; it needs to explain fully the meanings which actors confer upon violent practices. Motives are explained in political terms, but strong fan collectives are produced and reproduced through shared experiences of confrontation, which are described according to the social rhetoric of *aguante* (strength). *Aguante* has a wider meaning than its strict etymological definition; this includes a complete rhetoric of the body, and a collective resistance towards others (be they fans or police or officialdom). Therefore policies must be designed which recognise the complexity of violence, and which avoid or reduce public action to repressive practices, as certain proposals that copy the 'British approach' seem to prefer. The recent transfer of responsibility for this 'problem', to the Security Bureau of Executive Power, indicates such a tendency. Their first proposals include the installation of surveillance cameras (the old panoptical illusion), and the suppression of the 'ends'.

Argentina cannot respond effectively to the problems presented by globalisation. How can it mark out its local position and still retain a sense of national identity within the context of transnational media discourses? Instead, a collision of discourses occurs. A hegemonic neo-conservatism, which proclaims Argentine entrance to the First World, daily co-exists with the everyday experience of the lower and the middle classes. Their lifeworld reflects the acute deterioration of living standards, the increase in poverty, and the damaging effects of entry to the global market, such as the depreciation of the value of goods, unemployment as a world phenomenon, and drug trafficking. Football, is perceived as the last haven of enjoyment – like Barthes's *jouissance* (Armstrong and Giulianotti 1997: 26) – whilst also a window through which one can view the wealth of developed nations. That tension, at this time, seems to be resolved in favour of capital, in spite of the passionate recovery of the supporters. The violence manifested around the game may enable the lower classes to feel separate from the hegemonic classes. In football, the signs of this Gramscian excision are numerous; they occur when opposition to hegemonic control is at its maximum level. In Argentine football, one cannot defeat this power from the inside.

Acknowledgements

This work was financed by University of Buenos Aires. The author is grateful to Sally Scott and Susan Wildridge for their secretarial assistance.

7 The Brazilian Style of Football and its Dilemmas

José Sergio Leite Lopes

Football was introduced and played by members of Brazil's elite as a way of confirming their distinctive position against other social groups. Yet football's popularity spread extraordinarily from the end of the 1910s. In the following decade, in Rio de Janeiro and São Paulo, highly talented players emerged among the working classes. They opened the way to the professional age, despite a strong defence of amateurism mounted by most directors at the leading clubs. The defence of professionalism and its subsequent developments helped to forge a sense of national identity through football. This sentiment was related to the creation of a style of play that owed much to working-class players. Paradoxically, the same players' characteristics were criticised whenever a defeat was anticipated or actually occurred. The specific qualities of these players were seen as weakening the nation's status vis-à-vis European nations or Brazil's South American rivals, Argentina and Uruguay (cf. Leite Lopes 1997). Often, these criticisms emphasised the lack of physical and tactical discipline which supposedly influenced the results, even if an elegant style of playing had been exhibited.

There is thus a tension between the emphasis, on the one hand, on tactical and physical discipline and the role of coaches and physical trainers, and on the other, on the talent and creativity of the players' personal style (over and above any new tactical concepts that may be introduced). This tension relates to a basic contradiction within Brazilian professional football. The influx of working-class players brought a spontaneous and enjoyable football style, the kind played on improvised football fields (*peladas*) and by small-town and suburban teams. Conversely, the professional game requires physical, tactical and disciplinary preparation, but this does not eliminate the spontaneous, self-acquired skills of the working-class players. Instead, their ability is channelled into a style of football that is both aesthetic and competitive.

The issue of professionalism also relates to the balance between social groups *within* the world of football. The spread of football and its social function as a catalyst for national identity is due not only to the growing participation of athletes from the working classes and their subsequent professionalism. It is also influenced by the creation of new technical positions in football, which provided opportunities to former players with a higher social and educational capital, as well as to new *professionals* such as physical trainers. The appearance of new professionals in football, such as sports journalists and broadcasters, had an enormous impact upon the creation of an ever-growing multi-class society.

A significant number of these professionals (such as journalists and writers), began to oppose the traditional racist arguments that were applied to Brazilian football by the editors. They proceeded to demonstrate that what is striking and specific to Brazilian football, relative to other nations, is the creation of bodily techniques or skills which have their origin in the black and mulatto sectors of the working classes.

THE ORIGINS AND PROBLEMS OF A DISTINCTIVE PLAYING STYLE

A unique and distinctively Brazilian way of playing football began to be recognised during the 1938 World Cup in France. Then, for the first time, Brazil had a team of professional players, with two black stars, Leônidas da Silva and Domingos da Guia. In contrast to the championships of 1930 and 1934, Brazil chose a team of professional players, incorporating the technical richness that working-class players had brought to the leading clubs for the past fifteen years. French sports journalists recognised what a few isolated Brazilian writers had been saying at that time; Mário Filho, for example, had long advocated professionalism and the inclusion of black players who would act as creative 'outsiders'. In all this, the exhibition of a style of playing which led to improvisation – an ability well demonstrated in certain acrobatic moves, such as Leônidas's *bicicleta* ('bicycle-kick') – was critical.

International recognition strengthened a local perception of the originality of national players. This originality was taken up as a theme by Gilberto Freyre, who saw football as a manifestation of his historical interpretation of Brazilian society: the wealth of the cultural contribution of blacks and the importance of the racial mixture of Brazil's population. The 1938 World Cup permitted an intellectual such as Freyre to appreciate the importance of what was happening in this new and unknown area, connected to the 'sportification' of Brazilian society through football. In 1933, the year when he published his innovative book *Casa Grande 3 Senzala* (translated into English as *Masters and Slaves*), professional football began to emerge. For the first time, the winner of the Rio de Janeiro championship was a factory club with a team of workers – a team from Bangu, a textile factory founded at the end of the nineteenth century which had previously been a sugar mill characteristic of the patriarchal society studied by Freyre. These facts indicate that a strong process of functional democratisation had been in process since the early 1920s, thus coinciding with the formation of Freyre's ideas. When Freyre wrote the preface to Mário Filho's book *O Negro no Futebol Brasileiro* ('Blacks in Brazilian Football') in 1947, he acknowledged that the facts, descriptions and suggestions of Filho were an agreeable *surprise* (Filho 1964).

Freyre's work shows a concern with daily life, intimacy, the body and fashions (within the perspective of a macro-historical analysis). Yet even he had difficulty in realising what was occurring at that time, as an upper-class pastime became an element of popular culture. At the 1938 World Cup, Freyre was able to explain the Brazilian team's success and the public's fascination with the leading players.[1] This team, which earned third place at the tournament, made the best possible impression in the country. The team had come close to winning the title, in contrast to the failures at the earlier finals. It had only lost in the semi-finals to Italy, in a way that could be explained to protect Brazil's footballing superiority, e.g. a bad refereeing decision or a penalty, the effect of external pressures on the players, or the privileged status of Italy in this match against the only South American side in the tournament. The feeling of being *victimised*, of having won a 'moral victory' remained strong in sports journalism and among the growing public of football fans. The prestige of the great black players in that tournament was enormous in Brazil, and it contributed to the popularisation of the clubs where they played. Both Leônidas da Silva and Domingos da Guia were transferred, in 1944, to football teams in São Paulo, resulting in a consecration, in the other important centre of Brazilian football, of the style which had been created fundamentally by the working-class players in Rio de Janeiro.

During the 1940s and 1950s, the clubs that grew most were the ones that adopted professionalism. Some clubs were formed to draw new players from the working classes. Others brought these players into their teams, following the lead of Vasco da Gama, the first club to recruit coloured players during the 1920s, or Flamengo, an elite club which by that time had become the most popular team in Rio. On the other hand, there were clubs which had originated from the Italian immigration to São Paulo, Belo Horizonte and Curitiba; all of these clubs were named Palestra Itália, but were pressed to change their names and nationalise themselves when Brazil entered the Second World War on the Allies' side. The clubs adopted new Brazilian names such as Palmeiras, Cruzeiro and Coritiba; to signal their nationalisation, they began to admit a few black players. The rivalry between the clubs at this time was characterised by a competition between the elite clubs and those connected to middle-class groups, secondary elite and outsiders. Elite clubs remained in professional football but tried to control or arrest the entry of black players into their teams – the others were open to players from the working classes, including blacks.[2]

It should be noted that in the 1940s, Fluminense, an elite club from Rio, used to recruit white players from São Paulo to play against teams like Vasco and Flamengo, which were then selecting black players. The Rio team of Botafogo also resisted the inclusion of black players and struggled to compete; as a result something similar happened with Palmeiras, from São Paulo, and Grêmio, from Pôrto Alegre. The latter had a very explicit policy of excluding blacks, and lost ground to their city rivals Internacional, which adopted professionalism and produced an excellent team that was open to the best players from the lower classes. During the 1950s, the elite clubs finally accepted the results of football matches as evidence and opened their teams to black players: Fluminense signed Didi and other black players; Botafogo recruited Garrincha, who was then paying for a factory team, and later signed Didi from Fluminense; Grêmio recruited Tesourinha, who had first been picked by Brazil while playing for Internacional before transferring to Vasco in Rio.

The good showing at the 1938 World Cup encouraged Brazil to bid to host the next World Cup, which took place after the war. In Rio de Janeiro, a large municipal stadium was built capable of holding 150,000 people (cf. Moura 1998). Throughout the 1940s, Brazil was able to continue practising football while Europe was uprooted by war. Moreover, football's popularisation in the major cities, in terms of working-class players and growing public interest, made Brazil an emergent power in the game. The new generations perfected a national style of playing that was tested in international competition. Flávio Costa was chosen as national team coach. During the 1940s he had worked for Rio de Janeiro's two main clubs Flamengo and Vasco. The latter formed the basis of the national team, complemented by players from São Paulo and a few players from other Rio sides.

During the 1930s and 1940s physical education also developed rapidly. Starting in the military domain it spread to the new universities in São Paulo and Rio. Physical education was debated among educationalists; during the authoritarian regime of 1935–45, it became strongly associated with the civic good, with bodily health and discipline, all for the benefit of the nation. Arguments based on eugenics and on the 'racial development' of the Brazilian people were widely used in texts to promote physical education courses (cf. Negreiros 1998). During the 1910s and 1920s, the eugenist arguments were taken as a political foundation to defend the development of sport in Brazil, particularly football, which was becoming very popular. These arguments were used to justify the creation of clubs, including those in working-class neighbourhoods (cf. Pereira 1998). They were even more widely used in the 1930s and 1940s, when state institutions were created to regulate sports, and also during the debates about the building of municipal stadia in São Paulo in 1940 and Rio in 1950. From the late 1940s onwards, football team coaches – many of whom were former players – would only be accepted by professional football clubs if they had obtained a university degree in physical education.

During the 1950 World Cup, the results of the Brazilian team improved after a difficult opening game against Switzerland in São Paulo, when the players were booed by the fans. In Rio, the fans in the Maracanã stadium tried to encourage the team as a show of opposition towards their São Paulo counterparts. The Brazilian team improved to the extent that in the quarter-finals and in the semi-finals opponents were massacred leaving Brazil in a very favourable position over Uruguay in the final. The shock defeat of Brazil in this final transformed the happy and boisterous fans inside the world's largest stadium into a mourning multitude. The result also obfuscated the merits of a style of playing which was then being perfected and recognised by international journalists. The defeat reactivated the old elitist racist beliefs that had dominated Brazilian social thinking during the first half of the century (when they were challenged by Gilberto Freyre), and which were used to explain the supposed inferiority of the Brazilian people relative to Europeans and North Americans. Confidence in the specific qualities of Brazilian football was shaken; European football became overvalued, thereby inverting the situation that prevailed from 1938 to 1950. There was an explicit revival of the racist arguments that had been common in Brazilian social thinking at the beginning of the century (cf. Seyferth 1989, 1991, 1995), as they reappeared through the reports by Joãs Lyra Filho, the head of the Brazilian delegation to the 1954 World Cup (who, nevertheless, in later writings assumed more 'Freyrian' positions). According to Lyra Filho the subsequent failure of Brazil in 1954 was attributable to the composition of the Brazilian people.[3]

The Brazilian style only received national and international recognition with Brazil's unexpected victory at the 1958 World Cup finals in Sweden. The influx of players from the working classes continued strongly throughout the 1950s. During this decade, the last great elite clubs – tied as they were to the vestiges of amateurism and the racist recruitment of players – resigned themselves to the exigencies of competition; they began to scout for the best players – their social origin or race notwithstanding – while trying to attract the largest base. All this enhanced the quality of Brazilian football. The experience accumulated by generations of professional football players was very important. For example, Pelé's father was a former player during the time of Leônidas, Domingos and Valdemar de Brito (the coach of a small-town team, who 'discovered' Pelé). The new balance of technical and physical discipline, as demanded by coaches and club directors was also vital. This factor allowed Brazilians to develop a specific playing style that was not inhibited by defensive tactics; nor did it undermine individual initiative, which is a traditional signature of these players.

NATIONAL IDENTITY AND CONTRADICTORY PARTICIPATION

Shortly before the 1970 World Cup, a book was published in which a group of Brazilian coaches discussed their working conditions, evaluated Brazilian football, and put forward their views regarding the Mexico tournament (Pedrosa, 1968). The coaches pessimism reflected the general mood after the Brazilian team's performance at the 1966 World Cup.

The book also gave brief curriculam vitae of the coaches. Some had started playing as amateurs before going into professional football and then turning to coaching. Ademar Pimenta, for instance, was the coach at the 1938 World Cup when the Brazilian team excited the country and became a benchmark during the enormous popularisation of football in Brazil. Pimenta was born in 1896 and studied at the Pedro II School, a federal high school in Rio where many children from the city's elite were educated. Pimenta started playing football at school when he was fourteen. Afterwards, during football's amateur period, he played for several small clubs, ending his career at the America Football Club, supported by the wealthier families from northern Rio. Pimenta stopped playing just as professionalism was becoming the rule, as the interdependency networks of football's various social agents were becoming more complex. With his social and educational capital, Pimenta was able to become coach at small and medium-sized clubs such as Madureira and São Cristóvão, then technical director at the Rio de Janeiro Football Federation; he then coached the Brazilian team during the South American championships and at the World Cup in France. From the late 1940s, he took up a new position in the football world, as sports journalist and radio broadcaster.

Brazil's World Cup coaches between 1950 and 1966, had been amateur players and studied in reasonably good schools just like Pimenta; but in contrast they also had gone through PE university courses before the First Division clubs formally required this level of education. Both Flávio Costa, coach of the famous 1950 team, who was born in 1906, and Zezé Moreira, born in 1908 and coach of the 1954 team, and also his brother Aymoré, born in 1912 and coach of the 1962 and 1966 teams, obtained their degrees from the Physical Education School at the Universidade do Brasil. This school was originally linked to the army, before it was taken over by the university. Vicente Feola, born in 1909 and coach of the 1958 champion team, had a similar career, but was from São Paulo. He also received his degree in PE in the 1940s, from the São Paulo Higher School of Physical Education and Sports.

The trajectory of coaches such as Flávio Costa, Zezé and Aymoré Moreira, Vicente Feola and others shows that professionalism opened up new perspectives for players. The new age also produced coaching positions for former players who had a higher social background, better secondary education and had been accepted for degree courses in PE. With the demise of amateurism and its attendant social tensions, players from wealthier backgrounds stopped practising football and turned to other sports, or began to play in a different way. Some clubs in São Paulo, such as Germânia Paulistano, and São Paulo Athletic abandoned their football teams after the arrival of professionalism (Caldas 1990). This process is similar to what occurred with even greater intensity in other countries (for example in England and France with the establishment of rugby union). In Rio, most of the leading clubs maintained their football teams after the arrival of professionalism, but there were changes to the structure and meaning of these clubs' internal forms of association. Football became a professional dimension of the club distinct from its other activities. The players became the club's employees, not its members. A distance also emerged between the new players and the former elite amateurs who stopped playing. However, some players from the middle classes (from outside the elite of São Paulo or Rio, but with a comfortable social status and good education) stayed in professional football and filled the technical positions which had become more prevalent in an increasingly progressive and serious sport.

New tactical schemes were adopted, often with a lag of many years since their first introduction in Europe. Some players viewed the new schemes as an attack on the traditional styles of playing. This seems to have been the case when the Hungarian coach Kuschner introduced the 'W–M' system to the Flamengo team in Rio. Kuschner sacrificed the talented Fausto, a central midfielder, by forcing him to stay in defence. Flávio Costa, who was Kuschner's assistant, introduced a greater flexibility to this tactical system when the Hungarian left. Costa became the most important coach in Brazil during the 1940s and up to the 1950 World Cup. Subsequently, Zezé Moreira valued defensive tactics and discipline, even though he introduced the concept of zonal play (instead of man-marking opposing players), and favoured long pass in midfield, such as Didi. Others such as Feola and João Saldanha (who coached up to the 1970s World Cup finals) gave the players more autonomy, the former in a more implicit and less intentional way, the latter in a more committed and clear way. Their preference for freedom may be attributable to the fact that both had been given the national team position because the football authorities had experienced difficulties in making their final choice.

Feola was an unknown coach from a club in São Paulo when he was chosen to occupy the leading position on a technical committee that included people from São Paulo and Rio. He was chosen because he was considered as a 'neutral' in the traditional football rivalry between the two cities, which had undermined the national team at previous World Cups. With his low-profile style, and as the central figure within a wider committee, Feola seems to have lent greater weight towards the experience gained by players involved in previous World Cups. These players expressed their desire for space, to show the talent of Brazilian players, instead of emphasising defensive tactics and discipline. This viewpoint was given particular exposure through support for the selection of the talented but unpredictable right-winger Garrincha. In the following tournament, Feola was substituted by Aymoré Moreira, but continued to collaborate with the technical committee.

João Saldanha, born in 1917, was an ex-amateur player with the main football teams in Rio, and was a former beach-footballer as well. He was used to this spontaneous and popular kind of football, where social contacts and communication were established between lower-class athletes and those of the middle classes. Even though he had enjoyed an elite education, at Pedro II and the city's Law School, he became a left-wing activist, did not finish his university courses, and lived a troubled life, with periods as a clandestine activist and as an exile abroad. Saldanha came from a wealthy family from southern Brazil, and as an amateur always gave technical support to the Botafogo club. The club directors at that time (the 1930s and 1940s) were abandoning their position as the last defenders of amateurism to become belated advocates of professionalism. In this context, Saldanha was appointed as the reserve coach at Botafogo; he was the chief coach when the team won the championship in 1957 with players such as Garrincha, Didi and Nilton Santos.

Saldanha thus became linked to the creative phase in Brazilian football which led to the 1958 World Cup victory. After that, he became a sports writer and broadcaster, enjoying the freedom to defend the talents of Brazilian players and criticise club directors and coaches. He was appointed Brazilian team coach for the qualifying games for the 1970s World Cup, at a time when most other coaches had been discredited by the defeat at the previous tournament. Paradoxically, as a long time communist (since his law school days in 1935), Saldanha became the national team coach under a very repressive military regime. This unfavourable wider context was compounded by disputes within Brazilian football; he was replaced before the World Cup in Mexico, even though he had been responsible for structuring the team. Saldanha returned to sports journalism until his death (see Máximo 1954).

Saldanha is one of the journalists and intellectuals who possessed a high level of social and cultural capital, and who defended the creative football of working-class players. Before him, there were journalists like Mário Filho and Ary Barroso, and social commentators like José Lins do Rego and Nelson Rodrigues. Mário Filho can be said to have reinvented sports journalism in the 1930s and 1940s. He promoted this genre under very difficult political conditions, having inherited a newspaper that was persecuted by the dominant political forces after the 1930 revolution. Filho later became an influential political journalist protecting himself under the cover of sports journalism. He understood that by following what was happening in football, he could have as much access to national issues as he would if he focused directly on political themes. Filho became the chief advocate of professionalism in football, explaining that the issue was opening the way for black players to take part in an initially elitist sport (cf. Leite Lopes 1997; Leite Lopes and Faguer 1994).

According to Mário Filho, this nationally authentic style was related to deep and unconscious bodily techniques (which folklorists also valued in popular dance), and to something as modern and international as a sport. When he advanced this view, Filho became a sports counsellor to the central powers, especially to Getúlio Vargas in the 1940s, and later, when Vargas was elected president, between 1950 and 1954.

Ary Barroso was brought up in the provinces and, as a student at Rio's Law School, took an interest in football and popular music. He felt uneasy as a member of Fluminense, the aristocratic club, and switched his support to Flamengo, which in the 1930s was establishing itself as a highly popular club. He became a successful broadcaster promoting popular music (he was a *samba* composer); and later a radio commentator at football games, with his trademark bias towards Flamengo, even though politically he was a right-wing liberal opposed to the politics of Filho and Vargas's second term.

José Lins do Rego was a writer who became known for novels that focused on the North-East region of Brazil. In a late novel, written in 1941, he introduced a main character who was a football player. He also maintained an open and intense support for Flamengo from 1945 to 1953, during which he also wrote for Mário Filho's sports newspaper. The playwright Nelson Rodrigues, Mário Filho's brother, wrote about football between 1956 and 1958, supporting the inversion of the elitist and racist arguments which were employed against the Brazilian people and Brazilian football.

This process benefits from a kind of energy aimed at social *emancipation*, a subconscious energy related to the body and to hidden social conflicts over inclusion and exclusion from fields of power. This energy results in the mobilisation of a very wide cross-class public movement, including elite sectors, particularly in the post-1958 period when Brazil began to win international championships. While the influx of working-class players was critical, so too was the involvement of other social classes with a higher social and cultural capital, in contributing to football's greater general acceptance within the population as a whole. On the other hand, it is interesting to follow the tensions between the defenders of discipline in sport, who emphasised the new tactics learned in Europe, and the advocates of alternative tactics that would enable a competitive and aesthetic style, embracing the working-class practice of football and ultimately becoming linked to national identity itself. These tensions become even more interesting as football and other sports come to be used as an increasingly pedagogic procedure for poor children and youngsters with little prospect of finding regular employment.

Thus, in Brazil, the transition from amateur to professional football had real consequences: it created a diversified labour market for players, coaches and related professionals; it resulted in football's enormous popularisation and in the formation of a national identity with this sport at its centre; it also consolidated a characteristic style of play. Both this style and this national identity have as a reference point the debate about the racial mixture of Brazil. The 'racial mixture', that was a cause of self-criticism, became a basis for valorising a Brazilian style of play, specially since the 1958 World Cup in Sweden.

Yet, the democratisation of football did not lead to a complete distancing of the elite or the old amateur players, because they reserved a space as directors (in the clubs, the federations, and the government organisations responsible for this sport), or as coaches in the teams. The results of the unconscious struggles between the coaches (moulded in the physical education schools) and the players (formed by popular football, with its spontaneous body techniques) favour at certain times the development of a Brazilian style of play, which owes much to the working classes' appropriation of football.

Notes

1. In an interview before the Tournament, Freyre announced: 'I believe that one of the conditions for the Brazilian victory in Europe is the fact that this time we had the

courage to send a clearly Afro-Brazilian team. Let the Aryanists write that down' (*Correio da Manhã*, 15 June 1938). After the Cup, he completed his analysis: 'Our style of playing football seems to contrast to the European style because of a set of characteristics such as surprise, craftiness, shrewdness, readiness, and I shall even say, individual brilliance and spontaneity, all of which express our "*mullatoism*" ... Our passes ... our tricks ... that *something* which is related to dance, to *capoeira* [an Afro-Brazilian dance/martial art], mark the Brazilian style of football, which rounds and sweetens the game the English invented, the game which they and other Europeans play in such an acute, angular way – all this seems to express, in a very interesting manner for psychologists and sociologists, the *flamboyant* and at the same time shrewd (*malandro*) *mulattoism*, which today can be detected in every true affirmation of Brazil.'

2. On the case of southern Brazil, see Damo (1998).
3. If on the one hand the racial mixture and the contribution of blacks enable Brazil to play an aesthetically distinguished brand of football, on the other it also leads to great difficulties in obtaining results, because of the lack of discipline, collective playing and emotional balance during the decisive games (cf. Guedes 1998; Lyra Filho 1954).

Part III
Waiting in the Wings:
Marginal Players

8 Making the Maltese Cross: Football on a Small Island

Gary Armstrong and Jon P. Mitchell

Even in a winner-loser culture that is football, it is in the interests of the good of the game that frequent losers sometimes win. At the level of world competition small nations know their chances of victory against larger ones are negligible, but their fans will expect the occasional drawn game and certainly a victory over countries of similar standing. When such logic does not realise itself, problems set in; the spectators become disconsolate. As we write in 1998, the followers of the Maltese national side are some of the most disconsolate fans in the world. A World Cup qualifying campaign was concluded in September 1997 with Malta having lost all 12 games, conceded 37 goals and scored only two. Consecutive 6–0 defeats at the hands of Yugoslavia, Slovakia and the Czech Republic might have been expected, but losing home and away to the Faroe Islands (population 43,000) was not.

Such was the disdain of the Maltese that for the final game at home to Yugoslavia only 300 attended – a record low in the history of the European section of the World Cup competition. That same evening, however, half the population of Malta was glued to TV sets watching the Italy–England decider in Rome. At its conclusion more people took part in a motorcar cavalcade celebrating England's qualification than were leaving Malta's national stadium. An outsider could legitimately ask, 'What was going on?' The Maltese, without a World Cup qualifying victory in twenty-three years, legitimately ask, 'Against whom can we win?' For thousands of football fans in this island, the status of the national team has ceased to concern them. Their emotions are invested either in the parochial emnities of the domestic leagues or they have abandoned the local for the attractions of English and Italian teams provided by inter-terrestrial TV and the annual trips membership of supporters clubs offer them.

EMPIRE STADIUM, GZIRA, OCTOBER 1979

Compacted sand, not grass, provided the surface on which this European Championship qualifier was played. Although not officially permitted under its regulations, UEFA turned a blind eye to Malta's lack of a grass pitch, as it had done since Malta joined both the Federation in 1960 and FIFA the year before. The ramshackle stadium built in 1922, and privately owned, but leased to the Malta FA, had seen better days. Located in the heart of a densely populated area,

99

the stadium had hosted some great games and had regularly held crowds of over 20,000. British engineers had constructed a greyhound racing track around the pitch in emulation of the Wembley stadium in London, and the ground was known as the Empire Stadium. Surrounding apartments and their occupants enjoyed the game free from their windows and roofs. The ubiquitous extended TV aerials dominated the sky-line.

What emperors there were sat in the few hundred seats provided in the grand-stand. Here officials of UEFA sat with government ministers. To their left were around 20 Turkey supporters, one waving a large national flag. The scheduled 3.00 p.m. kick-off passed without any sign of a start, the Malta team squad arrived at the ground 15 minutes late because torrential rain had caused flooding which had delayed their journey from their hotel. The same rain produced huge puddles across the pitch and behind one goal-post lay a puddle at least a foot deep and ten yards wide. Standing between the changing room and pitch, this little pond presented the players with their first obstacle. The Turks negotiated it well, most merely getting soaked to their ankles. The Maltese who followed them ran out purposefully only for one to trip and fall head-long into the water. Soaked, he tried to retain a dignity as the crowd laughed at both his misfortune and what was to become, because of the water and the pitch, a farce of a match.

A scrappy contest played in teeming rain saw Turkey 2–0 ahead by half-time. Illicit (and illegal) bets were being taken in the usual corner of the ground for those in the know. Emulating the adults, young boys from poor backgrounds tried to make money as they heaved heavy baskets of small bags containing 'karawett' (nuts). One dominant hoarding advertised Pepsi-Cola, another sign erected in the popular enclosure questioned the need to use bad language. The police stood in a group smoking and watching the match and ignored those who had climbed on a corrugated iron roof of one side to get a better view.

Towards half-time chants of 'Dragut, Dragut' reminded the Turks of Maltese disdain for their part in the 1565 Great Siege. At half-time a few dozen locals taking exception to the presence of the Turkish flag, grabbed it from a flag pole, and threw it on to the pitch. Returning for the second half, the visiting players were met with a hail of stones thrown by a Maltese mob. After ten minutes, the police moved into one section of the crowd, their presence succeeded in keeping missiles to a minimum for the next 45 minutes. One stone hit the foot of the lines-man who complained to the referee. The match was allowed to continue and the score-line remained 2–0. Both teams were booed off the pitch.[1]

EMPIRE, NATION AND RESISTANCE

Malta's strategic location in the centre of the Mediterranean, 65 miles south of Sicily and 90 miles north of Tunisia and Libya has made it a valuable fortress for a succession of empires. The last of these was the British, which ran Malta as a colony from 1800 to 1964. Before that there had been a brief two-year visit by Napoleon's troops who had taken over from the Order of the Knights of St John (Blouet 1993). The Knights ran Malta from 1530 to 1798. Originally set up in Jerusalem as a hospital order to tend Christian pilgrims, the Order was ousted when Jerusalem fell to the Ottomans, and eventually moved to Malta. It initially entertained crusading ambitions but was eventually forced to adopt a more defensive position, as the southern 'shield of Christendom' (Bradford 1972). The Great Siege, which saw Knights and Maltese successfully defending the island against Sultan Suleiman III's troops, was a defining moment in national history. After months of hardship, the siege was lifted when the Turkish general Dragut was killed by one of his own cannons, and reinforcements arrived from Sicily. This military own goal set the agenda for the ridicule of Turkey and the maintenance of Maltese honour against these eastern Mediterranean adversaries on the football field.

Only 17 miles by nine at its extremities, Malta is one of the world's most densely populated countries, with 325,000 inhabitants. Its own language – a unique fusion of Roman-Italian and Arab-Semitic – gives its people a strong sense of national identity. In return they have to tolerate annually up to a million tourists who visit the island to enjoy Malta's greatest assets – a very warm climate and a famously friendly people. But as Dragut found, not everyone who arrived here departed in peaceful circumstances, and aside from religion, the game of football has manifested various antagonisms over the decades.

Football in Malta developed as a consequence of British colonialism. The first records of football in Malta date back to the 1870s. At that time, the game was being played among British servicemen stationed at the Malta garrison, but was introduced to the Maltese by a group of British Jesuits in 1877. The early success of the game took hold among the Maltese elites who attended colleges such as that run by the Jesuits. An official league did not begin until 1909, but institutions, gentlemen's clubs such as the Malta Athletic Club and the Equality Club, were also playing the game.

At the same time that football was taking hold, however, so was anti-colonial politics. The Equality Club as dedicated to equal rights – and particularly suffrage – between the Maltese and the British. Malta's struggle for nationhood against British colonial authority was a largely bloodless affair. In keeping with the status of the main agitators for change – who were mostly members of the legal profession – the struggle was mainly conducted through petition. It was also led by precisely the same class of people who were involved in the early Maltese football teams. The first party political meeting in Malta was held in 1879, and this set the nationalist ball rolling. From that time until the Second World War, the main issue for Maltese politics was culture – and particularly language. The struggle against the colonial powers became one against British cultural hegemony, as represented in the use of English as an official language. Partly because of the elite origins of Maltese nationalism, and partly because the indigenous language, *Malti* was not yet fully standardised, and the focus of Maltese national-ism became the Italian language. This was the language of the courts, of the Church, and of the early football pioneers.

At this time of burgeoning anti-colonial opinion, football became another way of demonstrating both equality and opposition. Indeed, this is a central paradox of competitive football – that it simultaneously produces equality and hierarchy; equality in the sense that the game is considered a contest between equals; hier-archy because despite this, one side must win. Early games pitted the newly formed Maltese teams against the established British regimental teams. Beating the regiments was all-important to the early Maltese teams, and a number of regular fixtures and trophies were established which had the status of semi-representative matches. Support for the club sides – some of which in the early years of the twentieth century were locality-based – became support for the Maltese against the British. The stakes were national(ist) stakes.[2]

However, anti-British feeling was not unequivocal because the British, as well as being opponents, were also patrons. Alongside the development of anti-colonialist nationalism was a corresponding movement – largely among the new industrial proletariat centred on the dockyards – in favour of British hegemony, as an opportunity for Malta to participate in the wealth of the British Empire (Frendo 1979: 20). The notion of British patronage over Malta, and its advantages for the nation, was being played out at a smaller level with regard to football. Following the establishment of football, other clubs emerged catering for the dockers (Baldacchino 1989). British support was essential in their development, particularly to give the clubs access to land for use as pitches. Teams were allowed to compete on the British parade grounds, and on sand pitches developed by the services. Later, land was donated by the colonial Governor, but the best pitches – particularly those with grass surfaces – were reserved for use by the British. By the 1920s, dependency on British patronage was reduced and local business inter-ests saw the value in developing football pitches. However, the continued use of sand pitches, and the difficulty of cultivating grass in a hot and largely barren island, militated against the quality of the local game, and does so today:

> There's a shortage of grass surfaces. You train in slippers and skid – which doesn't relate to grass, it's a different bodily function. (local club coach)

DUAL IDENTITIES: THE MARCH ON ROME

The political tension between pro-Italian and pro-British interests escalated in the first three decades of the twentieth century. Party politics polarised around this issue of cultural identity, and the so-called 'Language Question': whether Malta should speak Italian or English (Hull 1993). At the same time, support for inter-national football outside Malta polarised along the same lines. A key turning-point in the entrenchment of pro-Italian/pro-English football support came in 1933, during the tense years leading to the Second World War. The pro-Italian Nationalist Party had become increasingly associated with Mussolini's fascism and powerful irredentism. Their opponents, the pro-British Constitutional Party, fought against these moves to Italianisation. In the midst of this political upheaval, an international match was scheduled in Rome between Italy and England. A tour from Malta was organised for English Supporters. In the event, some 100 Maltese English-supporters travelled to Rome to cheer 'their' team. Because of the intense interest in Malta, radios were set up in the band clubs found throughout Maltese towns and villages and other social centres, and crowds gathered to listen to the commentary. In the dockyard town of Paola, a public address system was rigged up, and a table football game on the main square was used to demonstrate the movements of players and ball. As the first goal went to Italy, the assembled Nationalist crowds cheered, but as England equalised, the pro-British Constitutionalists retorted, mocking their political – and now football – opponents.

The occasion established the tradition of Maltese support for English and Italian teams, that in post-Independence Malta has become more important than support of the national team itself. Major tournaments such as the World Cup or European Championships, in which the two teams figure, are occasions for huge celebration, with public televisions surrounded by massed enthusiastic crowds. Following the games, cavalcade of cars set off around the roads of Malta, blowing horns and waving flags and scarves.[3] Support is as much demonstrated against the other team as for one's own. When Italy lose to Germany, for example, carcades of England fans circulate to mock the Italian fans. Such loyalty is no longer entirely political in post-Independence Malta, although many fans of Italy state that their support comes from their parents who were staunch Nationalists during the days of the Language Question. However, biography also plays a part. Where a person or their family was employed by the British, they will often tend to support England, even if they were Nationalists otherwise.

This orientation to Britain or Italy explains the existence of supporters' clubs in Malta for a variety of teams from the English and Italian leagues. The clubs emerged in the 1960s, and organise weekly meetings to watch videos of their favourite team or meet visiting players. The supporters' clubs with the highest membership are Manchester United (1,500), Inter Milan (900), AC Milan (1,000), Juventus (800), and Arsenal (600). However, not all fan clubs pursue big and famous sides. Clubs exist in support of the Sardinian side, Cagliari and English first division club Port Vale.

FOOTBALL AND THE EMERGENCE OF NATIONAL IDENTITY

After the Second World War, a more decidedly local national spirit emerged, that eventually led to the country's genuine independence as neither a satellite of

Britain nor of Italy. The war was a time of great hardship. From 1940 to 1942 Malta was subject to a second 'Great Siege'. As the island was blockaded by the Axis fleet for many months, food became a scarce resource during a period now referred to as 'the time of hunger' (Montserrat 1973; Vella 1985). Simultaneously, relentless bombing left many Maltese homeless as well as hungry. The island came close to capitulation in 1942, but eventually the siege was lifted and as reward Malta as a whole was awarded the George Cross – for gallantry. The rhetoric, both then and now, has the Maltese and British in joint defence of the island, unified by a single purpose and single effort. The reality was less clear cut. Prior to the war, prominent nationalist opponents of the colonial regime were deported out of the way to Uganda, but even those who remained were often less than convinced about the purpose of their ordeal. If Britain had not been in Malta in the first place, then the British would not have had to suffer alongside the Maltese. Malta was an important strategic centre, but only in the context of the British Mediterranean fleet and the Allies' southern campaigns. In and of itself, Malta was of little consequence (Frendo 1979).

The opposition to the wartime rhetoric of unified defence alongside the British was again represented through football, in an event that has now become central to the narrative of the nation. It features in school textbooks and is well known in all circles. On 25 March 1945, a Maltese representative team were to play against the Yugoslavs of Hajduk Split. Before the game, two anthems were played – the Yugoslav and the British. The perversity of this, particularly following four years of intense Maltese suffering and hardship, was recognised by the crowd, which protested. The national anthem, *L-Innu Malti* ('The Hymn to Malta') was written in the 1920s by Malta's national poet, Dun Karm ('Father Carmel'). First performed in 1923, it was adopted as the national anthem in 1941. It was expected at this representative match, and its omission marked the beginnings of post-war nationalism. To commemorate the events, the popular poet Ruzar Briffa composed a piece, *L-Innu ul-Kotra* ('The Hymn and the Crowd'), which begins 'The crowd suddenly awoke, and cried "I'm Maltese!"' (cf. Portelli 1993). By the late 1950s, both the Nationalists and the Malta Labour Party (which had replaced the Constitutional Party as one of the two main parties) were committed to independence from Britain. In 1957, the first full Maltese international match was played, against Austria. The Austrians won 3–2, which was an auspicious start for a small nation.

Some, however, were not unanimous in their support for the national team, as local allegiances and antagonisms continued to manifest themselves. The barracking of rival team players in the Malta side was such as to cause some observers consternation and appeal to fans of one club (Sliema Wanderers) not to get involved in such behaviour (DeCesare 1960). A decade later a massive Maltese crowd were damning in chants their former political overlords. In a 1971 World Cup qualifier against England, attracting probably the largest ever attendance for a match at the Empire Stadium, a crowd of around 30,000 saw a form of nationalism manifested in one particular chant. Responding to ill-chosen comments in the British media that proclaimed before the game that the England side should not be troubled by a team of waiters, the crowd sporadically chanted '*We are the waiters, you are the bastards*'. Fearing disorder, the British military authorities confined all service personnel to barracks during and after the match which England won 1–0.

PARTY POLITICS, DEVELOPMENT AND DECLINE

Until 1981, domestic and international fixtures were played on compacted sand, and the Maltese national side faced continued threats of expulsion from FIFA for this reason. Possibly FIFA did not know about the grass pitch only a few miles away from the Empire Stadium at Gzira. This was the Marsa Sports Club, owned by the British forces and from the late 1960s a playground for the Maltese rich and sporting (Bonnello 1996).

The new Labour government, elected in 1981, decided to build a new stadium. The crumbling ground at Gzira with its indifferent owners combined with the necessity for a grass pitch saw a search for an appropriate site. This was eventually found at Ta'Qali in the centre of the island. Prior to this, sport and sporting facilities had not been priorities for Maltese governments. The Labour government elected in 1971 tried to spread socialism through sport, and as a result tried to take over the running of the game in Malta. The 1980s Labour Sports Minister, Lorry Sant, found stiff opposition from Dr Guis Mifsud-Bonnici, the MFA president known for his hard-line Nationalist ideas (his brother is today the President of Malta). The affair developed into a battle of personalities between the two which was only resolved when Dr Mifsud-Bonnici was finally replaced as MFA president by Dr George Abela (a Labour Party Vice-President).

Like many countries on the economic and political peripheries, Malta is preoccupied with modernity and modernisation. Building a new, purpose-designed national stadium was part of this preoccupation (cf. Baldacchino 1997). More cynically, it was also perhaps acknowledged that sport and sporting facilities can reflect well on politicians. This explains the Labour government's building of Ta'Qali, and in 1993 the building of an Olympic swimming pool, a water polo stadium, shooting ranges and an Olympic standard athletics track by the Nationalist government.

The Ta'Qali stadium serves as a reminder of a political dalliance which followed the departure of the British forces in 1979. Close relations between the Labour government and Colonel Gaddaffi of Libya produced the funding from both sources that paid for the stadium. Opened in late 1981, the stadium was considered by many as a monument to Lorry Sant, the first Minister for Sport in the Labour government. Others credit its construction to the former sprinting champion and Nationalist MP George Bonello-Dupuis, who while in opposition was considered to be the person who actually suggested that Gaddaffi fund the stadium, in a spontaneous retort to Gaddaffi's question of how Libya could help Malta materially.[4]

On the face of it, moving football from the shabby, sandy Gzira site to the new modern terraces and plush turf of Ta'Qali should have been universally welcomed by fans and clubs alike. However, the move has been blamed for exacerbating – if not actually causing – a widespread decline in support for Maltese football. Attendance at matches, both domestic and international, has dropped considerably in recent decades. In the 1970s crowds of 15–20,000 would enter Gzira Stadium hours before kick-off when the opposition were famous foreign teams. As recently as 1988 a Malta vs. Spain fixture could attract 25,000; the same game in 1996 attracted only 6,000. The final game of the World Cup qualifier in 1997 against Yugoslavia saw an astonishing crowd of only 300. There are many reasons for this, but the move to Ta'Qali clearly did not help. Whereas it used to be possible to walk to the stadium from many of Malta's more densely populated areas, it is now necessary to have a car, or rely on the infrequent bus services. The new stadium is also more expensive; tickets to the Gzira stadium were easily affordable. Now at Ta'Qali, attending a football match is something of a treat. Furthermore, with televised football from top European games available most nights on terrestrial TV, there is undeniably a feeling that the reduction in interest has been caused by a perceived decline in the quality of football played by the Maltese.

The Ta'Qali has been criticised on another level. Although the grass pitch is kept healthy, it is not properly cut:

> Grass is sacred out here, that's why they let it grow so high and are reluctant to cut it because the thicker it is the less chance of it getting damaged. But, it slows the game down so when our teams play in Europe we're miles behind the speed of the game. (local club coach)

The standard of Malta's international game has varied, but in the past decade it has definitely declined. Indeed, since independence in 1964, there have been no particular footballing glories. The early 1980s saw draws with Scotland, Portugal and Hungary and narrow home defeats by Germany and Italy. In 1994 Malta beat Belgium 1–0 in a friendly. However, in 1995 Malta was beaten by Luxembourg in the European Championship qualifiers and twice by Iceland a year later. With populations similar to that of Malta, such defeats were badly taken by football fans.

TA'QALI STADIUM, DECEMBER 1996

For the spectators on one side of this football ground, the backdrop behind the opposite covered side is one of the most striking of any football ground in the world. The citadel and fortress walls of the medieval city of Mdina stand still as the winter sun slowly disappears behind them. All seated, with a running track distancing the fans from the pitch, the ground has no intimacy. Today it is barely a quarter full, 5,000 or so spectators watch two First Division games and then go home in darkness. Outside the stadium thousands attend a car boot sale/flea market while dozens watch a four-wheel drive motor rally or fly motorised model aeroplanes. The ground was built on what was once an aerodrome for the military aircraft of the British colonial forces. Today, imperialism of a different kind is manifest. The League is sponsored by Coca-Cola, previously it was Rothmans cigarettes. The scoreboard is plastered with Rothmans' logos, fourteen large flags advertise Coca-Cola, the highest of which is partnered by the flag of the Malta FA. The half-time whistle heralds the beginning of tannoy adverts which begin and end with jingles for Coca-Cola. The name of a bank is inlaid in seats behind one goal. Other hoardings advertise Pepsi, Lowenbrau, Daewoo, Nike, which vie for attention against local products – milk, beer, pizza and batteries. Behind each goal stands a warning sponsored by a government ministry about the dangers of drug-taking.

The matches are played on grass that appears too long and slows the game down. The crowd is fenced and segregated. Most men who enter have their pockets searched by police. Women are allowed half-price entrance. During the match members of the Task Force – a special police unit – occasionally intervene to eject or warn fans who swear or perpetrate or provoke violence. Fans resist the urge to 'Enjoy Coke'. Maltese beer is more evident than Coca-Cola, eaten with the local snack of *hobz biz-zejt* (lit. 'bread with oil', a traditional sandwich with tomatoes and tuna fish). The fifty uniformed police on duty stand smoking in groups watching the match. The four mounted police nearby are surplus to requirements.

The sedate and quiet crowd is animated only by perceived injustices and contempt. Individuals shout introductions in a hybrid language: 'Ref, half-time', 'Ejja Blues c'mon' and 'Bastid … Justine'. Later, following missed chances on the pitch, come the inevitable accusations of match rigging, and shouts of 'Mafja!' a dozen juveniles make their own spectacle. Having brought a football they play a game at the bottom of the terracing. Their aim is occasionally erratic and they repeatedly hit a police officer who patiently smiles and returns their ball. Some of those watching have somewhat disparate loyalties. Juventus and Inter Milan baseball caps sit alongside team shirts of Liverpool and Manchester United. Dozens watch the pitch, but have radios to their ears listening to the match reports from Italian state radio covering the games being played simultaneously in Italy. On the pitch are players from seven nations. Few are adored like the Italians being listened to, albeit the joy expressed in some Italian scorelines reflects more on illegal Maltese betting syndicates than football loyalty.

MODERNITY, COMMITMENT AND CORRUPTION

The modernisation of football facilities has been accompanied by a modernisation of football funding itself. Professionalisation and sponsorship are key concerns in the contemporary game. But this modernisation is far from unproblematic. Although preoccupied with modernity, Malta is also caught between its apparently positive aspects – new wealth and consumption possibilities, new infrastructure, increased communications with the rest of the world – and its negative. Into this second category fall such familiar trends as the erosion of traditional values, the break-up of local communities, the increase in social problems of drug abuse and marital separation, and a generalised pollution or corruption of the spirit caused by the increase in wealth (Abela 1991). This has taken its toll, in particular, on football.

In a political milieu dominated by nepotism, favouritism and clientism, it is not surprising that there is widespread historical belief that some footballers are corrupt (cf. Baldacchino 1991, 1993). Although there are few cases in which a footballer has been prosecuted for match-rigging, it is nevertheless assumed that it has occurred for decades. The more prominent chants at the football ground include references to perceived corruption. When a player fails to make a particular play – misses a tackle, misses a goal or a save – the calls come: *Mafja* ('Mafia') or *Hallelin* ('thieves') or *Bil-guh* ('hungry', therefore easily 'bought'). These phrases connote a willingness to put personal financial gain over and above the performance of the team.

The actual extent of corruption in Maltese football is impossible to know. Our question on this topic produced the following responses:

No one accepts a defeat in Malta. It's always either because the ref was corrupt or the players were. (Maltese coach)

It cost me £4,000m a year in illegal payments to rival players and referees to win the championship! (Floriana fan reminiscing on the late 1940s)

It's betting syndicates. There's a café in Valletta where they all meet; they would bet on two flies walking down a glass bottle ... Some syndicate men are also on club committees. (life-long Sliema fan)

It's not down to betting syndicates. The problem is club committee men – they approach a rival player to lose a match; they play, do their job and get a bonus for losing! (club committee man)

How can they say the referees are impartial when in Malta everyone's related to everyone else! ... I used to play and one of the linesmen was the best man at my wedding. (player 1990s)

This situation is not limited to the local club game. The national team's most notable – and forgettable – performance came in 1983, when the Spanish, needing to score 12 goals to qualify for the European Championships, beat Malta 12–1 in Seville. Accusations that the Malta team were corrupt came primarily from the Netherlands, who lost out on a place in the finals on goal difference to Spain, but also from within Malta from ashamed fans. The defeat had two consequences; one was the establishment in Malta of a commission to examine the possibility of bribery and corruption. The other was the policy of inviting European coaches and players to Malta to improve the standard of play. The commission consisted of FA representatives, journalists, supporters and others, who were to investigate the extent (if any) of corruption in Maltese football. Chaired by a lawyer, the commission concluded that the defeat was due to the absence of adequate preparation and inadequate fitness. The defeat then was not attributed to corruption. The Dutch newspapers, however, published photographs of a villa newly purchased by the Maltese goalkeeper![5]

One of the consequences of the Commission's findings was the establishment of the Professional Scheme for international players. Starting in 1988, this scheme established a twenty-strong squad with a full-time coach and two-year contracts for the players. Their wages came from sponsorship or secondment agreements with former employers who agreed to accept them back into their jobs should they drop out of the scheme. A ten-man selection panel, consisting of the president, and the secretary of the MFA and eight others including representatives of the leading six clubs, select the squad. Such professionalism presented a double-edged sword. On the one hand, there is a feeling that professionalism is a good thing, because it encourages a more rigorous and systematic attitude to training and playing. On the other hand, there is a feeling that when players are paid, they cease to make the effort. As one prominent sports journalist put it:

> The professional scheme meant players could only train with their clubs twice a week. Some club coaches wanted them to play one way, whilst the national coach was demanding something contrary. Some players got a superiority complex; they were not trying, they were in the squad and probably thought with an income guaranteed why should I worry?

Around the same time as the Professional Scheme, and with the aim of improving standards, foreign coaches and players were recruited, tempted by sometimes lucrative contracts (Baldacchino 1990). That said the importing of football talent is almost as old as the game in Malta. The first foreign club coach in Malta was Leo Druker, a Hungarian-born Austrian international who led the Floriana side in the 1920s.

The first foreign national coach was the Hungarian, Janos Bedl who, in 1966, co-managed the national team for two games alongside a Maltese coach. Under his control, Malta played two games and won two! The next foreigner in charge was the Italian, Terenzio Polverini who appeared in 1974. His records read played 9, won 1, lost 6. The Bulgarian, Guento Dobrev appeared a decade later and in 21 games in charge managed one victory and 16 defeats. The German, Horst Heese tried in 1988; in 36 games he managed three wins and 25 defeats. Later again, in 1993, came the Italian, Pietro Ghedin, whose 18-game reign produced five victories and nine defeats – and his leaving. He in turn was succeeded in 1996 by the Yugoslav, Milorad Kosanovic. In his 18-month reign Kosanovic never won a single game out of 15. Pending the departure of Ghedin in 1992 the MFA froze the Professional Scheme and inquired into the sustainability of it because the costs were not matched by the results.[6] Ironically the national team has achieved less when professional than its predecessors had when merely part-timers. Perhaps the enormity of their disastrous World Cup campaign can be placed in context when one realises that Malta are probably the only national team in the world to train together every week throughout the year.

STYLISTIC DIVERSITY AND EXTERNAL INFLUENCE

It was not always thus. Malta's international side has gained some very creditable results and over the years has experimented with a variety of styles. Being a colony meant it was inevitable that foreign influence would intercede in the development of football in Malta. That said, the political hegemony of the British did not automatically transfer itself to the football pitch. Most considered the British style – a fast, physical game with a strong forwards and backs – was not suited to the Maltese physique and their love of ball players. In the absence of TV it was private enterprise that exposed Maltese footballers to new styles and tactics. As early as the 1920s, the owner of the Empire Stadium invited teams from Tunisia, Italy, Austria, Czechoslovakia, Yugoslavia and Hungary to play Maltese sides at Christmas and Easter. These games drew large crowds and a good profit for the ground owner, but also made new ideas and tactics available.

Some club sides subsequently emulated the close control and short passing game of visiting Czech and Hungarian sides in the 1940s–1960s (cf. Griffiths 1985; Baldacchino 1994). Others favoured the Italian system of the double stopper and 'Libero', and the ploy of deep defence with counter-attack. From the late 1950s and the advent of televised matches from Italy local coaches were able to watch and practise new ideas. The post-1961 participation of Maltese clubs in European competitions widened technical and tactical possibilities even further.

Foreign players have been influential in the success of Maltese club sides, although in recent years they do not appear to have stimulated the overall quality of the national game. In part this is due to impulse buying and in part to the difficulty of attracting quality players to Malta. The presence of foreign players is as old as Maltese football itself. Initially British forces personnel turned out for local sides. Later in the 1930s numerous players from central Europe arrived, and from the late 1960s Malta became the last pay day for players both famous and unknown from Britain. In the 1980s former England Internationals, Paul Mariner, David Johnson, Peter Barnes and Tony Morley appeared. In the 1995/6 season there were 26 foreign-born players in the ten First Division teams, drawn from England (5), Yugoslavia (4), Albania and Bulgaria (3), Libya and Nigeria (2), and one each from Bosnia, Italy, Iceland, Hungary, Montenegro, Sweden and New Zealand.

It has to be said that the 1980s idea that foreign players would improve the standard of Maltese football has not really worked. Top-class players at the peak of their game will not come to Malta, and in what was regarded as an admission of this failure, the President of the MFA implemented the 'two foreigners only' rule for Premier Division teams (albeit the permissible number is five at Under-18 level) believing that foreign imports were stopping the progress of local football. A logical solution would be for native players to play abroad in good leagues and return with knowledge of techniques and tactics. However the presence of Maltese players in foreign teams is a rare occurrence. Since the 1940s Maltese players in Europe have numbered only *three*. The first being the legendary figure of Joe Cini who, in the late 1960s, played seven games in the English First Division for Queens Park Rangers. The next Maltese player to play in England was John Buttigieg, who had three years with Brentford in the English Second Division in the late 1980s. The longest lasting player in Europe was Carmel Busuttil, whose five years with Belgian club Genk saw him as captain for two seasons.[7] All were to return to finish their football careers with Maltese clubs. Why so few Maltese ever succeeded abroad provoked the following cultural analysis from a respected Maltese coach:

> We're a small island and we don't have scouts coming over. Then there's the island mentality – who wants to leave? The Maltese are big family people, they like intimacy – who would go somewhere cold in Europe and be alone?

Constant defeats suffered by the national side provoked in 1992 a controversy when the president of the MFA was reported to have suggested that Malta's future might be as a national side playing in the Italian 'C' division. The subsequent furore from a variety of sources prompted the president to claim that his comments were misinterpreted. That said, the debacle against the Faroe Islands prompted sports writers to suggest Malta withdraw from international competition to avoid future shame.

VICTOR TEDESCO STADIUM, HAMRUN, DECEMBER 1996

The two First Division games played out to the winter sunshine as the year ended provided for a variety of entertainment, not all of it limited to the standard of football. The crowd of around 2,000 sat themselves on one of the 14 concrete steps that constituted the terracing on the one side of this newly constructed (and unfinished) football ground. Segregated into three, this terrace held rival fans at each side and in between them was the VIP enclosure distinguished by its location near the centre of the field of play and by the presence of a dozen wooden chairs placed there for journalists and the president of the Malta FA and his guest from UEFA.

Named after the benefactor of the ground and former President of Hamrun Spartans, the ground was well-intentioned, but no deadline for the resumption of building was available. Behind one goal were a pile of two dozen sacks of sand and a low wall built from the limestone blocks available throughout Malta. At the opposite end the tiny space available between goals and perimeter wall witnessed only the lovingly tended wall garden of the groundsman whose nearby shed doubled as the half-time snack bar. On the side opposite the terracing sat only the team managers and their substitutes on the two benches. Behind them were a few spectators who watched free of charge – since their bedroom window were higher than the wall. Those that paid the £2m admission did not expect much of a spectacle. Their parochial loyalties, however, were vociferous – the two teams representing districts separated by only one mile. Almost exclusively male, they watched as the overgrown grass produced a very slow game and either cheered or grew resentful as the goals began to go in.

Players, spectators and managers were to leave the stadium in a manner they did not choose. One player, following a touchline run and cross, had gained such momentum that he ran into the low wall which stood only three metres behind the goal. The limestone slabs showed no mercy and he was taken away on a stretcher. Later an Irish-born forward was sent off after a late challenge to a Tunisian-born opponent. For the former England international managing one side this was to be his last game in that capacity. He flew home two days later. For a Bulgarian manager and two of his compatriots came the realisation that their side was not good enough at this level. With three goals conceded their task was made more difficult when a colleague was dismissed. The supporters were infuriated and moments later surged towards the referee and opposing player they held responsible as the players and officials made their way to the changing rooms for half-time. The police, two-dozen strong, previously stood in a group smoking then moved into the baying mob and arrested one man in his 40s – a relative of the player dismissed!

The fast and gifted winger of one team spent the match taunting and tormenting the young full-back in front of his partisan supporters. When an opportunity presented itself the same winger aimed gestures at the now infuriated fans. No doubt aggrieved at losing by a five-goal margin and the antics of both rival players and referees, a group of fans waited outside the ground after the game, one wielding an iron bar. Police intervened to prevent injuries. The official and player left unharmed, but unwashed – there being no water in the showers.

AN UNCERTAIN FUTURE?

Football now competes with new imported sports, as well as the ever-popular sport of water-polo and horse racing known as 'trotting'. Some sports lose their attraction only for new ones to appear. Thus the Maltese can today choose to watch or participate in judo, tai-kwondo, body-building, tennis, athletics, triathalon, cycling, swimming, basketball, volleyball, and lately even rugby and baseball, the latter now having a league of eight teams (Abela 1992). The expansion of higher education and the pursuit of academic credentials had forced many parents to stress the need for study over the perceived frivolity of football. In response the government has begun to introduce exams and qualifications in sports in an attempt to placate such parental attitude. With more distractions on offer young men do not turn to football as their sole leisure pastime and the traditional areas that produced footballers – Gzira and the Cottonera – are not supplying them in such great numbers.[8] Street football is dying replaced by the coaching provided by the nursery schemes, but with it perhaps 'heart' that makes good players and sets them apart from the technically superior, but somewhat detached players.

The nation has won its position on the world football stage, and now must justify its status through results. The future for football in Malta, it would seem, lies in the development of coaching and international financial markets. Every club today has junior teams for every age group down to the age of eight. While the clubs are responsible for the player, the nurseries have separate committees and secretaries responsible to the main club committee. They are producing players, and in the last ten years the national team has consisted almost entirely of products of such schemes. However, for some reason standards have not risen. Yet the abilities of the coaches are unquestioned. The two most recent foreign national coaches have left Malta for very good jobs in football. The Italian Pietro Ghedin is currently the assistant to Cesare Maldini, manager of the Italian national side, and the recently departed Kosanovic left Malta to take the reins at Red Star Belgrade. On arrival, Kosanovic accused Maltese players of lacking even basic skills, thereby enraging local club coaches. Others concur:

There's been very little or very poor coaching in schools for decades ... There's no discipline, look at the way they drive! Look at the litter all over the beaches. (foreign player)

The future seems to lie in the willingness of people to fund the continued pursuit of professionalism:

As it is, we compete against the same opponents each week. We need innovative coaches, experts, technology, long-term planning, good administrators and medical personnel. This needs to be financed but tax evasion is the national characteristic and meanwhile nine out of ten foreign players disappoint – but who who's any good will come here ...? (sports journalist)

Despite falling attendances money is still thrown at the domestic game. However the leading club sides are dangerously dependent on the patronage of rich fanatics whose fortunes lie variously in: imports, tourism, plant-hire and petro-chemicals. These benefactors sustain wages and transfers – sponsorship cannot compete with what they contribute. One club president annually pays from his own pocket £30,000m (£50,000) towards his team and rejoices in it by explaining that the team is his hobby!

The top club sides are seeking ways to generate income. As Valletta City launch their 'Official Beer' and a new souvenir shop opens with daily photo opportunities for fans to pose next to trophies, Sliema have produced a variety of merchandise. Two other teams – Hibernians and Hamrun – now play at their now much improved home grounds for the first time in Maltese football history. Financial problems may arise for the Malta FA, as they have yet to resolve who the admission proceeds from such matches go to. Plans are afoot to build a stadium for the Under-21 national team and for matches played at Division Two and Three levels. Inevitably funding will prove to be a problem; the president of the MFA has offered to contribute £100,000m if the 50 clubs affiliated will contribute the rest.

New world developments continue to impinge on the parochial. Two players – Nigerian and British – have recently obtained Maltese citizenship and now train with the national squad. The first-ever positive drugs test produced (in 1997) a peculiar arrangement whereby the Maltese player was banned from the domestic competition for two months, but was available for the national side! The nouveau riche side, Birkirkara has an impending stock market flotation and plans to build its own stadium. Women's football is expanding; thirteen 7-a-side teams now constitute a league which began in 1993. Women are in many ways the unsung heroes of the nursery committees. The interest in the game remains, and expansion defies economic logic – but can and will Malta win a match?

Notes

1. No love is lost between the Maltese and the Turks. This emnity goes back to the Middle Ages when the Turks would plunder the islands and take the Maltese away to use as slaves. The Maltese always believed their teams suffered whenever a Turkish referee controlled European games involving Maltese teams.
2. This emergence of a sense of national identity in football mirrored developments in other sports. It was the 1928 Olympic Games and via water polo that Malta first achieved a sporting team of international status. This, however, was a struggle achieved against British wishes. Nine years earlier four Maltese had been shot dead by colonial forces while rioting in Valletta against poverty and bread prices. Before this there had been pre-war agitation for the island to be allowed the status of a Dominion, and not a

colony. Continued political agitation produced the first (but very limited) constitution in 1921. Three years later Viscount Plumer, then Governor of Malta, following his enthusiastic spectating for the game, suggested Malta enter the Olympics with a water-polo team. Retiring soon after, the idea was taken up via the Maltese Water-Polo Committee by Meme Buscetta, the island's best water-polo player at the time. Politics then became involved. Following the formation of the Amateur Swimming Association in 1925, the committee decided to apply to participate in the 1928 Olympics in Amsterdam. The reply from the Olympic Organising Committee was that, since Malta was a colony, it could not partake as a nation, but could be part of the Great Britain contingent. A lawyer argued, however, that Malta was a Crown Colony with a degree of self-government. The Dutch decided that Malta was eligible to participate as a nation; they were thus invited and competed under the name of Malta for the first time.

3. The cavalcades of cars containing rival supporters either celebrating the victory of 'their' adopted country go back to the 1960s. Following the defeat of Italy by South Korea in the 1966 World Cup in England, supporters of England created a mock funeral cortege to ridicule their humbled rivals. During the 1980 European Championships the Italian victory over England produced a 60-vehicle cavalcade which drove for three hours along the busiest roads in the island. A few days later the defeat of Italy by Belgium saw a cavalcade half the size ridiculing their former tormentors with only one car containing Belgians.

4. With the stadium completed in 1981, the Government leased the ground for a nominal sum, although the MFA annually spends thousands of pounds on its upkeep. The admission costs to games at Ta'Qali are not taxed, thus the MFA takes all the gate revenue and gives a percentage of it to the ten local First Division clubs. Other income is provided by TV transmission rights.

5. Over the past thirty years, only one player has ever been suspended on charges of corruption. In 1993, he was banished from the game for life and a colleague jailed for two months. There were instances in the past when players were accused of selling a match. The famous Ruggieri Friggeri, considered as the greatest-ever Maltese player, was in the 1920s accused of corruption and went to court, but the charges were never proven. In the 1950s, Effie Borg of Hamrun Spartans was convicted by the Maltese courts of corruption and sent to prison. The same thing happened to Farrugia of Floriana during the same period who was also jailed. The latter was a full-back of international standard, reported to the MFA by his own club and taken to court. The lack of corroborated evidence has not lessened the belief among fans, journalists, coaches and club presidents that football matches in Malta are bought not won, and that this state of affairs is nothing new.

6. The scheme was ressurrected two years later under the newly-appointed Yugoslav on a two-tier basis of professionals and semi-professionals. This caused a dispute amongst the players which resulted in three quality players withdrawing from the national squad, refusing to play for the team. By 1997 24 players were chosen for the Professional Scheme.

7. On the recommendations of an Italian player, who spent a season in Malta, 'Busu' was bought by Verbagnia in the Italian 'C' division. Then the Maltese national coach, Horst Heese, recommended him to the Belgian club Genk.

8. The term Cottonera is used to describe the geographical areas consisting of the forti-fied towns of Vittoriosa, Cospicua and Senglea. Known as the Three Cities, such areas are renowned for housing an industrial proletariat with staunch political sympathies towards the Labour Party.

Acknowledgements

The authors are both anthropologists and have spent considerable time in Malta. Gary Armstrong was resident in Malta for one year (1979–80), and has returned annually since. Jon Mitchell conducted two years of ethnographic fieldwork in Malta (1992–4) and also returns annually.

The authors are indebted to many people who answered their questions and made the research task enjoyable. Particular thanks are due to Carmel Baldacchino, Lewis Portelli, Mark Miller, Joe Cini, John deGray, Father Hilary Tagliaferro, Joe Grech, Tony Nicholl, Sammy Nicholl, James Calvert and Tony Pace.

9 Beyond Edirne: Football and the National Identity Crisis in Turkey

Can Kozanoglu

Both the optimism and pessimism of Turkish society are reflected in the statement 'Nowhere else in the world'. Many Turks will claim that their country's natural beauties, hospitality, political scandals, outbreaks of public disorder, and perceived degeneration cannot be found in such intensity elsewhere in the world. Such claims are exaggerations usually reflecting an ignorance of other countries and cultures. But, as is frequently said, 'The love for football in our country may be found nowhere else in the world'; such an assertion is worth considering. For Turkish people, the epitome of good football is the Brazilian style; similarly, the idealised form of football passion is Brazilian. Yet Turks visiting Brazil often return disappointed with the reality, airing the above familiar statement.[1] Indeed, one can ask is there any other country in which a World Cup qualifier against minnows San Marino could transform vibrant cities into dead ones for the duration of the game? In which other country is the ratio of active club supporters per capita so high?[2] Can another place be found where intellectuals, workers, peasants, 'yuppies', the rich and the poor, power elites and ordinary people spend so much time engrossed in football, and where around significant fixtures the whole country speaks only of football for days?

EAST-WEST: EMULATION AND TENSION

Football was brought to Turkey in the latter decades of the nineteenth century by English merchants who played the game informally on the meadows of Istanbul and Izmir. Following debates over whether football was contrary to Islamic codes, the first Turkish team was established in 1901 with an English name – the Black Stockings. English migrants in 1904 founded the first schedule of games and, ultimately, what became known as the Istanbul Football League which lasted 47 years until 1951. In the decade 1905–15, Turkish teams began to establish themselves; Galatasaray, Fenerbahce, Beykoz, Vefa and Besiktas in Istanbul, and Karsiyaka and Altay in Izmir. Towards the end of the Ottoman state in 1918 with Istanbul under the military occupation of the Allies, Turkish victories (particularly those of Fenerbahce and Galatasaray) against British forces teams helped popularise the game among Turkish people. Particularly notable was the establishment, in 1923, of the Turkish Republic and the establishment of the Turkish Football Federation and football league competitions in Ankara and Izmir. A Turkish national team played its first ever game (against Romania) and by the 1930s football had become Turkey's most popular sporting attraction.

According to the official proclamations of sports bureaucracies, Turkey's national sport is wrestling. In reality, football has been Turkey's national sport since the 1930s. The state has made its biggest financial investments in football, and men ranging in age from five to fifty-five play football on any vacant lot, empty street, school garden or impromptu football field in every city. Until the late 1940s all players had amateur contracts. Many, however, were de facto professionals, a status recognised officially in 1959. From then on players began to attain the status of public heroes, attendances at matches grew and Turkish players were in demand from European teams. In the latter half of the 1950s most of the national side were to be found playing in the Italian leagues. The game grew at home with the formation of a Turkish Second Division (1963), and Third Division (1967) which gave every city a team and, hence, a footballing interest. That said, the three Istanbul clubs – known as the 'Three Greats' – Fenerbahce, Galatasary and Besiktas have dominated domestic success. The mid-1970s then brought forth another team now ranked among the greats in the shape of Trabzonspor from the Black Sea coast and the only team that has succeeded in breaking the 'Three Greats' monopoly.

Successful clubs have mostly preferred to employ foreign coaches, be they Brazilian, British, German or Croatian. Consequently, it is difficult to speak of a definitive Turkish style of play. Thus, while there is no dominant style there is undeniably a unique Turkish football culture. Despite the level of interest and popularity, the international performances of both the national and club teams were usually disappointing until the mid-80s. Occasional successes, such as the national team's 3–1 win over the legendary Hungarians in 1956, and Fenerbahce's elimination of the then mighty Manchester City in 1968 brought consolation for years. But tournaments typically began with grand assertions and ended with disappointment; the constant refrain that: 'We do not exist beyond Edirne' could be heard. Edirne is the western most city of Turkey; it is Turkey's European border.

Throughout the 1980s, Turkey experienced very rapid economic, social and cultural changes under the political aegis of the New Right. In spite of some partial economic improvements, social inequalities have increased, and for some Turkish cultural and social values have been ruined (Boratav 1991). What is known as the 'Kurdish problem' in Southeast Anatolia (a 'low density conflict' in official discourse, but in reality a conflict which has much graver dimensions) has greatly affected domestic political balances. Alongside the rise of Islamic and nationalist movements, the Turkish government has attempted to become closer to Western Europe. Consequently, a national identity crisis, reflected in symptoms of social schizophrenia, has been experienced. This complex process has (not coincidentally) occurred during a period when Turkish football began to achieve relative successes in the international arena. Football has thus become an arena where the national identity crisis is felt most acutely; and where the tensions between East and West, the regional and the international, have emerged in their most intense form. The game remains a test area for Turkey, but now more importance and greater attention is paid to social relations 'beyond Edirne'.

Since the early Republican era, an ancient Turkish culture has continued alongside attempts at Westernisation, the roots of which may be found in the mid-nineteenth century (Cengiz 1993). Until the changes of the 1980s, Western life was, for the majority, something only heard and read about. When the slogan of the new economic order, 'opening the economy', coincided with general global trends, Turkey began to play up to the West (or the 'North'), and became part of a small economic ring in the international consumption chain, particularly through foreign trade. With the explosion of European and American oriented media channels, and the rise in ownership of domestic televisions, the West became more directly seen, known and imitated by Turkish citizens.

However, the new economic system caused inequalities. Concomitantly, urban overcrowding was created as a consequence of heavy domestic migration, and the Kurdish problem intensified. Such problems conspired, on the one hand, to strengthen Islamic movements, and on the other to promote the popularity of nationalist-racist movements (Cakir 1994; Tanil 1995). Such disturbing processes fatally undermined the traditional political centre its public discourses and its realm of solutions. The social response to these problems led people of differing political opinions to a cultural centre, an orientation interpreted by some academics as 'the threshold of a new synthesis'. However, this was a centre housing similar, but not united people; violence, both political and public had reached a frightening degree.[3] People who did not hesitate to act violently towards one another competed to consume as many different delicacies as possible from the 'open buffet' at the cultural centre. This buffet offered Westernism, Easternism, regionalism, radical secularism, exaggerated religiousness, conservatism, liberalism, modernity, nationalism, violence, war cries and olive branches. Many tried to possess various cultural identities, within a general framework of 'modernisation', provoking unusual discursive styles reflecting both the tension of this burden and the contradictions inherent in the abundance of choice. It was possible in the poorer districts of cities, for instance, to see young Islamic militants wearing American style clothes. The militant cadres of the fascist Nationalist Movement Party (MHP) called themselves 'idealists', abandoned their traditional conservative attitudes, and began to adopt a multiple identity which would not be incongruous in mosques, discos, army barracks and rock concerts.[4]

GETTING INTO EUROPE

One important part of this complex process was Turkey's endeavour to become a member of the European Community. Although full membership was not in sight, the coming threshold of this union led a previously unperturbed society to show concern. No one except radical Islamists openly opposes Turkey's membership of the EC, yet only a narrow group of liberals support such membership unconditionally. The great majority fall between these two; nationalists are especially confused, alternating between modernism/Westernism and traditionalism/regionalism. EC membership is anticipated to require changes in Turkey's social values. Hence, many political speeches emphasise the transition with the phrase 'In these days we prepare to enter the EC ...'; on the other hand, the same politicians complain daily about Europe's support for activities seen as against the interests of Turkey (see Laciner 1994; Gogus 1991). Though this contradiction has recently deepened, its roots may be found in the distant past. Although not emphasised in official discourse, throughout the Republican era Turkish society could not decide whether the West (or Europe) was a friend or an enemy. The desire to westernise carried admiration and appreciation within official policies; but there were also speeches proclaiming the Turks' superiority to Europe, full of slanderous words and suspicious attitudes (Murat 1993).

Since the mid-1980s the relative successes of football teams in the international arena have deeply influenced Turkey. The three Istanbul teams had a monopoly over the championship for many years; the first and only champions from Anatolia, Trabzonspor, have not brought major changes except to join this monopoly. By the mid-80s, Turkish football was beginning to overcome disappointments in Europe; Galatasaray advanced to the semi-finals in the European Champions' Cup in the 1988–9 season, eliminated Eintracht Frankfurt in the European Cup Winners' Cup in 1990–91, and advanced to the Champion League, eliminating Manchester United in 1993–4. Later, in October 1996, Fenerbahce ended Manchester United's 30-year undefeated home record in Europe. Trabzonspor, meanwhile, could have scored four goals against Lyon in France, and almost eliminated Aston Villa. The national under-21 team won the European championship and, most important of all, the national team qualified, for the first time in its history, for the finals of the 1996 European Championships in England. These successes represent the fruition of specific long-term football strategies, including investment in the public infrastructure as far back as the 1970s. The successes were a source of great pleasure throughout Turkish society, though they never diluted its schizophrenic relationship with Europe.

One unchanging drama amidst all these opposing perspectives is the effort to win Europe's approval, and the anxiety that Turkey might 'fall into disgrace before Europe'. Hence in 1991, a Fenerbahce-Atletico Madrid match, organised as a testimonial for the serving German goalkeeper Schumacher, was left unfinished because the electricity was cut off. A sense of great public shame was reflected in newspapers headlines, such as, 'We fell into disgrace against Germany and Spain' and 'Europe laughs at us'. It was not considered so important for 30,000 Turkish citizens in the stands to be deprived of watching a match; the real problem being humiliated in front of Europe.

One man in particular was regarded as a symbol of Turkey's European advance. Mustafa Denizli, contributing greatly to Galatasaray's advance to the Champions' Cup semi-finals, later became the manager of Aachen, a German Second Division team in 1991. Denizli's reign with Aachen saw them relegated, but his first few matches as manager had produced brilliant results. These successes became part of Turkey's news agenda, to the extent that the state television interrupted its broadcast to announce an Aachen victory as a 'newsflash'. At the same time, a long interview with Denizli was serialised in a newspaper under the heading 'All Europe Talks About This Man'. Of course, the matches of a team in the German Second Division were not high in Europe's public agenda. But this fantasy boosted national morale.

The words 'football' and 'Europe', when combined, touch a sensitive nerve for Turkish society, because successes on the football field were recurring at the same time as advances in public organisations at the European level. Through these organisations, the fiercest reflections of the national identity crisis emerged in the stands. One slogan chanted incessantly at both international and European games symbolically explained many issues: 'Europe, Europe, listen to us / These are the footsteps of the Turks / No one can master the Turks / Europe, the "gay", protect yourself.' The accusations of being 'gay' is one of the most offensive insults in the machismo culture that dominates football in Turkey. When their clubs reached the next round of European competition, fans would insult the supporters of eliminated Turkish clubs by asking: 'We are European, where do you play?' The slogan 'Do you still use your mother's margarine?' taken from a margarine advertisement was modified by the fans of Galatasaray (who had qualified for the Champions' League) to provide the slogan 'Do you still play in your mother's league? / We are European, we play in the European League'.

But, we need ask in all of this, what was Europe? Was it a friend, or an enemy? Was being European a good or a bad thing? Furthermore, was Turkish football's success at the European level a positive step or should it be seen as heralding a campaign to seize the enemy's land west of Turkey? Intellectuals opposing or supporting the regime could not decide what Europe was or what was the meaning of Western relations, so how could football spectators, confused by the changes of the 1980s and experiencing a deep national identity crisis, give exact answers to these questions? Both the engagement with 'being European' and the hostility towards Europe became apparent within the same fiery attitudes:

Perhaps the clearest reflection of Turkish national identity in football emerges in the attitude towards Europe. The pressure to prove itself against the West, the desire to be accepted by the West is a clear 'national' characteristic of Turkish football (Bora and Erdogan 1993: 231).

Such a contradiction was not peculiar to discussions about football. The large media institutions dominating Turkey's agenda, most of which are inclined towards the New Right, displayed the same contradictions in headlines, articles, and television comments about relations with Europe or with the West. The importance of good EC relations was emphasised, and with it the notion that acquiring a European identity would no longer be a dream 'if we put ourselves in order'. Conversely it was also argued that 'Turks have no friends other than Turks'; that Europe harboured hostile attitudes towards Turkey, that there were alliances against Turkey from European politicians who wanted to intervene in the country's internal affairs. In the Turkey of the 1990s, this social schizophrenia became more widespread; optimistic and pessimistic waves followed one another nationwide.

In reality, these moods originate in part from the special conditions of Turkey; the widespread political violence, the Kurdish problem, economic instability, institutional corruption, political disturbances. In Turkey, a 'great crisis' can occur at any moment and after each crisis pessimistic winds blow. The statement, 'This country has come to an end, it is finished; our future is very bad' dominates the streets. But, the effects of each major crisis last only a few days, due in part to media practices, and an atmosphere of optimism soon appears. The days of intense pessimism are days when Europe or the West is damned. When moments of optimism return, Europe or the West begins to be viewed more moderately.

As the air of optimism reinforces sympathy for Europe, and the air of pessimism precipitates hostility towards Europe, a mentality regarding the winner as European and the loser as Asian acquires the upper hand. In the 1994–5 season, Trabzonspor were drawn against Aston Villa in the UEFA Cup, and Trabzonspor's manager Penol Gune was asked in a television interview: 'It is said that your rivals Aston Villa regard you as an Asian team, what will you say?' Gune answered, 'Let us first play with Aston Villa ... You will see then who is the Asian and who is the European.' After a period of unsuccessful results, one hears the statement 'We do not exist beyond Edirne.' Football thus becomes a field in which the national identity crisis is played out. For the same reasons, the international matches of the Turkish team become more and more important.

REMEMBERING SÈVRES

The European matches of club teams can dominate the public agenda of Turkey. This interest is shared by all sections of society, horizontally and vertically. The week before, the mass media allocate extensive broadcasting time for news on these matches. As match day approaches, coverage increases; forecasts, interviews and analyses mention 'the strength of the Turks'. During live broadcasts the streets are emptied. When the match is in Turkey, the stands are jam-packed. Even high-scoring away defeats do not dissuade people; for example, a packed ground watched Galatasaray eliminate Neuchatel in Istanbul with a 5–0 win after losing 3–0 in Switzerland. Such optimism sometimes brings great disappointments. Following Fenerbahce's 4–0 defeat in the UEFA Cup against Cannes in France, ten of thousands watched the return match and chanted 'We'll score five'. When the team lost 5–1 they set fire to the stands; the players were unable to leave the ground for hours after. Following a victory, especially when the Turkish team qualifies for the next round, the streets are full of celebrations until the early hours. Prime ministerial attendance at European matches in Turkey has become a tradition in the past decade. Some politicians even attend matches abroad, sharing their 'away trips' with the rest of society. Until 1996, to travel abroad each Turkish citizen had to pay 100 US dollars. The few exceptional cases in which this obligation was lifted included supporters travelling to international football fixtures. Thanks to such facilities and the vast number of Turkish migrant workers in Europe, Turkish teams play overseas matches with a mass of supporters in attendance. In 1994, even after Fenerbahce had beaten the Azerbaijan team Turan 5–0 in the preliminary round of qualifying matches, the fans still filled many aeroplanes for the away leg. Two weeks before that, the Avenir-Beggen versus Galatasaray match was played before Luxembourg's record crowd of spectators, most of whom were Turkish. Turkish football thus exists beyond Edirne; sometimes with its football, but always with its fans.

Until a few years ago, victory celebrations were no different from the ones which took place throughout the world. The national identity crisis, however, made the international matches more significant; the rise in nationalist tendencies and fascist sympathies has altered the processes of celebration. Supporters of the fascist MHP, known as the 'Idealists', have become the most militant and aggressive football fans, and have changed the nature of street demonstrations. Militant activists displaying Idealist symbols have begun to direct the crowds. These demonstrations can go awry; celebrations with pistols caused six deaths the night Galatasaray eliminated Manchester United and three deaths when the national team beat Switzerland. The beating of motorists who refuse to blast their horns has lately become commonplace. Moreover, such celebrations can turn into political demonstrations, slogans are shouted, and demonstrations are organised in front of foreign embassies. The same song, 'Europe, Europe, listen to us …' accompanies these demonstrations.

The Idealists constitute one of the groups which experiences the national identity crisis most acutely. This political movement tries to appear modernist and open to the West (despite hesitating over the fine details), and supports both Turkey's integration into Europe and full membership of the EC. Together with the Islamic bloc, however, they simultaneously lead the discourse and actions against the West of Europe. Although they appear in the stands from time to time, Islamic militants do not attach the significance to football that the Idealists do. In Turkey, the Sèvres treaty of 1920 is seen as a symbol of submission to Europe before the War of Independence. This is said by the fascist movement to be a situation which the West (or Europe) is keen to restore. Consequently, Idealists unfurl a banner with the message 'We'll demolish the Sèvres images.' Across the football stands. Under pressure from Idealist groups, the singing of the national anthem before each league match has become a ritual. According to UEFA regulations, the singing of these anthems before European club matches is forbidden. Hence a compromise has been found which complies with European demands and suits the nationalist ideal, while still preventing Turkish clubs from being punished. The national anthem is sung one hour before European club matches in Turkey.

The presence of fascist–racist movements in the stands is not peculiar to Turkey. If we discount 'natural enemies' such as the fans of other teams, and the teams and citizens of other countries, who are the 'others' in the eyes of Turkey's racist groups? This is a complex subject, but consider the following point. When they find the level of support at matches is insufficient, fans chant, 'Turks, stand up – Turks, stand up!' This recurs not only at internationals, but also during league matches in an attempt to get the whole stadium shouting. According to the logic of Turkish nationalism, each citizen of the Turkish Republic is a Turk; mention of sub-national identities according to ethnic groups is not tolerated. Within this framework, everyone is the same out of necessity. According to the fascist–racist movements, there is only one compulsory identity, no alternative existence is possible. Though they do not always declare it, there are various groups of 'others', hence millions exist where club and national identities intersect or are in opposition. The rise of fascist nationalism from the 1980s onwards was greatly influenced by the Kurdish problem and the support given to the biggest armed Kurdish group, the PKK, by many Kurds in the south-east. But this collective of 'others' is mentioned only indirectly. A citizen should either proudly say that he/she is a Turk, or he/she does not love the country. Banners reflecting MHP's 1995 slogan, '*Either love, or leave!*', can be seen both in the streets and the football stands.

Great hostility exists between the fans of club teams, especially the three Istanbul clubs, Fenerbahce, Galatasaray and Besiktas. Idealists, constituting the biggest group among fanatics, stab and beat each other in the stands and in street fights. When the leaders of the largest organisation of Idealists tried to reconcile the Idealists in the stands of Fenerbahce, Galatasaray and Besiktas by saying 'You are friends of the same cause', these sentiments and attempts at arbitration were refused in all three stadia. A fascist organisation found such a refusal difficult to tolerate, but it showed significantly that the club identity was regarded as superior to the national identity, and indeed to the nationalist identity. Hence this ideology does not appear to comply with the dominant conception of nationalism.[5] These fascist supporter groups legitimise their attitude within their own logic. During the Fenerbahce–Galatasaray match, before a Champions' League match between Galatasaray and Barcelona, Fenerbahce fans shouted 'Barcelona, Barcelona', and were answered 'PKK is proud of you.' Besiktas fans shouted 'Tiran, Tiran', the name of Fenerbahce's Albanian opponents, and this time Fenerbahce fans answered with the slogan 'PKK is proud of you.' Within the logic of such groups, their team represents the national identity, and the rivals are the team of 'others'; if we evaluate according to current political developments, they become a Kurdish team that denies their Turkishness.

These fans may see their rival as others and give their team the right to represent the national identity but they also know that such approaches are not very meaningful, but who is looking for a meaning? The important point is that 'others' are created and exist to be discriminated against. Though the fascist movements – reinforced by the national identity crisis – gain the sympathy of the masses, their actions remain marginal. When their violence or hate exceeds a certain limit, they are publicly damned. International football provokes less intense but confusing hysteria. Racist, discriminating attitudes are not always evident. On some occasions 'we' are happy to become closer to 'the others', paradoxically 'we' celebrate by swearing at 'the others'. On other occasions, 'we' are proud of being different, so that 'we'll never get close to the others'. At other times, the football superiority of 'the others' can provoke depression among us.

The problem thus remains: Who are we, and who are the others? Are we European, or Asian? Are we Eastern, or Western? Are we on the threshold of a perfect synthesis, or in a complex that destroys our dual personality? Should we come closer to others in the West, or should we distance ourselves from them? In the words of the classic statement, Do we exist beyond Edirne, or not? The answers to these questions are not known; more truly, the answers change according to the daily moods of a Turkish society that is experiencing a national identity crisis. And it is football that affects the mood of Turkish society most deeply.

Notes

1. Perhaps, in reality, Brazil is not the 'true' country for such a camparison. In John Humphrey's words (1986: 128), 'Active club supporters in Brazil, or elsewhere, are male and a minority of the population ... When the national squad takes the field in the World Cup, however, the picture changes completely.' In Turkey the level of active club supporters is among the highest in the world, so that they can never be called a minority.
2. A Public survey carried out by PIAR/Gallup in 1993 found that 76 per cent of the population actively follow football, with this majority heavily skewed towards the modern, educated social groups. While barely half (53.2%) of the 'non-educated' followed football, graduates of primary school (80.2%), high school (86.7%) or university (83.1%) were committed fans.
3. Reliable data on this rise in violence is difficult to acquire, particularly due to the lack of comparable data from earlier periods. In any case, the 'climate of violence' is as much something that is experienced as it is a set of statistics.
4. See Can Kozanoglu (1995) for a fuller analysis of the 'open buffet' available within Turkey's modern cultural centre.
5. A minor section of supporters outside these 'hooligan' groups do not support the other clubs in international matches for a variety of reasons. They are heavily criticised and sometimes unjustly insulted by the great majority which actively supports every Turkish team in international matches without any differentiation.

10 View from the Periphery: Football in Indonesia

Freek Colombijn

Around 1900 football was introduced into Indonesia by a colonial power, the Netherlands, and quickly captivated the indigenous people. The diffusion of football in Indonesia followed that of the Netherlands in remarkable detail. The Haarlemsche Football Club, the oldest club in the Netherlands, was established in 1879 by a Dutch schoolboy, who had attended an English boarding school. Sixteen years later a schoolboy, who had learned the game in Great Britain, founded the first club in Indonesia. His name, John Edgar, suggests the possibility of a British father. In England, Holland, and the Dutch East Indies, football spread from the elite, via the middle class, to the workers, at which point the upper class began to seek other sporting pastimes (Berretty 1934: 161). Pursuing a strategy of divide and rule the colonial power conquered and ruled the indigenous population that was split into some 300 different ethnic groups.

A nationalism that united all Indonesians did not emerge earlier than the 1920s. Since gaining independence in 1945 nation building and suppressing regional disparity have been important items on the government's agenda (Cribb and Brown 1995; Dick 1996). However, within Indonesia there is a clear distinction between core (the medium-sized but densely populated island of Java, on which the capital Jakarta is situated) and periphery (the rest of the country, referred to as Outer Islands). This is a colonial legacy; the European elite dominated the indigenous people of varying ethnicity, a clear majority of whom were excluded from political and economic power. The elite, however felt isolated and looked to the home country for a lead in culture. As far as football was concerned, the Indies were at the periphery of the periphery, for the Dutch felt inferior to the British.

Home to the world's fourth largest population, Indonesia was considered to be a potential 'economic tiger' until the financial and political unrest in Asia during the late 1990s. Were the whole archipelago to be projected on the map of Europe, it would stretch from Ireland to the Urals. This sheer physical distance restricts regular inter-regional contacts. Its first president, Sukarno, convened a number of Asian and African nations in the first meeting of non-aligned states (1955), and its long term president, Suharto, aspired to play a leading role in the Southeast Asian ASEAN and the Trans-Pacific APEC economic organisations. The national football team, however, continues to play an insignificant role both in Asia and globally. This marginality is reflected in the sport journals. The popular weeklies *Bola* (Ball) and GO (*Gema Olahraga*, Sports Echo) carry scores from a dozen European and South American leagues, and photos of world football stars rather than Indonesians.

DIFFUSION INTO A COLONIAL SOCIETY

Colonial Indonesian society was juridically classified into three categories: indigenous people; non-indigenous Asians; and Europeans, which rather oddly included Americans and Japanese (Fasseur 1992). The racial undertones of classification had far-reaching consequences for civil obligations and rights, salaries, marriage preferences, and residential patterns. People labelled themselves and others in ethnic terms, and constructed ethnic groups to which they ascribed certain characteristics (Bruner 1974; Schefold 1988). In order to understand the importance of ethnicity for the colonial football associations, analysis will focus on one particular town, Padang (Colombijn 1996). As the provincial capital and port town of West Sumatra, the most important of the Outer Islands, Padang, is truly a peripheral place. Economically, the west coast is considered the 'wrong' side of Sumatra. Padang's biggest rival city on the east coast, Medan, profits from a vast natural hinterland, a location on the busy Straits of Malacca, and proximity to Singapore.

In colonial Padang the three most important ethnic groups, each from a different juridical category, were the Minangkabau people, the various Chinese groups, and the Dutch, many of whom were of Eurasian descent. Long before the introduction of football, Minangkabau boys played a juggling foot game with a plaited bamboo ball (Van Hasselt 1882: 126). The first football team in Padang was established by Dutchmen in 1901, and called Padangsche Voetbal Club. In the next few years six other teams were formed, including three Minangkabau teams and an army team, Sparta. This nomenclature referred to the, tough and belligerent ancient Greek state and was a popular name for army teams throughout the Dutch East Indies. At first the teams arranged occasional matches, or played against scratch teams from local trading houses or visiting German warships. Old residents recall that most matches were played with a *rago*, which was lighter, smaller and less expensive than official leather balls.

In 1905 the seven teams united in the WSVB (West Sumatran Football Association). For a long time, the WSVB remained the only football association in which Minangkabau, European and Chinese residents ever gathered together, be it on the pitch or around the football league conference table. The association organised a proper league competition, and matches were played on the Plein van Rome (Rome Square), a very wide, grass-covered army parade ground. The WSVB association profited from entrance fees necessitated by their erecting a bamboo fence around the field to obstruct the view of non-payers. Gate-money was meant to cover costs, but the local journal insinuated obliquely that profits were spent in an 'improper way' (*Sumatra Bode*, 24 December 1915).

Many teams did not survive for long for two principal reasons. First, many clubs were composed of employees of trading firms, or soldiers and civil servants, who were regularly transferred elsewhere in the Archipelago, thus hindering continuity. Secondly, teams fell apart when recurrent violence hampered matches. Following early disorder the initial interest in football began to wane and in 1915 the WSVB disbanded. Consequently, only occasional challenge matches were played. In 1921, after much lobbying from local newspapers, the WSVB was revived, but this time with an exclusively European board. A new league was organised which included three teams drawn from the mountainous hinterland and four teams of Europeans. Three military teams, however, were of mixed ethnic composition; professional (military) loyalty over-ruled ethnic boundaries.[1] A special train ran between the urban centre and harbour before and after matches. There were different entrance fees for non-indigenous spectators and 'natives'. Since the WSVB organised everything, the board decided it was entitled to all the gate-money.

One issue was whether teams consisting exclusively of indigenous players should be allowed to join the league. Outside the league jurisdiction, Minangkabau–European challenge matches were played, which were characterised by fair play and a paying attendance of up to 2,500. However, when one such game ended in disorder the die was cast. The WSVB members concluded that teams of indigenous players should form their own league. The existing indigenous teams reacted by resigning from the WSVB and in August 1922 founded their own association, the SVM (Minangkabau Sports Association), provoking the local journal to comment that two football associations in one town was ridiculous. The small and now exclusively European WSVB succumbed after a couple of years, completely outclassed by the indigenous teams. Europeans then organised football matches merely for charitable local causes, and moved their efforts to the elitist sport of tennis. Unencumbered by the Dutch elite ethos of amateurism, the indigenous teams began to pay their best players, while others were given work outside football.

While those who controlled the football association had access to the profits of the gate-money, the pressing problem was material; namely, the association needed access to a pitch. Basically there were two: Rome Square owned by the Dutch Forces, and the Justitieplein (Square of Justice) owned by the municipality. By 1930, the Minangkabau association (the SVM) was monopolising Padang football by renting both, and thus enjoyed the income from both. The SVM organised tournaments, in which star players turned out for more than one team, and while it paid the players it also kept the majority of the takings; it also cooked the books to avoid paying in full the local entertainment tax. Some indigenous clubs expelled from the SVM established a new association – the PSV (Padangsche Sport Vereeniging, The Padang Sport Association) – but neither it nor the European and Chinese teams had access to the pitches, and so could not play any matches.

The PSV sought to resolve this dilemma by preparing a third field. This proved to be too uneven, and only further increased tension between the two football associations. This was epitomised when the PSV organised a match against a Javanese team, thus provoking the SVM to arrange for another Javanese team to play on exactly the same date. Competition over crowd-pulling opponents (and implicitly turnstile profits) led to the pre-war highlight of a visiting Singaporean team in 1931. This first international match in Padang attracted many spectators despite greatly inflated entrance fees. A similar game also inspired fraud: one Penang (British Malaya) team turned out to be from Medan (East Sumatra).

The rival associations eventually merged under the PSV title in 1935. Immediately a crisis erupted resulting in two teams, Sparta and SIOD, leaving the league and withdrawing the use of fields. Sparta, the military team, controlled Rome Square; SIOD, the railways team, had built the first regular pitch in Padang, complete with changing rooms and a small grandstand. Only the Square of Justice, the least suitable pitch, remained in use. Into this deadlock stepped Th. Van der Lee, consul of the national federation of football associations, the NIVU (Nederlandsch–Indische Voetbal Unie, The Netherlands–Indies Football Union). In 1936, he established a new association called the VPO (Football Association Padang and Environs). Perhaps the link between Van der Lee and the national federation, and through this a perceived influence in FIFA, gave him sufficient prestige and leverage to control all pitches in Padang. All clubs joined the VPO. Shortly before the Pacific War a regional umbrella association for the VPO and other football associations in West Sumatra was established. NIVU's successful intervention reflects the advanced political and economic integration of the Dutch East Indies on the eve of war. The VPO, whose leadership was in Dutch hands, spelled the end of an independent Minangkabau football association. The institutionalisation of NIVU was proven when Van der Lee left Padang in 1940. His successor as consul of NIVU was elected VPO chairman without a hitch.

NATIONAL INTEGRATION

These changes were typical of many other places in colonial Indonesia, including the capital Jakarta, then called Batavia. There the first team, the Bataviasche Voetbal Club, was founded in 1903 and played on an undersized pitch inside the city zoo. Batavian clubs started a league in 1904, which was similarly troubled by club closures and frequent player transfers to elsewhere in the Indies. In 1912, the local association bifurcated and teams from either side were banned from playing each other. For financial reasons, the two struggling associations were united again after a year. Matches against visiting foreign teams attracted large crowds, despite increased prices, and brought large profits. In Batavia, as in Padang, a bamboo fence surrounded the ground to ensure all spectators paid.

During another match, where fifty fans had climbed a tree to obtain a free view, the tree collapsed; thirteen were injured and two killed (Berretty 1934: 18–49, 138, 194). Foreign teams came from as far away as British India, the Philippines, China and Australia; a professional Austrian team visited the East Indies twice.

Amid the similarities there were also contrasts with Padang, due mainly to differences in scale. There were more teams and the league had several divisions with regular promotion and relegation. Several clubs had their own pitch, some even with a semi-permanent grandstand. Owing to the constant influx of experienced players from the home country, the standard of play was higher.

One crucial difference remained between football in the Outer Islands and Java. High population density, relatively short distances between cities, and a good transport network enabled the development of a supra-regional organisation in Java. In 1914, during the Colonial Exhibition at Semarang, a cup was contested by teams from the local associations of the four major cities in Java: Batavia, Surabaya, Bandung and Semarang. Most teams were usually composed of one ethnic group, but the representative teams of these four towns were multi-ethnic. These matches were deemed such a success that they were repeated every year at Pentecost, in one of the four cities in turn. At first these so-called *stedenwed-strijden* (city matches) were organised by ad hoc committees drawn from one of the four local associations. In 1919 the first umbrella association, the NIVB (Nederlandsch–Indische Voetbal Bond, The Netherlands–Indies Football Association), was formed to organise the annual city matches on a permanent footing. Gradually other associations in Java joined, so that qualifying rounds were played to determine which associations could send a squad to the final round. In practice, it was always the big four who qualified (Berretty 1934: 211–25).

The NIVB stabilised the life of the local associations. Separatist associations found it increasingly difficult to maintain an isolated existence (Berretty 1934: 63, 81–2). Integration of local associations, however, simply entailed new schisms at national level. After disagreement in 1935 about the federation's future, the whole local association of Batavia resigned from the NIVB and established the NIVU, mentioned above. One after the other, local associations went over to the new, national federation and soon the old NIVB was discontinued. The NIVU extended its role beyond city matches, adopting member associations outside Java, such as Padang in 1936. It joined FIFA and then sent a national team, of mixed ethnicity, to the World Cup in France in 1938. The team was soundly beaten by Hungary in the first round. It then played an even more important friendly against the national team of the mother country before a crowd of 40,000 spectators, losing to the Dutch team 9–2 (Baumgarten et al. 1949: 43–52, 133–42). The NIVB also encountered another rival which survived both the NIVB and the NIVU. This brings us to the interplay between football and nationalism.

NATIONALIST STRUGGLES

Throughout the twentieth century nationalist feelings steadily gained ground in Indonesia, and found expression in various organisations. During the 1930s, in an increasingly tense political atmosphere, the more radical organisations were forbidden, and their leaders exiled. The Japanese conquest of Indonesia in 1942 overturned Dutch control. Then in 1945, immediately after the Japanese surrender, Sukarno and his co-commander Hatta proclaimed the independence of the Indonesian Republic. The Dutch responded by trying to crush the republic by military force. When this proved untenable because of international pressure on The Hague, the Dutch endeavoured to contain the Indonesian Republic within Java by creating a series of states in the Outer Islands. This was a forlorn idea and in 1949 the Dutch transferred sovereignty to the federal Republic of the United States of Indonesia, of which the Indonesian Republic was but one constituent, although by far the most important. Within one year Sukarno dissolved the federal United States of Indonesia and the new nation became a unitary state. Overcoming regional rebellions, nation-building, and placing Indonesia on the world map were items high on Sukarno's agenda. Creating a favourable economic climate was neglected and the redistribution of wealth took precedence over economic growth. In 1965 the army seized power and the communist party was crushed, with an estimated half a million people killed. General Suharto established the so-called New Order and became the second president of Indonesia (Cribb and Brown 1995; Ricklefs 1981). Football followed both nationalist resistance before Independence and nation-building afterwards and played its own minor part in each.

In Java a number of football associations with teams consisting of indigenous players preferred to stay outside the NIVB. In 1930 seven founded their own national association, the PSSI (Persatuan Sepakbola Seluruh Indonesia, The All Indonesia Football Federation). The Malay name indicated its exclusively indigenous membership, but even more notable was the confident use of the word 'Indonesia'. This designation, instead of 'Hindia Belanda', the Malay translation of Netherlands East Indies, betrayed their nationalist sympathies (Van Miert 1995: 188; PSSI 1955: 9–14; PSSI 1980: 24–5, 79). Despite their anti-colonialism, the PSSI saw itself as parallel to the Dutch NIVB and a similar Chinese association, and, in fact, the PSSI did mirror the NIVB. Constituent local associations also organised leagues with club teams, and delegated their respective association teams to annual inter-city matches.

The PSSI memorial volumes (1955, 1960, 1980) probably tend to overemphasise the nationalistic aspect of what was essentially a football association. They stress its all-Indonesian character and downplay its actual limitation to Java (cf. Henley 1996: 1–5). Occasionally, their nationalism was expressed explicitly, for instance in speeches during the annual congress (PSSI 1955; PSSI 1980). All member associations, numbering 40 in 1941, came from Java, but by then the PSSI had NIVB-style consuls in three towns in the Outer Islands, including Padang (PSSI 1960: 39). The definition of the PSSI, and of the NIVB, as an all-Indonesian organisation, and the realisation of every team in the boundaries of the colony as the remit of the football federation, must have had a role in imagining the nation as a community (cf. Anderson 1983; Houlihan 1997: 120).

The NIVB opposed any rival associations, particularly those with nationalist tendencies. Apart from a short-lived gentlemen's agreement in 1937, the NIVB forbade members to play against PSSI teams, threatening them with suspension if they did. The best Indonesian players, who attracted the largest crowds, preferred to play under the NIVB. Moreover, the NIVB denied the PSSI access to pitches, forcing it to play on makeshift pitches, such as fallow paddies on the urban fringes where few spectators turned up (PSSI 1955, 1980). The PSSI's income suffered, but they survived and stunned the NIVB and even gained a moral victory when a strong team from China arrived by invitation in 1937 and only managed a 2–2 draw against their select eleven (PSSI 1980).

Future Imperial impositions delayed the development of the game. During the Japanese occupation (1942–5), both the PSSI and the NIVU were disbanded. The Japanese established the Tai Iku Kai, a general sports organisation for martial arts and other semi-military exercises. Even it, however, observed the custom of city matches (PSSI 1980: 27). After the Republican proclamation of Independence, both Dutch and Indonesian sides made football part of their struggle. The Dutch Commander-in-Chief, S. H. Spoor, welcomed matches on the central square of 'freed' towns. The harmless sight of Dutch soldiers kicking a ball would, it was hoped, counteract Republican propaganda that pictured the Dutch as terrifying creatures. In late 1946 the NIVU was re-established, and in 1947 the Dutch had such large parts of Java under military control that the first city matches began again. To many Europeans it must have been a symbol that life was returning to normal. In 1948, after a secret meeting with Dutch officers and high-ranking civil servants, the NIVB decided to change its name to the VUVSI/ISNIS (the Football Union for the United States of Indonesia). The new name, and its bilingual form, brought the federation into line with the revised policy of the waning colonial power. At the same time, the board co-opted more Chinese and Indonesian members (Baumgarten et al. 1949).[2]

On the Republican side, where a whole state apparatus had to be developed, the value of sports propaganda was emphasised. In 1947 the young government founded an Olympic Committee and the PORI (the Federation of Sports in the Republic of Indonesia) a football department. The latter applied for FIFA membership in an attempt to enter the 1948 Olympics at London, but VUVSI/ISNIS blocked the bid (PSSI 1980: 105). In 1950 the football department was transformed into a resurrected PSSI. Member associations of VUVSI/ISNIS merged in each town with the PSSI's local rival, soon the former became a shell and in 1951 disbanded. This allowed the PSSI to join FIFA the same year (PSSI 1980: 105–6). The transfer from a federal to a unitary organisation had been as smooth in football as in the state administration. Further integration is reflected in an ever longer list of regional consuls on the national board, the transfer of PSSI's headquarters from Yogyakarta to the capital Jakarta, and, most of all, a growing number of affiliated associations, 289 in 1977 (PSSI 1980). In the mid-1950s there were still local associations outside the PSSI which competed with PPSI affiliates for official status. For many regular income was still a problem (PSSI 1955).

After the transfer of sovereignty, the priority of Sukarno and the young nation shifted from the struggle for Independence to nation-building. If a successful national team makes citizens – who would otherwise have few opportunities for participation in national politics – identify with the nation (Houlihan 1997: 121; Stokvis 1994), then the national football team played its part. FIFA membership enabled several successful international performances. In 1953 the PSSI team, the national squad, made a successful trip to the Philippines and Hong Kong. The next year the team beat reigning champions India in the second Asian Games, but was itself defeated in the next round. In 1956 they toured East European Communist countries and then at the Melbourne Olympics held the very strong Soviet Union to a 0–0 draw. The climax should have come in 1962 when Indonesia hosted the Fourth Asian Games. President Sukarno was in the midst of a grandiose building programme in Jakarta (Leclerc 1993). For the Games he ordered the construction of a new football and athletics stadium, to be named Senayan, and capable of holding 100,000 spectators. Smaller stadiums for other sports, the first-class Hotel Indonesia, and the Welcome Monument were all part of the preparations. The buildings were impressive, but success was dependent upon an Indonesian football triumph. Training started years in advance and friendly matches were promising. But not long before the tournament, the team was disrupted by a case of corruption which became known as the Senayan scandal. This event epitomised the prevailing atmosphere at the end of Sukarno's reign, and forced a purge of the team players (PSSI 1980: 107–8). In the final, the team lost 2–3 to rivals Malaya, of all countries.

After the 1965 coup Senayan became, like a number of other stadiums in the world, a mass prison for the detention of adversaries of the military regime. When the army emptied it in 1970, six teams from abroad were immediately invited, including the Australian junior team. Indonesia's changed Cold War position was manifest by the 1974 European tour with matches against such countries as West Germany, France and Sweden. In 1979, 1987 and 1997 Indonesia hosted the South-East Asian Games; in 1987 Indonesia won the tournament.

THE NATIONAL LEAGUE OF CLUBS

The New Order Government of Suharto embarked on a policy of social stability and economic growth. Until 1998 the economy was dominated by a number of conglomerates run by Suharto's family, army officers, and some of his civilian partners. The state had become strongly centralised and rampant inter-regional tensions seemed by and large to have been domesticated (Cribb and Brown 1995; Ricklefs 1981). The New Order Government also known as the Pancasila regime had its ideological foundation in the multi-interpretable state philosophy known as the 'Five Pillars'. The Pancasila and the motto *Bhinneka Tunggal Ika* (Unity in Diversity) was an attempt to define Indonesia as a culturally diverse state, but also one with a geographical and national organic whole. Via this law making, references to the constitution, and parliamentary elections made by the rulers were invested with a legitimacy (Van Langenberg 1990).

The PSSI emulated the New Order government. Where the state had Five-Year Development Plans, and a Broad Outline for the Direction of the State, the PSSI had Four-Year Development Plans, and Broad Outlines for the Direction of Football. The published decision to accept the Four-Year Plan 1974/1975–1978/1979 derived its paper size, layout, and style of language from published government by-laws. The proclaimed aim of the PSSI was to develop football throughout the country (thereby integrating all regions) based on the Pancasila. This general aim is elaborated into five principles, the sacrosanct number implicitly showing allegiance to the Pancasila, and hence to the New Order state (PSSI 1974, 1991). Conversely, the state was committed to football as a matter of national prestige. The paradox that all aspiring nations face is that, to project a sense of national unity and identity on the world stage, they must adjust to an increasingly uniform set of strategies, including a good performance in dominant sports (Houlihan 1997: 120). Whereas Indonesia has idiosyncratic sports, like the martial art of *pencak silat*, and also excels in badminton, it is forced by football's globalisation to seek to make a good impression. As recently as 1997. President Suharto warned the PSSI leadership that the national team of a country of 200 million inhabitants ought to perform better (*Kompas*, 20 April).[3]

Unfortunately for the New Order government, the national team declined during the 1970s, and sporting performance became a matter of public concern (PSSI 1980: 12, 42). A radical solution was offered in the creation of a national league, mimicking European football. The league, it was proposed, would provide players with prolonged competition and exercise at the highest level, which was otherwise offered only briefly during city matches. The national league named GALATAMA began in 1979 (PSSI 1980: 12, 109). However, the clubs relied on a sponsor for both funds and professional management. When the sponsor withdrew, the club often collapsed, so the national clubs have proved to be as unstable as local teams before Independence. Even once famous clubs that played in Asian cups disbanded. At the end of the 1990–91 season no less than six league teams were dissolved (PSSI 1991: 35).

The local associations (and their long-standing financial interests) were not so easily swept aside. They continued to organise local leagues and nationwide inter-city matches. In 1994 the professionalism of the club teams and the enthusiasm of the local associations were combined in one league that has replaced

GALATAMA. This has resulted in the peculiar combination of club teams and association teams playing together, in about equal numbers, in one league. The association teams, free of sponsorship pressures, are much more secure than club teams and they seem to attract larger crowds. Today, association teams also recruit players from outside their own territory.

A regular league with promotion and relegation has not yet been established; organisation is decided only from year to year. Three issues have to be resolved annually. First, considering the shaky financial position of the clubs, the association must decide which clubs and how many will be admitted to the league. Second, there is a recurrent debate about whether the league will be national, or split into two or three zones to cut transportation costs. All options have been tried. Whatever the format of the league, it always ends in play-offs, semi-finals and a final played in Senayan. This is the old formula for city matches. Third, there is a confusing, irregular schedule of other league and cup competitions which are additional to the national league. Despite the improved transportation network with domestic flights, the league's functioning is handicapped by distances. To cut travel costs, teams usually play a series of away matches in a brief tour of one particular island; however, the players become exhausted, so results often go from bad to worse. Moreover, players lose heart due to hostile crowds as none of their own supporters can afford these trips. Pertinently a team that starts its tour usually falls down the league table, whereas a series of home matches means a quick ascent.

Considering the history of football associations in Indonesia, money-making was undoubtedly a league aim (not counting the rather predictable cases of selling matches for gambling purpose). GALATAMA has offered promotional opportunities to the big Indonesian conglomerates and other enterprises, and so it has always been sponsored by various cigarette brands. Sponsors have also supported individual teams, with the aim of creating a good public image rather than merely promoting a brand name.

Whatever its merits, GALATAMA did not improve the national team's results. Seeing themselves on the periphery, Indonesian football leaders understandably have sought direct contact with what they see as the core, to raise their level of play. A tested method was employing foreign trainers whose nationalities have reflected varying political influences. In colonial times some Java clubs jointly employed an English trainer, until they ran out of money. In 1950, the first national team was coached by a Singaporean Chinese. When Sukarno became involved in the non-aligned movement, the PSSI used a Yugoslav trainer. Today Western European trainers are popular for the national and club teams (Berretty 1934: 62; PSSI 1980: 105, 107; PSSI 1991: 29). One recently implemented and interesting experiment is to send promising young players to top Italian clubs as apprentices. Another way to establish direct contact with core countries is to attract foreign players. This had happened occasionally in the past, but in 1993 the PSSI took the formal step of admitting foreigners to the league. This has led to a flood of foreigners who either are third-rate, come from nations where players can be obtained cheaply (the former Yugoslav republics, Africa, Brazil), or are fading football stars, such as Cameroon's Roger Milla and the Argentinian Mario Kempes. Most are no better than Indonesian players, but nevertheless their presence keeps local players out of teams (*Kompas*, 14 and 16 April 1996).

Television has brought football to every corner of the Archipelago and Indonesians have maintained an intense interest in European and South American football. One peculiar feature is the standard application of nicknames for national teams in newspapers. The Azzurri (Italy), Samba (Brazil) and Lions (Cameroon) are more or less global names, but there are Indonesian inventions too, such as the Toreador team (Spain) and the Union Jack team (England), and, for the Germans, the Panzer team. The international orientation is also evident in a dictionary containing foreign words in Indonesian sports discourse, which has entries for, among other phrases: 'corner ball', 'quarter-final', 'centre forward/ centervoor' (thus also giving the Dutch phrase), 'hungry for goals', 'banana shooting' and 'jumps at an opponent' (Syariffudin 1985: 340–55).

VIOLENCE ON THE PITCH

Violence has been connected with Indonesian football from its beginnings. The violence in colonial times should not be examined via modern theories about hooligans, but in the context of a plural society. Football was a pastime that drew together different ethnic groups which otherwise met only at the market (Furnivall 1944: 446–64; King 1994: 183–4). At the same time football was an opportunity to express ethnic identity in opposition to other ethnicities: most teams were ethnically assembled and matches were a way of venting personal feeling against other social categories. The impression gained from newspapers – that most fights occurred during inter-ethnic games – is confirmed by interviews with old residents. The exception was of course the ethnically mixed army team, Sparta, whose strong, drilled, corporate mentality could override ethnicity. However, the garrison consisted predominantly of Minahasans and Ambonese, who came from outside Sumatra and certainly did not consider themselves one nation with the Minangkabau (Henley 1996).

Although the urban elite was sometimes worried about fighting, we can see with hindsight that during these matches people probably worked off social tensions. The result must have been that ethnic distinction with the concomitant social inequality was reinforced rather than upset. The same 'Durkheimian' effect of football has been noted in more colonial societies or those with strong and static social inequality (Giulianotti and Armstrong 1997: 5; Lever 1983: 146, 157; Tuastad 1997: 118–20). The question remains whether the colonial government played on this latent function of football or not. In colonial Java, *main Padang* (to play the Padang way) was the expression for foul play (Van Miert 1995: 89).

But fights were by no means restricted to West Sumatra. For instance, in West Kalimantan, another Outer Island, the first inter-ethnic cup final ended in a massive fight, starting between European and Chinese teams, and ending between Chinese and indigenous spectators. Fights similarly took place in the core island, Java. In Batavia, a match ended prematurely due to disorder for the first time in 1909 (Berretty 1934: 38, 243–7). In the GALATAMA league and its successor, fights on the pitch between players, or with the referee, were and remain rife. As in colonial times, fights are a spontaneous reaction to the events on the field.

Travel costs impede 'away' supporters from following their team, thus reducing the possibilities of inter-fan disorders. However, the public often hurl stones and other small missiles at the referee and visiting players. Mass fights among spectators occur usually for two reasons. First, for popular matches too many tickets are sold, leading to restricted views, hence individual squabbles can quickly lead to brawls. Second, the final round of the GALATAMA and other tournaments resembles the old city matches and the Senayan stadium in Jakarta is attended by rival supporters. Jakarta is a multi-ethnic society with many immigrants and a team from any corner of the Archipelago can expect to find supporters from their region living there. Furthermore, for a semi-final or final a sizeable group of supporters will follow their team. The dividing line in these fights is not ethnicity, as in colonial times, but region of origin. To prevent any suspicion of referee bias, foreign referees officiate the final.

A cultural explanation can explain fan violence. The numerically dominant group in Indonesia, the Javanese, have strict ideas about order. The deeply internalised feeling of public shame fosters conformity, behavioural controls and social harmony. Overt conflict is avoided at all costs. The normal reaction to a conflict is avoidance and mediation by outsiders (Geertz 1961: 47–8; Magnis-Suseno 1997: 42–62, 71–83; Mulder 1989: 21–6, 42, 52). Where there is a conflict, however, especially when insults are exchanged, it is difficult to ignore, as this is felt to be losing face and shameful. With such an attitude towards human interaction, playing football is problematic. Football is an explicit conflict with losing an intrinsic part, where it is easy to feel insulted (a ball played between the legs, a rough tackle by an opponent), and where the culturally prescribed reaction of avoidance is simply impossible. However, this tension is exacerbated by the fact that any insult is not just in public, but before crowds of hundreds or thousands. A typical reaction for a Javanese under such strain is an outburst of rage and violence.

This explanation is partial and hypothetical, for the same argument is less convincing if applied to other ethnic groups in Indonesia, who are less culturally reserved, but fight just the same. It is interesting to note here that a *pencak silak* master visits the players of the west Sumatran team, PT Semen Padang, every fortnight to teach the players stamina and self-control. Perhaps the cultural explanation can be extended, by drawing a speculative parallel between football and the political culture, to which all players and spectators, from every ethnic background, are subjected. In a true democracy, losing and having a fair chance are all part of the game. In a non-civil society, however, the idea that competition implies conflict has not yet been transcended, and sporting behaviour is considered foolish. According to many people, Indonesia is closer to a non-civil than to a democratic society.

Notes

1. In 1910, the army command in Java forbade soldiers of different ranks to play in the same match, believing that such fraternising would undermine the military hierarchy. Army teams were thus restricted to one rank. When their civilian opponents had army personnel in their line-up, the latter had to remain standing on the sideline (Berretty 1934: 38).
2. The presence of Chinese and indigenous Indonesians on the board was not in itself new. In 1942 the chairman of the NIVU was Chinese (Baumgarten et al. 1949: 52).
3. Suharto, like his predecessors Sukarno, and the Dutch Governor-General, willingly lent his name and photo to the memorial volumes (Berretty 1934; PSSI 1955, 1980). At lower administrative levels, mayors and governors often take charge of local football associations, which is regarded as an astute move to further their public careers.

Acknowledgements

The author would like to thank Bart Barendregt, David Henley, Ed van Hoven, Andryas Mawardi, and Mestika Zed for their advice and suggestions, and Rosemary Robson for her ideas when correcting the paper for omissions and errors in English.

Part IV
Contested Decisions:
Disunited Players

11 The Generation Game: Football among the Baga of Guinea[1]

Ramon Sarro

Since 1989 the Baga people of Guinea, West Africa, have celebrated an annual football tournament that they like to compare to the masquerades performed in the old days (that is, when the old people of today were young men and women). This tournament proves to be one of the best occasions to assess the dynamics of intergenerational competition. While football is indeed a 'new' thing, a modern activity for young people away from their elders, the elders behind it are increasingly taking control of the situation and are not letting it be just a youth activity. By revitalising ritual activities long since disappeared and by reinforcing age structures mediated by the demands of the elites in Conakry (the capital city) the elders are indeed 'domesticating modernity' and using football matches as a context to retain the power youth were in principle trying to escape from.

The Baga are an ethnic group of some 40,000 living on the coast of the Republic of Guinea in West Africa. As happens with other groups elsewhere, it is difficult to determine whether Baga is one single ethnic group or a cluster of groups. Historically speaking, it is apparent that there have been several discrete ethnic units along the Guinean coast named 'Baga'. Yet, in today's Guinea, the proper Baga are conceived to be first and foremost the people living in the territory called 'Bagatai', a word that stems from *Baga tae*, 'Baga villages' in Susu (the lingua franca of coastal Guinea), situated between the prefectures of Boffa and Boké. Linguistically speaking, there are three different groups in the Bagatai: Bulongic,[2] Baga Pukur and Baga Sitem. Whether other groups living on the Guinean coast but outside this territory, such as the Southern Baga Koba and Baga Kalum near the capital Conakry, are also 'Baga' is a matter of contention. In general, it seems that territory is increasingly becoming a significant (and sufficient) criterion to determine ethnicity, and these Southern groups, even if they are called Baga, are left out of activities intended to express cultural unity, such as the annual football tournament. In 1994, when the representatives of some Baga Koba villages asked for inclusion in the tournament of Mare, they were refused admission on the grounds of not being Baga enough and of living too far away from the Bagatai. The late J. Camara, President of the Youth Committee of Mare in 1994, when I inquired about this refusal, explained: 'Maybe they were Baga in the past, but they are not so in the present.'

Baga people are said to be one of the oldest groups on the coast. According to their oral traditions, they settled on the coast after the Muslim pastoralist Fulbe chased them away from the Fuuta Jaloo highlands of the hinterland, which they claim to have been their homeland previous to the arrival of the Fulbe in the early eighteenth century. Although there is room to presume that the settlement and ethnogenesis of the Baga is more complicated than their migration narratives say (see Hair 1997 for a sceptical view about migration narratives), what remains interesting for analysis is that the pressure of the Fulbe slave raiders forced the Baga to hide more and more in the coastal mangroves and to build an impressive ritual system that helped protect them against external forces by producing a stereotype of sorcerers and 'savage' people much feared by raiders from the hinterland (see Fanthorpe 1998).

Yet, this stereotype of the Baga as pagans and masters of ritual powers ended in 1956–7, at the end of the French colonial period, when under the leadership of a charismatic Muslim preacher backed by anti-colonialist political parties, Baga youths cleared sacred bushes, burned sacred objects and masks, and converted to Islam. This movement, explored elsewhere (Sarro, forthcoming), was but a prelude to the years of oppression that were to come. In effect, under the rule of Sékou Touré, first president of independent Guinea, all forms of indigenous rituals other than the official 'national folklore' dictated by the Party were to be banned and ethnic particularisms repressed in the name of 'nation building'. While some groups on the border with Liberia and Sierra Leone could continue their forbidden initiation practices in these neighbouring English-speaking countries, the Baga, whose territory does not stretch over any other neighbouring country, could not return to the sacred bushes and to the initiations that they had abandoned in the late 1950s. It was only after the inauguration of the second Republic by President Lansana Conté and the growing democ-ratisation and decentralisation of Guinea that specific ethnic groups could engage in reappropriating what they perceived as their own cultural traditions (see Hoejbjerg 1991).

The Baga have attempted to revitalise their traditions (Lamp 1996a). Yet, what is surprising among the Baga is the contradiction between the intentions and the actions of the active 'nationalist' youths. What they intend and would like to do is indeed to bring back forms of traditional (or perceived to be such) masks and dances that have disappeared since 1956. This intention is very clear when one speaks with the intellectual representatives of the villages, who insist that their fellow villagers should engage in cultural activities, most notably in what they call 'carnivals',[3] festive celebrations with displays of dances and masks. Yet, the fact that initiations ceased to happen in the fifties has created a situation in which initiated elders possess ritual knowledge while young people do not. The objects, dances, and other cultural manifestations that the youths would like to see in public displays are considered by the elders to be sacred and secret, not to be publicly displayed or only to appear under their strict control. The process that I, following the German anthropologist Hermann Bausinger, would call 'folklorisation' (Bausinger 1990)[4] – that is to say, the process by which living elements of a culture become ideological, frozen items to be displayed as 'folklore', 'tradition' or 'custom' of a particular ethnic group – is for the Baga a difficult one to engage in because the generational gap between elders and juniors is bigger than the one found among other groups in Guinea.

THE FOOTBALL TOURNAMENTS

The best occasion to assess the dynamics of cultural revitalisation and of generational conflict were the annual football tournaments that the Baga youths have celebrated since 1989 and the 'carnivals' with which they open them every year. The football tournaments were created in 1989 by the Jeunesse Agricole Catholique, which had been reactivated in 1985 by the French Fathers when they were reaccepted in Guinea.[5] The cup given to the winner of the tournament was accordingly baptised *Coupe Bienvenu* in honour of Gustave Bienvenu, the charismatic Superior Father at the Mission of Katako (the biggest Baga village). In principle, so they say, the Missionaries wanted an occasion for Baga people to gather and 'know each other' and to reactivate ties among villages. When talking about this tournament, the comparison with old times is always present in people's minds. They conceive of the tournament as having the same function as old masquerades, especially the famous *Nimba*.[6] Similar to football matches today, masquerades once would bring the whole Baga country together.

As my Baga adoptive father told me when pondering the virtues of the tournament: 'People no longer know which their corresponding lineages[7] in other villages are, because we have been too isolated for too long. Now this football tournament forces young people to go to other villages and know their people there as they have to stay in the house of their corresponding lineage when they go to another village.' The tournament does indeed bring to life kinship and other ties among villages. But it not only reactivates a common identity that has been for many years dormant or resilient; it also gives expression to a constant redefinition of moving identities that increasingly take on a territorial dimension, although they do not ignore blood links. Thus, villages that were before considered Baga are nowadays left out of the tournament (even if they ask for inclusion) because they are 'too far' for the majority of Baga youth to attend, or simply because they are not considered as being Baga enough (in fact, 'Baganess' seems to be something achieved gradually). The football tournament also creates divisions and alliances between villages or clusters of villages, which may have a kinship rationale, but are more strongly marked by a politico-territorial element than by a kinship one.

CARNIVALS AND REVIVAL

Every year it is announced that the opening of the tournament will be accompanied by what we would call a folkloric celebration (although 'folklore' is not a word Baga themselves would use, except for a few found amongst the Catholic elite). They call it 'carnival' and in theory it involves the exhibiting of different Baga masks and dances. That masks will appear is insisted upon by the elite groups of Conakry, who play a very important role in the tournament, especially in finding financial support. The youths in the villages are also excited about the masks, but they are more sceptical about the reality of the promises made by their intellectual spokesmen. In fact, masks belong to the elders of the villages, who had been initiated in the old, pre-Independence times and who do not allow youths to 'play' with them. They do not recognise the ideological importance that the youth and Conakry-based Baga people give to the public display of a 'Baga culture' and they do not see why football and masquerades or dances should go together.

Every year the social process of the preparation of the tournament consist of an endless dialogue between the youth, the elders and the elites. At first, elders did not really want to become involved in the games. These were considered as things kids did and therefore should not concern them. Yet, little by little they began to realise the importance of the tournament for the common development of the villages, and the elite groups (who normally are very respectful and fearful of elders actions) were more and more insistent that the games should happen with the help of the elders, or under their instructions. The elders thus gradually became involved, and started to make sacrifices to empower the young players of their respective villages. The situation we find nowadays is that both youths and elders are involved in the tournament. While the youth play the football, the elders become instrumental in making sacrifices and prayers to ensure that the games will happen in the best conditions, and that their boys will win the matches. Youths play for the cup and for the possibility of promotion to better Guinean teams; elders become involved, because the honour of their village is at stake. I will come back to the dual activity of youths and elders later. Meanwhile, if we look at the three last tournaments (in Mare 1994, Bukor 1995 and Kawass 1996) a picture emerges of the processes of revitalisation.

MARE '94

The preparation for this tournament coincided with my ethnographic fieldwork in the village. Many people were insistent on the 'folkloric' aspect of the tournament. One of the most active Baga intellectuals in Conakry is Maurice, a theatre manager from Mare. He announced with such an insistence that the tournament would be opened by a folkloric seance that it even attracted a few curious Europeans based in Conakry, who in the event were disappointed to learn that football and not masks was what the tournament was all about. A *Nimba* headdress was danced in a rather unstructured way, but that was all. Maurice had even written a long text on the history and culture of the Baga that he promised to read on the occasion, but to my disappointment he did not. I imagine that once in the village, under the pressure of his elders, he realised that 'history' and 'culture' are secret things not to be given away in public speeches.

This lack of 'folklorisation' and of reflexivity (i.e. the use of the occasion for the Baga to explain themselves their history and culture) was accompanied by a recrudescence of incidents of sorcery and witchcraft gossip. Thus, the death of a young boy who fell from a tree while observing a match was said to be a sacrifice made by the people of Bukor to win the cup. The fact that subsequently Bukor (a village particularly feared for its witchcraft, especially in 1994) did win the cup reinforced the belief in witchcraft. Someone told me that this death had probably been a sacrifice to *Amanco ngopon*, the highest male spirit of Baga cosmology. A year later, I learned that while the tournament was taking place, a few elders, away from it, were making important decisions as to where and by whom the few ritual objects that they still have in the village would be kept. They chose the moment when all the young people (and anthropologists ...) were in a football stadium to freely discuss their most secret and important matters.

BUKOR '95

The preparation of the tournament in 1995 was even more interesting. To start with, people were afraid of going to Bukor because of the perceived presence there of witchcraft. A solemn sacrifice to *Amanco* involving many cows was still performed in Bukor in 1986, whereas in other villages ritual activities associated with him seem to have been completely abandoned, albeit the belief lingers. Some young people from Mare and other villages told me that they would not go to the tournament. People from Bukor had to take action against this predicament (the point of the tournament being, of course, to gather as many people as possible, not to scare them away). It so happens that Bukor is the only Baga village where the social tissue still consists of a very structured age pyramid with the *alipne* or council of elders at its apex. The *alipne* (lit. 'those who have finished') consist of a group of men (one from every lineage of the village) who have completed the initiation cycle. They are always present, but silent (and at a distance) in daily village meetings, but very active in nightly ones. They also meet secretly in a special grove situated in the middle of the village, that nobody else can visit. It is common knowledge that masks and other objects are kept there. Even in distant villages like Mare I have been told that 'there is a bush in Bukor that should be cleared' referring to that grove and the trees surrounding it.[8] The *alipne* of Bukor are regarded by other villages with both fear and admiration.

Bukor elites in Conakry decided that in order to avoid witchcraft attacks during the three-week tournament, they would ask the *alipne* to take care of the situation. The *alipne*, accordingly, performed a series of rituals known as *kaenger* ('the closing of the land'), closing it for as long as they wanted to, sometimes for up to six months. These solemn actions whilst very rarely performed theoretically makes it impossible for people to die from witchcraft attacks. In the days when the Baga had long initiation rituals, the closing of the land was linked to these rituals and to the appearance in the village of the high spirit *Amanco* (these two things going hand in hand).[9] To my knowledge, the last time the land was closed in the Bagatai was in 1986. As mentioned above, it was also closed in Bukor when a *kaebok*, or solemn sacrifice to *Amanco* was made in order to stop an increase of witchcraft deaths. On that occasion, so people say, the voice of *Amanco* was heard coming from the forest, although he was not seen.

The closure of the land in 1995 had nothing to do with *Amanco*, but rather with prevention of witchcraft during the tournament. The association between the two elements (that is, this ritual and *Amanco*) occupied the minds of all the Baga, that the *alipne* of Bukor dared to close the land in order to hold the football tournament frightened many people. The outcome was that some villages did not allow their children to compete in such a potentially dangerous village. This may seem contradictory, since *kaenger* is not intrinsically bad, but we have to understand that the elders of these other villages were afraid that their 'irresponsible' kids would not know the importance of a *kaenger* and would not respect it, having to pay deadly consequences later. (When a village is in *kaenger*, for instance, unmarried people are not allowed to have sex. Yet sex is obviously one reason youth go to other villages on such occasions as a football tournament ...)

It was also decided that the *alipne* should be in charge of the preparation of the carnival. They were particularly upset about the unstructured way their youth had danced the *Nimba* headdress the previous year in Mare. This year it had to be done properly. When the opening day arrived, there were a few dances and masks: *Nimba* and *Sibondel* danced under the direct control of the *alipne*, 'in the old way'. But for the elites of Conakry this was not enough. They insisted on the inclusion of the old initiation dance (*kaekenc*), which had not been performed in the village since the late 1940s. They sent a special commission to Bukor to discuss the issue with the *alipne*. These ones, at first, did not show any open opposition to the idea. A group of young people had already been chosen in order be taught how to dance the *kaekenc*. But then, as the tournament approached, the *alipne* refused to teach the youths. They said that football is just a game and that in consequence only games may be played: *Nimba* and *Sibondel*. The Baga make a distinction between what we could call 'secret' masks or *tolom*, which can only be seen by initiated people, and other masks or *powolsene*, a word meaning 'toys', although these may also be referred to sometimes as *tolom*. Nevertheless, the carnival was considered a success by the whole of the villagers, with the visit of the first lady of Guinea (the wife of President Conté, a Baga herself) and national TV coverage into the bargain.

KAWASS '96

Whereas Bukor is remote and during many months accessible only by boat, Kawass is only 8 km from Kamsar, on the main road between Kamsar and Conakry. Kamsar hosts a major bauxite port and factory, run by the international CBG (Compagnie de Bauxites Guinéennes). It has 30,000 inhabitants (many of them American or European) and is the focus of modernising forces in the hinterland and near coast. The little airport of Kamsar (proposed to become an international one) is in fact in Kawass. Catholic missionaries are very active in Kawass. Half the population of Kawass is Susu, and the Baga element has not retained the structure based on age and ritual knowledge evident in Bukor. The tournament of Kawass was accompanied by a 'carnival', but a rather poor and short one. Three masks were shown and dances around them performed: one represented an aeroplane, another a helicopter and the third a boat. That people from Kawass had to show such masks was criticised by those from other areas, as though they had 'forgotten their roots'.

BOFFA vs. BOKÉ: THE RISE OF NEW IDENTITIES

One important characteristic of the Kawass tournament was that it very soon became a fight between two different geographical regions: 'Arraponka' and 'Kakande' are the vernacular names of the territories around, respectively, the Rio Pongo (the region of Boffa) and the Rio Nuñez (that is, the region of Boké). Boffa and Boké are nowadays different prefectures. It so happens that Boké is the prefecture where Kamsar and its modernising elements are located, while the Baga villages in Boffa are untouched by these development agencies, and are geographically remote. While most villages in Boké are Sitem, villages in Boffa are mostly Bulongic, except for Bukor, Kalikse and some lineages in the village of Yampon. The crudeness of the opposition between Arraponka and Kakande was new to me – as was the use of these two words. The previous year the cup had been won by Kuffen, which in terms of kinship and migration narratives is a very close village to Bukor (Kuffen is 'the younger brother' of Bukor). Yet, because administratively Kuffen belongs to Boké and Bukor to Boffa, people from Bukor were very disappointed and considered this victory a betrayal of their brothers from Kuffen. In fact, it was somehow 'decided' by people in Boffa that in 1996 the *Bienvenu* cup had to 'come back' to Arraponka (Boffa). During the first days of the tournament, I visited Bukor and attended a night meeting where the *alipne*, together with a group of old women, reassured the rest of the population that the cup was to come to Boffa prefecture; whether had to come to Bukor itself or another village in the prefecture was of secondary importance (but Bukor was preferable, of course).[10]

The fact that, despite their linguistic and other characteristics, Sitem people from Bukor feel closer to other Baga villages in Boffa (which are not Sitem) than to their 'brothers' of Boké reveals the importance of new territorial policies on the shaping of identities. The 1996 tournament was also the first time that I heard about the project of making a prefecture out of Kamsar and the Baga villages around it, that is, the villages in Boké prefecture. People call it the 'Baga Prefecture', although of course it will have to include (if it ever comes into existence) many people other than the Baga. People in Boké certainly take advantage of the presence of Kamsar in their prefecture. For example, a new road and a bridge inaugurated on April 1994 opened up a few villages and has made it possible for inhabitants (especially women selling fruit and rice) to go to Kamsar in a few minutes for a relatively cheap price. An important French agricultural project based in Kamsar is now improving the rice fields of the area. Even the twin engine aeroplane of the CBG makes it possible for a few, well connected Baga people to fly to or from Conakry in less than an hour. The Boffa villages, on the contrary, have the feeling of being left out, and realise their chances to be 'opened up' and to enjoy wider resources do not rely on Boké, Kamsar or on development projects based in Kamsar, but rather on the Boffa prefectural authorities.

DIFFERENT PERSPECTIVES ON BEING BAGA

One aspect of this new opposition between the Boffa and the Boké villages is their respective outlooks towards what they consider their culture. Although they envy the modernising element of Boké, people from Arraponka (Boffa) are very proud of being considered more traditional than their Boké neighbours. I think this is what they tried to prove with the relatively spectacular carnival in Bukor '95, which, as stated, was broadcast on national TV and reported as a token of the *Bagatai profond* (deep Bagatai). The same people consider the carnival of Kawass '96, with its aeroplanes and helicopters, as a preposterous travesty, an abandonment of their 'Baganess'. I recall one occasion when I saw a group of people in a Bulongic village refuse to greet some visitors from the region of Boké. That was rather surprising to me, and when I asked why, they answered that these were not their relatives, but *tubabs* (white people). It has to be said that Baga Fore (the Susu word to refer to Bulognic speakers) means in Susu 'Black Baga', and that blackness is a matter of pride among the Baga in general. (The discourse about blackness intermingles with the discourse about purity. 'When the skin of a Baga is clear, his origins are not clear' someone told me, suggesting that a fair skinned person would be a descendant of slaves.)

As one might expect, people in Boké do not share this view. They do not consider that Bukor or the Bulognic villages of Boffa are more 'Baga' than them, but rather that they have not been successful in eradicating witchcraft and evil-doers, that is, the bad aspects of Baga society. Even the fact that Bukor people still have *alipne* is strongly criticised. For them, and not without reason, *alipne* and witchcraft go hand in hand. They consider the Baga of Boffa as the under-developed side of the Bagatai.

It would nonetheless be untrue to say that Baga people from Boké have completely lost interest in their cultural past. In fact, if a visitor (say a white employee of the CBG during a weekend around the region) wants to see a 'traditional' Baga masquerade (and if he or she is ready to pay for it), the chances are that they may get a good one by the *troupes de théâtre* installed either in Katako or in Kamsar itself. These will perform either *Nimba, Sibondel* or any other 'toy'. Yet, these public displays of masks, albeit clearly 'folklorised' in the sense discussed above, do not occur as often as one would expect, and certainly not as often as the Baga elites would like. We did not see them in Mare '94 (although they had been announced), we did not see them in Kawass '96 (although, again, they had been announced). We only saw one of them in Arraponka, in Bukor '95, and although it was obviously conceived as a public show, the exhibition of the masks was also surrounded by a climax of ritual solemnity, in that it was directed by the respectful and fearful *alipne* and done over a closed land. It could perhaps be said that Bukor succeeded in doing it because the generational structure allowed for a preparation of the tournament in which the *alipne* made decisions and the youth executed them. In the Boké villages, on the other hand, the generational breach is enormous and seems irreversible. Youth refuse instructions from the elders; preferring to dance to images of aeroplanes and helicopters they thereby escape the control of the elders.

ARE YOUTHS DOING ANYTHING REALLY NEW?

As seen elsewhere in the world, many youths saw in football a means to escape from their village, to be promoted to regional and maybe even national teams. But the process as it stands nowadays is that the tournament has become too important an occasion for the whole village to be left to the young. Elders are really behind it, it is they who are playing – albeit certainly not football. Baga elders normally say that 'the youth are never responsible for a success, but always responsible for a failure'. There is no way the elders are going to say something like 'our boys have won the cup'. If the much envied *Bienvenu* cup comes to the village, that's thanks to the elders' play (that is sacrifices, prayers, witchcraft, etc). If it does not, then it is because 'our kids are lazy and irresponsible and they have not done what we ordered them to do'.

An interesting account of this assumption of control by elders was given to me by one of my male elder informants in Mare, who suggested that the reason why they (i.e. men) started to care about the football games was the increasing involvement of women in the games:

> Women started, especially in Monshon tournament, to perform drumming and dances in the fields, during the matches, behind the goals. ... [*Authors note: The final match of Monshon '93 was cancelled due to the fears these dances*

induced in the opposite team. Also in 1994 in Mare I could some nights see the women going to the field to bury secret substances and 'prepare the soil' with dances and drumming.] ... Women could not realise that all this is just a game, they are too proud of their children and they would do anything to help them succeed. That's why we then decided to do something about it.

But this is just one version of events. As stated earlier, in Bukor I was told (by one of the *alipne*) that elders decided to take control of the games with sacrifices and prayers because the whole honour of a village is at stake. We can identify other factors: the fight for resources, pressures from the elites, and on top of it all a wonderful occasion for elders to empower themselves.

Whenever I get old people to talk to me about the days when they danced the *Nimba*, they always insist that this was a dance for young people, done by young people away from elders. But then again they admit that they could only dance it thanks to the instructions given by the elders and by the sacrifices they made for them. If young people today thought they would escape from the elders by 'playing' football, they were certainly wrong. In fact, the football tournament is reproducing and reifying the very structure they were trying to escape from: one that makes elders the decision makers and sacrificers, and youths the more or less irresponsible executors of the decisions. And as for the elites of Conakry, if they thought that the football tournament would revitalise the 'folkloric' aspect of their culture (masks and dances for a tourist public) they also seem to have got it wrong. If there is a revitalisation, it is a revitalisation of power structures and practices attached to these structures: that keeps secret what has to be secret and public what can be public, and sustains the elders' control of everything. Exactly as it was when these elders in the late 1950s were young and tried to escape from their elders' control by converting to Islam, clearing their secret forest and burning their sacred objects.

The general conclusion is directly applicable to the villages of Boffa prefecture (especially to the Bukor case), but probably less so to the more 'modern' villages of Boké prefecture. However, my feeling after conducting interviews in 1997 one year after the Kawass tournament, is that the 1995 Bukor tournament preparation provided an example for all the other villages. The future will probably see an increasing involvement of elders in all tournaments, even in Boké prefecture, and is the issue that future research must address.

Notes

1.   I am grateful to Nick Argenti, Marie-Nathalie LeBlanc, Mike Rowlands and Will Rea, as well as to Peter Mark and Robert Leopold for their comments.

2. As it is common usage among many Africanist linguists, I use the symbol *c* to transcribe the voiceless alveo-palatal affricate consonant that other authors transcribe as 'tch', 'tsh', or 'th' (similar to the 'ch' in 'cheap'). In doing so I am following the more recent works on Baga linguistics. See Voeltz et al. 1997; Ganong 1998.

3. I suspect it is the proximity of Guinea Bissau, a former Portuguese colony, why people on the Guinean coast use the word 'carnival' to refer to various forms of celebrations.

4. To my knowledge, the theoretical framework and terminology outlined by Bausinger was first applied to African celebrations by Peter Mark (Mark 1994), who in his research on Jola 'folkloric' dances combines Bausinger's ideas with other works concerning the rise of self-conscious activities among other African groups, most notably those of Karin Barber on Yoruba popular arts.

5. The French Catholic priests had been expelled from Guinea by Sékou Touré in 1966 and only reaccepted when he died in 1984.

6. *Nimba* is a huge female headdress that Baga used to celebrate joyful occasions and in performances to gather people from many different villages. See Lamp 1996b and Curtis and Sarro 1997.

7. A corresponding lineage is a lineage that an individual can consider his own in the full sense. Every Baga lineage of any village has a corresponding one in any other single Baga village. In the past, when the links among the villages were much stronger, individuals always knew all their corresponding lineages (or such is the idealised version given by informants). Today there is a high level of anomie and individualism and many Baga villagers, especially young people, do not know many people outside their own village.

8. This remark reveals the ambivalence of Baga people towards the pagan element of their culture. The fact that Bukor still has a sacred grove where the *alipne* meet is seen by other villages as a source of evil that should be destroyed.

9. *Amanco* was represented by a very high wood and raffia construction with a mask at its apex, and would appear at the end of initiation rituals. The last *Amanco* masquerade took place in the early fifties. Frederick Lamp's book on Baga art and ritual (Lamp 1996b) is the best source of information regarding *Amanco*'s performances.

10. The cup did not 'go back' to Arraponka but stayed in Kakande, since it was won by *Ataent*, a new team composed by the young Baga boys studying in Kamsar (but belonging to other villages).

12 The Territorial Politics of Soccer in Northern Ireland

Alan Bairner and Peter Shirlow

It is in the realm of culture that communities come to understand themselves and to articulate this understanding to the wider world. There are, of course, numerous cultural forms and arenas within which this process can take place. In the modern world, however, sport has become one of the most important of these. As MacClancy suggests, sports are 'vehicles of identity, providing people with a sense of difference and a way of classifying themselves and others, whether latitudinally or hierarchically' (MacClancy 1996: 2). This does not mean that the resultant identities are either self-contained or immutable. Indeed, identities are more likely than not to be dual or even multiple (Kellas 1991: 15). Thus, one's identity as a player of a certain sport or a supporter of a particular team may or may not overlap with other aspects of one's identity. Nevertheless, sport plays an important role in the construction and reproduction of part of the identity of many (particularly men) in the modern world.

Much work, however, needs to be done if we are to understand completely the processes whereby this comes about. According to Werbner, 'the extent to which "fun" and the spaces of fun are constitutive of identity and subjectivity – whether ethnic, gendered or generational – remains to be fully theorised, although discussion of youth subcultures, and popular culture have highlighted certain dimensions of this conjuncture' (Werbner 1996: 106). What is certain is that of all the world's major games, soccer is one of the most powerful in terms of identity formation and reinforcement.

Writing about ethnicity in Australian sport, Jones and Moore observe that 'soccer is a public arena in which ethnic identities can be assessed and reinvented in changing circumstances' (Jones and Moore 1994: 18). While players may be able to detach themselves from the political and social context in the course of a game, for spectators, as Duke and Crolley remind us, football matches never take place in isolation:

> The participants (the fans) do not cut themselves off from external matters. In a sense, football does not cut out external factors but it acts more like a sieve than a solid wall, and the sieve is not only selecting but also modifying what it filters. (Duke and Crolley 1996: 126–7)

In reality, the relationship between the game and these so-called external matters may be even closer than Duke and Crolley suggest. Sport has been widely recognised as contested terrain. As a consequence, attendance at a soccer match can become an integral part of a broader social process. In this regard, academic attention has tended to focus on examples of soccer's counter-hegemonic role in the promotion of such things as working-class solidarity (Jones 1988) or self-styled progressive nationalism (Hargreaves 1992). Less interest has been shown when the cultural resistance expressed by soccer fans assumes more reactive forms, except insofar as hooliganism has been linked to right-wing extremism (Giulianotti et al. 1994). This paper seeks to redress the balance by revealing the complex nature of identity politics fought out on the abstract terrain of soccer support and in terms of the defence of real sporting spaces.

POLITICS AND PLACE

Clearly the socio-economic and cultural history (or historiography) of place is central to any narration or understanding of communal devotion, collective action and socio-cultural modification. Moreover, modes of socio-cultural resistance emanate from on-going and modified processes of socialisation which, because they are distinctive to place, give specific meaning to life and living in that place (Thrift and Forbes 1983). In turn, and in reaction to multi-layered forms of social precedent, place and its readings can also engender among individuals and communities an identifiable pool of resistance against the real and imagined processes of socio-economic and cultural modification which redefine the nature and composition of places and localities.

Comprehending how space has been either socially or culturally fabricated into a distinctive understanding of place, in relation to the manifestation of support for specific soccer teams, provides crucial insights into the production and reproduction of conflict and reactive resistance. However, a valid interpretation of how place and cultural identity are constituted demands an analysis which stretches beyond the nature and form of built environments (such as stadia), while embracing an analysis which includes the examination of other observable processes of socio-cultural modification and alteration (Beck et al. 1994). As such material, residual and topophilic relationships are saturated with expressive meaning as they are placed in the subjective and at times introspective context of the iconographies and landscapes of past and present occurrences (Shirlow and McGovern 1996).

What ultimately emerges is a geography of socio-cultural domination and/or resistance in which power relationships are spatialised and imagined in distinct and observable ways. In particular reactive ideological forms are primarily concerned with the definition and defensive reaction to particular cultural and social forms which are construed as alien, hostile and unacceptable. Undoubtedly, modes of reactive resistance which are played out through the medium of racist and ethno-sectarian discourses are excessively biased and tied to remorselessly negative forms of socio-cultural definition. However, the literature on theories of resistance has tended to ignore the manner, potency and direction of cultural forms of resistance which are located among communities, self-identified as being influenced by fascist or right-wing philosophies (see for example Pile and Keith 1997). Obviously, the omission of communities which promote highly reactive forms of resistance impedes a diagnostic interpretation of the multiplicity of power relationships and their varied locations.

In relation to an understanding of the relationship between resistance and reactive modes of resistance this paper is taken up with an examination of the extent to which soccer supporting in Northern Ireland interacts with external factors and plays its part in the construction of the political identity of certain working-class Protestant men. Specific attention will be paid to supporters of those clubs usually identified as Protestant, particularly Linfield. There will also be some discussion of the relationship between support for the latter and for the Northern Ireland national team, both of which play their home games at the same stadium. In assessing the extent to which these phenomena provide examples of cultural resistance, the paper draws on theoretical perspectives concerning space, place and territory which have not previously been used in the debate on the relationship between politics and sport in Northern Ireland (Sugden and Bairner 1993).

This paper conveys a sense of the localised nature of politics of territorial control and resistance, where the imperatives of communal difference, segregation and exclusion have predominated over the politics of shared interests, integration, assimilation and consensus. The paper charts and explains the relevance of space and topophilia in the reproduction of forms of highly politicised identities which are linked to notions of cultural 'besiegement' and cultural dissipation.

CULTURES OF REACTIVE OPPOSITION

In many instances reactive forms of cultural opposition are tied to notions of cultural dissipation, besiegement and disintegration. Obviously, and as noted by Spradley and McCurdy (1987), the reality and perception of fear which is tied to the cultural 'other' means that many individuals

> cling tenaciously to the values they have acquired and feel threatened when confronted with others who live according to different conceptions of what is desirable. Thus culture is like a 'security blanket' which 'has great meaning to its owner'. (Spradley and McCurdy 1987: 5–6)

In particular sectarianism and racist discourses are in themselves cultural constructions which are reproduced and reworked through time and space. It is in this sense, too, that the disquisition which constitutes sectarianism in Northern

Ireland, is reproduced through what are essentially 'lived experiences'. Obviously, the nature and potency of sectarianism in Northern Ireland is sensitive given the character and extent of socio-political segregation together with nearly thirty years of domestic conflict. The defence of boundaries or the perception that communally defined boundaries are or could be altered by the in-migration of the sectarian or racial 'other' means that a reactive consciousness is not simply reproduced through consciousness and ideology themselves, but also in physical and spatial terms (Bell 1990).

In this instance religious affiliations are established as primary demarcators of the 'collective other'. However, religion is not recognised as the 'subject' of conflicting interest but as the symbol of conflict, representing a method to distinguish, asseverate, and 'legitimate' rivalry and dogmatic asperity.

Evidently, defining the 'Other' leads to the imposition of negative and putative characteristics upon a 'Collective Other' whose lifestyle, culture and politics must be both resisted and repelled (Jenkins 1994). Ultimately, the culturally hostile manner of reactive resistance and the desire to challenge pan-cultural contact leads in turn to what are essentially cultures of besiegement, which, somewhat depressingly, focus upon imaginings which distinguish the 'we' from the 'they'. Such a conception of peoples undoubtedly fortifies group togetherness, on the one hand, and provides a rationale for group action one the other (Baker 1990; Graham 1994).

The biosphere of cultural opposition is firmly established upon the primary binary opposition, of the Collective Self and the Collective Other, and upon the construction of a necessary relationship between the two. The Collective Self, for the Ulster Protestant/Loyalist community, is subjectively defined in terms of 'Devotion' to what is imagined as a distinctly Protestant way of life. The Collective Other is the 'Menace', which can come from a range of social groups or agencies but which is particularly constructed in this instance as the republican-nationalist communities of Ireland. The mediating practice which defines the necessary relationship between the two is the notion of 'Defence'. 'Communal Devotion' in this sense is produced and reworked through animosity and identifiable defence strategies.

'Communal Devotion' is based upon ethno-political identities tied to what are imagined and perceived as the Ulster Protestant way of life and living. The 'Collective Self' is, in other words, built upon the sum of the social relationships experienced by someone growing up within a particular value system. At the same time, through the discourse of 'threat' any challenge to, or change in, the position of the 'Collective Self' is experienced within the context of traditional lines of division and conflict. More important is the perception that a loss of socio-economic or political status is tied not to the flaws within the character of the 'Collective Self' but rather is due to the encroachment of the 'Collective Other'. As a result, the potency of such interpretations means that both communities must defend themselves. 'Defence' and the protection of territory thus emerge as the primary discourse defining the mediating practice between the Self and the Other; the conceptual ordering of inter-communal relations.

It is in this sense that it is necessary to focus upon the relative autonomy of ideology and collective consciousness as a determining factor on social action; the way, in other words, material, political and cultural change is perceived within the context of a pre-existing, if discursive, ideological framework. The role of sectarianism clearly indicates how class relationships in Northern Ireland cross-cut politics, economics, ideology and culture. It also illustrates the manner in which class relationships are experienced and perceived as ethno-racial relationships.

CONTEXTUAL BACKGROUND

Highlighting the importance of sport for the construction and consolidation of national identities, Jarvie observes that 'it is as if the imagined community or nation becomes more real on the terraces or the athletics track' (Jarvie 1993: 75). Most sports fans cast their sporting heroes and favourite clubs in the role of 'proxy warriors', to use Hoberman's phrase (Hoberman 1986: 6). In Northern Ireland, this analogy is complicated by the presence of competing national identities and ethno-sectarian attitudes which are intimately involved in a 'real' conflict with real warriors who are also assigned heroic status by certain sections of the population, most notably working-class young men (Bairner 1997: 108).

The general relationship between politics and sport in Northern Ireland is already well established (Sugden and Bairner 1993; Sugden and Harvie 1995) although there remains considerable scope for more detailed analysis. The broad argument that the organisation of sport in the province not only reflects but can also exacerbate sectarian attitudes and the politics of division cannot be challenged despite the recognition that sport can also be utilised to promote cross-community reconciliation. To support the general thesis, however, it is important to examine particular manifestations of the interplay between sport and politics and to do so from a variety of academic perspectives. One such theme is the relationship between soccer and the construction of collective identities. For example, the importance to unionists (and specifically to unionist men) of the existence of the Northern Ireland national soccer team has been explored in some detail (Bairner and Sugden 1986; Sugden and Bairner 1994; Bairner 1997). It is clear that although Catholics in Northern Ireland are as likely as Protestants to play and watch soccer, a unionist atmosphere surrounds the game at its highest levels, including the administration of senior soccer as well as support for the Northern Ireland team. However, it is not enough simply to record this fact and to pass critical comment on it; what is more important is to uncover the reasons why Northern Irish Protestants persist in their attempts to exercise a degree of hegemonic control over soccer.

An obvious nationalist response would be that this phenomenon is simply a continuation of traditional unionist discriminatory practice which has been weakened in other areas, such as the allocation of jobs and houses, since the introduction of direct rule from London in order to replace the devolved parliament at Stormont (Clayton 1996). Adopting a rather different perspective towards the same evidence, it has been argued that, with the loss of self-government and given the fact that most sports are organised on an all-Ireland basis, the national soccer team and its administrative body, the Irish Football Association (IFA), are among the few visible indicators of the existence of Northern Ireland as a separate place (Sugden and Bairner 1993: 77). On its own, however, this explanation cannot explain precisely how significant soccer is in the construction and reproduction of a unionist identity although it points in a direction which, if followed, might lead to greater understanding of this process. The key idea raised is that of Northern Ireland as a place, both real and imagined.

Although Northern Ireland is constitutionally part of the United Kingdom, it is separated from the rest of Britain not only by a stretch of water but also by distinctive cultural patterns. Physically, it is part of the island of Ireland from which it is separated politically by the will of the majority of its citizens as well as by cultural differences. Within the six counties of Northern Ireland there are additional borders, both visible and invisible, most significantly separating Catholics from Protestants, but also dividing the country from the town and the middle classes from the working classes. As a consequence of these various boundaries, the constitutional impasse in the province can be said to be intimately bound up with territorial politics. As Anderson and Shuttleworth (1998) suggest, the intensifying controversies over Orange marches since 1994 serve to illuminate the importance of the symbolic 'claiming and re-claiming' of territory from which Protestants have retreated, or in which their proportion of the sectarian headcount has diminished. Claiming the right to march through areas against the wishes of a majority of local residents is justified in terms of 'tradition' and basic civil rights. For some, it is a way of demonstrating Protestant and unionist supremacy. Above all, it symbolically asserts that all Northern Ireland is British and that Protestants are the privileged upholders of the Union. It is sport's relationship with the territorial politics of space and place in Northern Ireland which needs to be recognised if soccer's role in the construction of the Collective Self vis-à-vis the Other is to be more carefully theorised.

Sporting venues, in Northern Ireland as elsewhere, consistently emerge as sites for the reproduction of a sense of alienation from the Other. The source of the alienation can be social class, with few working-class people feeling comfortable at rugby grounds, for example. Or, it might be gender, since women are unlikely to feel at ease at most sports stadia in the province. In terms of the politics of division, however, feeling alienated at sporting venues is intrinsically linked to ethno-sectarian identities. Three major examples illustrate the point.

First, there is the alienation of Protestants from nationalist sporting spaces. It is undeniable that Protestants can be made to feel unwelcome at certain soccer grounds in the province. The best example is that of Derry City's Brandywell, particularly since 1985 when the club began to play in the League of Ireland, having resigned from Northern Ireland's Irish League in 1972. Supported in the past by Protestants in the city, the club's following is now almost exclusively nationalist. The entire west side of the city, where the Brandywell is located, is nowadays regarded as a hostile environment by the overwhelming majority of Derry's Protestant inhabitants and to venture into it for the sake of attending a soccer match is virtually unthinkable. Here is a soccer club which now quite literally plays 'across the border' (Duke and Crolley 1996: 70–6) and which symbolises the estrangement of nationalists from Northern Ireland as a political entity.

Cliftonville's Solitude ground is also alien territory even when Protestants travel there to support their own team. Established as an amateur club in what was a predominantly middle-class, Protestant area of Belfast, Cliftonville only acquired a nationalist following after population shifts led to a marked decrease in the numbers of Protestants in the area. Into the vacuum stepped Catholics, primarily from the nearby Ardoyne and New Lodge districts, although also from other nationalist parts of the city and beyond. The impression of Solitude as nationalist space is further enhanced by the fact that, on police advice, Linfield fans are not expected to visit there at all. Instead, their team's 'away' games against Cliftonville are played at Windsor Park. As a result, Solitude is transformed into a place where, for Linfield fans, 'real' Protestants do not go.

However, Protestant feelings of alienation from sporting venues in Northern Ireland are by no means confined to soccer grounds. Arguably Gaelic sports grounds are even more alien to Protestants than soccer stadia are to either community. The games themselves are not usually part of the experience of growing up Protestant. Venues and clubs are often named after heroes of Republican historiography. The symbolism is nationalist with the Irish tricolour aloft and the Gaelic language being used, albeit less extensively than the founders of the Gaelic Athletic Association would have wished. Overtly sectarian comments are seldom heard, but one might argue that this omission owes at least as much to the fact that Gaelic games do not involve competition between the two major communities as to inherent political correctness on the part of the followers of Gaelic games. Certainly when nationalists turn their attention to soccer, as in the case of Cliftonville fans, there is far less hesitancy about sectarian chanting. However, as far as senior soccer is concerned it is Catholics rather than Protestants who are more likely to experience a sense of alienation at most major venues.

Indeed, a second obvious example of alienation experienced at sporting venues concerns the overwhelmingly Protestant or loyalist ambience surrounding most Irish League games. There are a number of related aspects to this situation. First, of the best supported clubs in the Irish League, only Cliftonville has a predominantly Catholic following. Of the other major clubs, Ballymena United, Coleraine, Crusaders, Glenavon, Glentoran and Portadown are all mainly supported by Protestants. In the case of Linfield, moreover, it would be reasonable to suppose that the following is almost exclusively Protestant. There are a number of reasons for this preponderance of Protestant support for Irish League soccer which persists despite the fact that all the clubs, including Linfield, have Catholic players. Among these are the British origins of the game which arrived in Ireland at a time when sportive nationalists were constructing a separate Irish sporting culture as a response to what was regarded as British cultural imperialism (Bairner 1996; Mandle 1987). This meant that, in the past, many Catholics viewed soccer with suspicion with the result that they were far less involved than Protestants in the game's early formal development.

This is directly linked to a second reason that most senior clubs tend to be supported by Protestants. Although Catholics today follow soccer with as much enthusiasm as Protestants, especially since the Gaelic Athletic Association has become increasingly less antagonistic towards a sport which is now more appropriately described as universal rather than British (Holmes 1994; Cronin 1994, 1996), most senior clubs were established in those areas where Protestants were and, for the most part, continue to be in the majority.

In this respect, the example of Cliftonville is instructive. The fact that nationalist soccer fans were in search of a team leads directly to a third reason for the disproportionate numbers of Protestants involved in supporting Irish League teams. Over the years, not only Derry City but before them, in 1949, Belfast Celtic, teams which did possess large numbers of Catholic supporters, were obliged to leave the Irish League. With the departure of these clubs, it has become all the more likely than in the past that Irish League soccer will continue to derive the bulk of its support from the Protestant, unionist community in Northern Ireland. Moreover, being a Catholic soccer fan is by no means an easy option.

For example, during the 1996–7 soccer season successful attempts were made on two occasions to prevent Cliftonville fans from attending soccer games at grounds which are regarded as Protestant territory. In response to efforts to have Orange marches re-routed away from nationalist areas, loyalists impeded the progress of Cliftonville supporters as they made their way to games in East Belfast and Portadown on 4 September 1996 and 19 October 1996. In this way, territorial politics became even more closely involved with sport than ever before and soccer grounds became even more alienating.

Catholics have also experienced increasing difficulties as regards supporting the Northern Ireland national team. Its home fixtures at Windsor Park provide a third and final example of the alienating capacity of sporting venues in the province. Only those Protestants who are absolutely repelled by vocal expressions of anti-Catholic sentiment would find Windsor Park on the occasion of Northern Ireland games a hostile environment. Catholics respond very differently. They have always represented Northern Ireland at various levels. In addition, it is undeniable that, in the past and even as recently as during the 1982 World Cup Finals in Spain, many of them supported the national team despite the fact that their political outlook would have led them to question the idea of Northern Ireland as a nation or even as a separate place. The fact remained that Catholics as well as Protestants were playing for the team and deserved the support of their co-religionists. This view was taken by large numbers of Catholics although, even at that time, many of the team's Protestant supporters chose to wear the red, white and blue of Linfield or Glasgow Rangers as opposed to the green and white of the national strip and to sing loyalist songs in preference to ones more commonly associated with football supporting. The situation today, however, is markedly different.

Very few Catholics now attend Northern Ireland games and, indeed, few would even admit to supporting the national team. They argue that the loyalist symbolism associated with the side is the main reason for their antipathy. Cynics would add that it cannot be a coincidence that their abandonment of the national team coincided with an upsurge in the fortunes of the Irish Republic's soccer representatives. For the first time, northern nationalists had a worthwhile alternative to supporting Northern Ireland and, given their own political preference for a united Ireland and the fact that the constitution of the Republic continues to lay claim to the six counties of Northern Ireland, for most of them it was a relatively easy choice to make. However, another reason for their growing sense of alienation from the Northern Ireland team brings us back once more to the question of space and its social meaning.

The national team plays its home games at Windsor Park which is situated beside the predominantly Protestant Donegall Road and Village areas of Belfast. The ground is also home to Linfield, the senior club with the most vocal loyalist following. Both because of its location and also its association with a particular club, Windsor Park has always been regarded by nationalists as alien territory. In addition, some fans of Northern Ireland and Linfield have intended it to be so. For many years, the slogan – 'Taigs Keep Out' – which had been painted on a wall close to the stadium represented a sinister warning that Catholics were not welcome at Windsor Park unless, ironically, they had arrived to play for Northern Ireland or, as is increasingly likely today, for Linfield. The message is clear. This is a Protestant place for a Protestant people and Catholics require special dispensation to be there. Furthermore, the message has arguably been communicated with an even greater sense of urgency as growing numbers of Catholics have moved into nearby residential areas in south Belfast. Windsor Park must remain Protestant despite and in defiance of changes in the surrounding locale. Indeed, for some Linfield supporters the stadium's symbolic meaning is altered not only by the presence of Catholics but even by the arrival of rural Protestants for international matches. The identification of Protestant Ulster with urban Belfast and its heavy engineering and shipyards appears threatened by the inhabitants of a related but different landscape. The fact that Linfield receives considerable support from outside the city, however, weakens the impact of this sense of a divided Protestant identity and testifies instead to the club's quasi-national status.

WE ARE THE (LOYAL) PEOPLE!

These various observations concerning soccer and territory are particularly relevant to the experience of young Protestant males as they seek to come to terms with the diminished status of the Protestant working class. Unemployed, socially marginalised and with deep-seated fears about the future of Northern Ireland as a separate entity, they look for channels through which to express their loyalist identity and, as a result, to restore their self esteem. One such vehicle, as Bell observes, are the 'Kick the Pope' bands which accompany Orange marches:

> The bands and their parades seem to provide for the dispossessed Loyalist youth of Ulster a sectarian habitus within which their generational concerns with communal identity and with winning public space become fused with the focal concerns with territoriality and ethnic solidarity. (Bell 1990: 100)

The political strength of Ulster loyalism historically has been its identification with a state which has been able to impose territorial boundaries, directly or indirectly, while being able to afford a relatively relaxed attitude to boundaries within the British Isles. In the last thirty years this state has been able to enforce a form of effective territorial control in the face of sustained armed resistance. But, Ulster Protestant ideology has an additional myth of siege which implies a contested sense of domicile, which cannot be shared with other British citizens but which also fails to find an exclusive 'homeland' in Northern Ireland.

Supporting a particular 'Protestant' soccer club, such as Linfield or Glentoran, who play at the Oval close to the shipyards of east Belfast, or the Northern Ireland team provides a similar kind of outlet to that offered by membership of a marching band (Bairner 1997: 100–1) and soccer stadia offer a context for the celebration of a wider culture. Wearing the colours and singing the songs, young men avail themselves of the opportunity to exhibit their sense of what it means to be Ulster Protestants. Thus, they sing about being up to their knees in Fenian blood or chant the names of loyalist paramilitary organisations in what are among the few public spaces where such behaviour is possible (Bairner 1997).

The identity of most of these soccer fans takes the form of a secular, non-Christian Protestantism, described by Gillespie and his fellow researchers as 'a mixture of selective theological dogma, anti-Catholicism and pragmatic loyalism' (Gillespie et al. 1992: 135). Despite the lack of religiosity, the commitment of these fans to their native Ulster is undeniable. Less certain, however, is their understanding of Ulster as a landscape.

As Graham has argued, the territorial definition which has traditionally been proposed by unionists has been essentially negative, with the place being understood not for what it is but rather in terms of what unionists do not wish it to be, namely a part of Ireland. For Graham, therefore, 'Unionism occupies not so much "a place apart" as "no place", a failure of legitimation which ensures that it is an ideology which commands little or no external support' (Graham 1997: 40). But soccer grounds are real places and, in addition, most of the venues for senior soccer in the province are Protestant places, hence their role in identity formation. The imagined community of Ulster as a Protestant place becomes more real for young loyalists as they express their affiliation at Windsor Park or the Oval and, in so doing, struggle 'to resolve at the level of the imaginary, the real contradictions confronting the Protestant working-class in contemporary Northern Ireland' (Bell 1990: 23).

In their own way, by supporting certain soccer teams, these young fans are attempting to defend their home territory and those traditions which make it what it is or what they imagine it to be. This reactive defensiveness is part of a more general 'siege mentality' which afflicts the unionist population and which derives from a sense that everything around them is undergoing fundamental and irrevocable change. Thus, theirs is a form of cultural resistance which remains linked to a parental tradition. The old industries have gone and along with them the sense of community which they helped to create. Political developments are all construed as concessions to the nationalist minority. Through all of this, however, the leading soccer clubs and the Northern Ireland national team have remained constant elements in Protestant working-class culture, although even they are not immune to the forces of change.

The presence of Catholic players, including ones recruited from the Irish Republic, in the Linfield team is a relatively novel phenomenon. Combined with the movement of Protestants from inner city Belfast and the growing number of Saturday afternoon distractions which have affected soccer crowds throughout Ireland and beyond, this has clearly had some impact on attendances. Similarly, the inclusion of Catholic players, or ones only tenuously linked to the province, in the Northern Ireland team does not meet with the approval of every loyalist. Overall, however, clubs like Linfield and Glentoran as well as the national team continue to provide a necessary focus for Protestant working-class identity. In this respect, they perform a similar function to that played by soccer clubs in other, less overtly divided societies.

Supporting particular soccer teams allows these fans to express their opposition to rival identities while celebrating their own. The places where they engage in these activities thus become quasi-religious sites, important in their own right but also as metaphors for the political territory which is regarded as being in need of defence (see Bale 1993). These stadia are, therefore, of vital importance in the production of certain identities and in the process of cultural resistance.

This chapter seeks to demonstrate the complexity of the relationship between soccer support and identity formation. It does so by emphasising the importance of place to soccer fans. In part, of course, this simply involves an affection for a stadium where their team plays and it should not be forgotten that many of the fans involved would regard their devotion to a particular club as the single most important element of their identity. It has been argued, however, that the love of a real place, the soccer stadium, is also linked to the construction of and loyalty to an imagined place, namely the nation as understood by the fans involved. By revealing this linkage as it operates in the divided society of Northern Ireland, the chapter also endeavours to say something more general about the relationship between sport and the formation of reactive, perhaps even reactionary, identities as a feature of cultural resistance.

The soccer fans under discussion feel themselves to be threatened by a variety of economic and social processes which are beyond their control. In response, they gather together in those spaces where they still feel safe and believe themselves to be able to exercise a degree of authority in terms of who is allowed to follow the team and what sort of ambience should surround matches. Those spaces, the stadia, in turn become metaphors for the imagined nation which must also be defended against internal subversion and foreign encroachment. In this way, the 'Collective Self' is transformed from a group of soccer fans into 'the people' and supporting a team becomes a perceived part of a broader movement of cultural resistance against threats to 'the people' and all its cherished places.

13 Team Selection and the Chosen People in Israel: The Case of Hapoel Taibeh
Yoram S. Carmeli and Iris Bar

Two teams were promoted from the Second to the First division of the Israeli football league at the end of the 1996/7 season. The elevation of Hapoel Jerusalem was a procedural matter, reflecting their status as Division Two champions, and merely a source of joy for the club's fans. By contrast the concomitant success of Hapoel Taibeh was considered in the Israeli sports world as a great novelty. In a country in a state of permanent civil war between its five million Jews and one million Arabs, it was the first time that a team from an Arab town had made it to the premier league. While the team represents the Arab town Taibeh, Hapoel Taibeh has a wider resonance, it is considered an 'Arab Team' representing the whole Arab population, despite the fact that Jewish and imported non-Israeli players were selected for the team. This chapter, therefore, seeks to analyse the complexity of meanings and functions that exist in football matches between an 'Arab' team and other (Jewish) teams in Israel.

THE ARABS IN ISRAEL

The State of Israel was founded in 1948 following a bitter war between Arabs and Jews on land previously recognised as British Mandatory Palestine. For the Jews the new state was regarded as variously: the fulfilment of a two thousand-year-old dream, a culmination of seventy years of Zionist effort, a victory in the heroic battle of few against many. For those Arabs who fled or were expelled, the creation of Israel was and remains a calamity which had to be resisted. Arabs who remained considered themselves part of the Palestinian Arab people, but had now to live as a minority within the Jewish state which was forced upon them and limited their liberties (Beshara 1993). The state's policy was, and remains, derived from Zionist ideology central to which is the building of a state for Jewish people.

Since its creation all Israeli governments have promoted the policy of 'Jewification' of the land, and to this end have confiscated land in Arab towns and villages. Consequently, the percentage of land owned by Arabs has diminished from about 20 per cent in 1976 to only 4 per cent in 1996. Furthermore, Israel's official agrarian policy ruined the lives of those Arabs involved in agriculture, and a variety of restrictions have limited the opportunities of the Arab middle classes. The result of these policies was a proletarianisation (but without industrialisation) of the formerly dominant agricultural Arab society, and subsequently an economic and institutional dependence on the Jewish state and its bourgeoisie (e.g., Zureik 1979). The Arab educational system and legal means of political expression were limited or controlled with the aim of making such ideology convenient to the state's requirements (Nakhle 1977).

The six-day 1967 war was a turning point in the history of the Palestinian Arabs in Israel. As Israel occupied the Palestinian centres of the West Bank and Gaza Strip, nineteen years of Arab isolation in Israel from the rest of the Arab world came to an end, bringing to the surface both the similarities and the differences between both societies. During the 1970s, two significant processes emerged among the Arabs in Israel. The first was the establishment of national institutions; the second involved economic and political integration into Israeli society. The former process can be traced back to both the establishment of the 'Committee for the Defence of Arab Lands' established in 1975, and to the 'Day of the Land' a one-day general strike on 30 March 1976, marking the first time that the Arab population in Israel mobilised itself around national political demands. The latter process began after the 1967 war when the middle class, which was beginning to develop among the Arabs in Israel, found its place as a co-ordinator between the Jewish administration in the capital and the cheap Arab labour force in the West Bank and Gaza Strip.

The abolition of 'military rule' over the Arabs in 1965 and the general economic prosperity in the country after 1967, contributed significantly to the limited improvement in the Arabs' socio-economic situation. In this context, Beshara (1993) suggests that the 'Day of the Land' uprising was a unique event, and with it came a growing awareness among the Arab population of the difference between their life circumstances and those of the rest of the Palestinian people. Most of the political effort was directed towards establishing co-ordinating organisations for the Arab minority, a process available due to the political and economic liberalisation of the state after the 1977 general elections. Although the winner was the nationalistic and militant Likud party, this victory ended twenty-nine years of Mapai (Labour party) government. The election changed Israel from being a de facto 'one-party state' to a two-party system and weakened the Mapai monopolies in the labour market, business sector, and means of communication (Beshara 1997).

Inside the Israeli political 'centre' there is no room for Arab equality or for integrating Arabs into a united identity (Smooha 1976; Rosenhak 1995). Starting in the 1970s various theories tried to address the contradictory forces and processes that influence the relationship between Israel and its Arab citizens. A thesis of 'radicalisation' (Palestinisation) was developed (cf. Rekhess 1976), entailing the empowerment of a radical Palestinian identity and the concomitant decline of the so-called 'Israeli' identity, as a result of renewed contact with the Palestinians in the West Bank and Gaza Strip and the strengthened international status of the PLO (Rosenhak 1995). By contrast, Smooha (1992) rejects the term 'Palestinisation' preferring instead to see Israeli political participation as a process he describes as an 'ethnic democracy' – a state in which two categories of citizenship exist. The hegemonic group – the Jews – determine the 'common social values', while the dominated group – the Arabs – are granted formal civil rights. He predicted that the Palestinian minority in Israel will be content with controlling its own institutions and partaking in some spheres of political life. More recently, Ghanem (1997) suggests that Arabs accept the Jewish character of the state because of a deep crisis derived from the stress and alienation of widening socio-economic inequalities between Jews and Arabs in Israel. He concludes that the Arab population never succeeded in developing a coherent identity, either Palestinian or Israeli, but are left instead with an injured and distorted identity. It is via this fractured identity that a football team can become significant.

LOCAL AND NATIONAL IDENTITIES

Taibeh, a town of 30,000 residents, is the largest Arab town in the centre of Israel, and one of the four biggest Arab towns located inside the 1948 border (known as the 'Green Line'). Taibeh is a long way from Galilee – the cultural and social centre of the Arab population in Israel – but close to Tel Aviv, the Jewish cultural and social centre, and to the Arab cities in the West Bank. The extended family is a basic social unit and the people of Taibeh can be divided into seventeen extended families. The biggest are the Haj-Yihia family, the next largest is the Massarwa family (Avizur 1978). Such families influence the political system in the town, particularly municipal elections. For the last seven years the Haj-Yihia family has controlled the municipality; the mayor is Rafik Haj-Yihia, one of the Labour party leaders in the Arab sector.

Similar to all other Arab townships, Taibeh receives a lower governmental budget than a Jewish township would. This limited budget is reflected in the elementary levels of physical infrastructure and services, chronic monetary deficits (estimated at $17 million) and unpaid municipality workers. Taibehans complain about the lack of funds, budget deficits, and seized treasury income, always blaming governmental discrimination. However, the mayor and municipality were also criticised on the grounds of personal incapacity. All Taibeh residents interviewed, however, agreed that a strong football team could challenge the negative image people held of the town and give positive motivation to young people, perhaps diverting them from crime and delinquency. As one respondent articulated:

> This is a way of restoring some lost honour. Taibeh has inside the Arab society, a negative image, an image of a place full of crime and drugs. Now, we have a team. It's the first Arab team in the National League. It gives us pride.

Most of the sports clubs in Arab towns and villages belong to one of the four big sports associations, all of which are connected with Zionist parties. This is the result of strong centralisation tendencies that dominated the state until 1977, and of a general policy that discouraged Arab organisations from operating outside the influence of the Israeli system. The football league in Israel consists of five leagues, all under the jurisdiction of the IFA (Israeli Football Association). The two lowest leagues consist of semi-professional teams, while the three above them are professional (Farbstein and Semyonov 1990). The National League (the top league) consists of sixteen teams. At the end of the season, the two bottom teams are relegated from the top league, and replaced by the two best teams from the 'country league'. The regular league fixtures (thirty per season) are considered to be most significant and are ranked above various cup matches.

The Hapoel Taibeh football club was established in 1963, as part of a sports association that belonged to the Israeli general workers union – the 'Histadrut' – and the Labour party. In 1989, while Hapoel Taibeh were in the Third division, the Haj-Yihia family won the municipality election and overthrew the Massarwa family, which had run the club via its control over the Histadrut's workers' council. The team then played three seasons in the Second division whereupon it began to be considered as a team 'representative of the Arabs'. By 1996/7, when they reached the first division, their mission was stated:

> Hapoel Taibeh is not a private achievement of the players and the town of Taibeh. It belongs to all the Arab population. This is the first Arab team in the Primary league. They brought us honour, a compensation for not being represented in official institutions ... They treat us as leaders, as a vanguard of the confrontation between Arabs and Jews, while we are just football players. (Taibeh players to *El-Senara* reporter February 1997 – the most widely circulated Arab newspaper in Israel)

However, in our interviews, members of the team management emphasised that 'more Arabs than Jews hate the team', explaining that such an attitude was due to jealousy and lack of self-confidence. 'People think that a team from the big centres in the Galilee, probably from Nazareth, should represent the Arabs ... we didn't find Arab sponsors ... all of them said "You will be relegated anyway" ...'

The main problem faced by Hapoel Taibeh was financial. The club receives income from four main sources: the sports association, ticket sales, municipal funding and private sponsors. Taibeh's inadequate municipality budget limited the local council's investment in the team. Moreover, there were no large and prosperous Arab companies comparable to the businesses that sponsored other football teams in the First division. Consequently, Hapoel Taibeh had a yearly budget of 5 million NIS (nearly $1.5 million), while the top teams' budgets were around 25 million NIS. The low income handicapped the team on an infrastructural level insofar as they lacked a suitable training ground, and were forced to move from place to place in nearby towns, paying the owners of different grounds and stadiums (both municipalities and sports clubs) between 5,000 and 15,000 NIS per day.

Inevitably there were problems with the players' salaries. Although conceived of as an Arab team, Taibeh never succeeded in attracting the best Arab players, some of whom openly refused to join. Due to the low budget, Taibeh players were paid irregularly – a situation that affected their motivation. When at the end of the season Taibeh were relegated, the best Arab players left and moved to 'Jewish' first division teams.

THE FIRST HALF OF SEASON 1996/7

Two months after the beginning of the season, Hapoel Taibeh lay in the middle of the league. Between 1,000 and 1,500 fans attended every match, which made Taibeh the fourth best supported club. In most matches Jewish fans were not openly hostile and were not considered as 'enemies' by Taibeh fans, but every incident, no matter how trivial, could provoke a defensive reaction. A typical example was observed in the match against Maccabi Haifa, one of Israel's top teams from the northern town of Haifa, and a club which has traditionally played talented Arab players and attracted many Arab fans from the Galilee area. In this particular incident a rival team player, in preventing a goal, collided with and badly injured one of Taibeh's players. The Haifa fans began to shout and clap in derision. In response the Taibeh's fans replied by chanting 'All of you are rightists, all of you are racists ...'. A similar attitude was evident in a match against Bnei-Yehuda, a team representing a poor, right-wing, nationalist area within Tel Aviv. The match began with a friendly greeting on the pitch between the players and the management of both teams. However, as some rival fans began to swear at the Arabs, Taibeh's fans shouted 'Cyprus, Cyprus', thereby mocking a recent defeat of the Israeli national team in a World Cup qualifier, and implicitly showing their support to anyone who is against or can defeat the Jewish state.

The concerns of Taibeh's fans are not limited to rival teams and their supporters, but also to the football 'system' and its representatives, as manifest in the figures of uniformed authority – the referee, the linesmen, and the police. The fans consistently complain that the 'system' is forever sympathetic towards rivals. In one game, a Taibeh Jewish player, perceiving injustice, shouted at the referee: 'You discriminate against us because we are Arab!' He was fined and later released from the club. The concern over police prejudice did have some credence. From our research observation, the police seemed to treat Taibeh's fans differently to Jewish fans. We witnessed two matches which ended with Taibeh fans being injured due to assaults by the police.

Ironically, in the mass media, Hapoel Taibeh received more coverage than any other team that was not at the top of the league. The attitude towards them, however, differed depending on whether the press was Jewish or Arabic. Jewish press coverage was not concerned with the team's achievements and was clearly political; one headline in the sports section read: 'I voted for the Likud party [the right-wing party in power in Israel] ... but in our state the Arab population should be represented in the national league' (an interview with one of the team coaches, *Ma'ariv*, the second most widespread daily newspaper in Hebrew, 13 January 1997). The Arab press, by contrast, covered Taibeh as its top team:

> Our duty as a paper is to raise the problems, difficulties, and achievements of the Arabs, because the Hebrew press neglects the Arabs in Israel ... We emphasise the achievements, even if they are small ... In football, the most popular sport, we didn't have any team on a national level, so this is a great achievement. (Interview with a member of the editorial board of *El-Senara*)

In describing Taibeh's matches, the *El-Senara* used the word *Jamahir* in its plural form [masses] which has primarily a political meaning, rather than the word *Jumhur* in single form [crowd], which is the ordinary word for describing football fans or supporters. Moreover, the chairman of the Taibeh supporters' club preferred to use the phrase *Jamahir Arabiya* [Arab masses], a phrase that carries deep national connotations.

That said, most of the shouts and slogans during matches were in Hebrew! Shouting in Hebrew is a common phenomenon even in lower leagues and even when two Arab teams compete and all spectators are Arab. The fans conceived of the league within an Israeli institutional framework; the match is an event that happens inside Israeli public space, and, as such, the accompanying language is Hebrew. However, at moments of high excitement the fans revert to their Arabic tongue, through nationalist mantras that express pride and self-confidence. They sing words about Taibeh and football to a popular tune, originally associated with the resistance in south Lebanon, and another song familiar to them from a political satire named '*October Village*', screened on Lebanese television.

ATTACKING FROM THE RIGHT WING

Beitar Jerusalem is one of the strongest teams in the Israeli First division. Most of its fans are residents of Jewish slums in Jerusalem and immigrants from Arab countries, called in Israel 'Oriental Jews'. The club is politically linked with the extreme right wing of the Likud party and is supported economically by the bourgeoisie of this sector. Antagonism between Taibeh and Beitar Jerusalem had started a few years earlier; as Taibeh became known as the best Arab team Beitar became known as the club with the most right-wing sympathies. A week before this fixture the most widely-circulated Hebrew newspaper, *Yedi'ot Akhronot*, published a provocative interview with Beitar's coach, who declared the match a 'war between Arabs and Jews'. This interview was followed by frenzied coverage in the mass media that built up the match as an impending 'real war'.

The match became a symbol, not only in the contest of Jewish-Arab relations, but also for the relations between the political left and right within the Jewish population itself. Labour party supporters, mostly a well-to-do elite in Tel Aviv and Haifa, were backing Taibeh against the blatantly racist Likud fans. Shaul Adar, the associate-editor of *Shem Hamishak* – the leading sports journal in Israel – described the Beitar fans thus: 'They are populists ... scum – Fascist, racist, a hooligan crowd that reflects to the utmost Israeli society ...'. However, the commentator himself added:

> The press used Taibeh to provoke Beitar ... The sports editors represent a western origin, petty bourgeois, secular, Labor party elite ... They hate Beitar because it represents an opposing social force ... Taibeh is an example of a team that represents a different social force, and I suppose that if they were not so weak, the attitude would be different.

The Arab press reacted and Taibeh's directors used the press to call for the mobilising of fans (*El-Senara*, 1 November 1996).

To prevent street confrontations and limit the number of fans, the match was moved to Haifa, more than one hour by car from Taibeh and almost three hours from Jerusalem; nevertheless, the game was well attended with 13,000 fans, their loyalties equally spread between the two clubs. Taibeh's terrace was full, mostly with fans from outside Taibeh. Youngsters wearing the green scarves of Haifa's team sat adjacent to 'The Arab fan club of Hapoel Beer-Sheva', who travelled from the south in two buses. The atmosphere was reported by *El-Senara*: '... After the racist declarations of Beitar's coach, we are all Hapoel Taibeh,' said Mr Muhammad Abu-Riash, a member of Hapoel Beer-Sheva's Arab fan club. 'It is the duty of all the Arabs in the Galilee, the Triangle, and the Nakab[1] to support Taibeh in this match' (*El-Senara*, 1 November 1996).

People who were not typical football fans, such as women and the upper-middle class, also attended this game. One supporter, an Arab lawyer from Haifa, presented himself as ordinarily a supporter of Maccabi Haifa's team, but summarised his attendance and the situation: 'Taibeh has a million fans ... ' (meaning all the Palestinian Arabs in Israel). Another Arab from Haifa said:

> [I came to the match] because of the advertisement ... Arabs against Jews and all of this shit ... The management 'sold' Taibeh as a representative of the Arabs and mobilised a lot of Arab fans ... don't forget, this is the National League, every ticket costs 50 shekels. Now, multiply 50 shedels by 13,000 and see how much money they earn in one game.

Around 100 Jewish fans sat on Taibeh's side, mainly to protest against racism; Taibeh's supporters understood this as a political act of supporting Arabs.

An inverse motivation was found on the Beitar side, the letter of a young Jew from a village in the north read:

On Friday, November 1, 1996, I was at the match between Hapoel Taibeh and Beitar Jerusalem. I'm a loyal fan of Maccabi Haifa, but I went to the match to support Beitar against Taibeh, who I consider as a representative of the Arabs. (*Shem HaMishak*, 1 December 1996).

In order to avoid crowd trouble, fans of rival clubs were directed to different stands and segregated. For this game each club was allotted three sections, whilst two empty sections were left between the rival crowds. On the Taibeh side, the most enthusiastic fans, mainly youngsters of working-class origin, residents of Taibeh and other Arab villages, were placed in the middle section. The sections located on the sides which were closer to the rival teams' fans, were occupied by older and more sedate supporters. The police prevented fans from entering the ground with bottles and cans. Their attitude angered Taibeh's supporters, who felt the police treated them harsher than Beitar's fans. In fact during the early moments of the match, Beitar's 'mob' destroyed the fences at the entrance to their section without any police attempts to disperse them.

At the beginning of the game, Taibeh supporters stood and sang a Palestinian nationalist song, 'Biladi Biladi' (My homeland, My homeland), in response Beitar fans screamed 'Death to the Arabs', and 'Kill all the Arabs'. The Beitar sections were decorated with large yellow flags ornamented with black skulls and the words 'Welcome to hell'. Most Beitar fans wore T-shirts and scarves coloured yellow and black. By a coincidence (?) the same colours had been adopted by a racist, fascist, political party in Israel, which called for the expulsion of the entire Arab population from Israel, and was officially outlawed. In reply some of Taibeh's fans waved a German flag. The Germans, or more exactly the Nazis, represent the ultimate murderous enemy in the Jewish-Israeli context. By waving this flag, the Arab fans did not present to the Jews their Arab identity, but instead reflected the expression of the other side's feelings: 'We are what you hate most'.

Only twenty minutes after the game had begun, Taibeh was already 3–0 behind, and the confrontation both on and off the pitch was effectively ended. The Taibeh supporters sat quietly, while Beitar fans constantly abused them, screaming 'Death to the Arabs' and 'Go on Bibbi' (the nickname for Mr Netanyahu, Israel's right-wing Prime Minister). Taibeh played better in the second half of the game. Their fans began to respond to the incessant screams and shouted 'Death to the Jews' and 'Fuck Bibbi'. Paradoxically, this slogan 'Death to the Jews' (in Hebrew) was just another proof of the hegemony of the Jewish discourse on football grounds in Israel, mirroring that of 'Death to the Arabs'. In itself, it never appears even in the most angry of Arab demonstrations or riots. When the match ended, outside the ground a short violent confrontation took place, causing injuries to both sides. The police intervened and escorted the groups on to separate buses. Skirmishing between supporters who remained in the area after in bars and cafés lasted for more than an hour.

The match was the first of a string of defeats for Taibeh, which saw them finish the season bottom of the league. One match later in the season was against another Jerusalem club, Hapoel. Taibeh were losing 2–0 when Hapoel scored another goal early in the second half. The Taibeh supporters began to shout at one Hapoel player, Bahjat Odeh, 'You Arab! You traitor!' – a shortened version of 'Remember that you are an Arab, you traitor!' Odeh's imagined 'betrayal' then spread from the football context to the national-political context via a terrace rumour that 'the Odeh brothers', two of the best players on the team, had sold games to their rivals. The rumours were proved to be lies after an investigation. In the last twenty minutes of the match, the fans were hanging on the fences, throwing bottles and cans. The players became frightened. When a fourth goal was conceded, the fans started swearing at the Jewish goalkeeper and Arab players who were not Taibeh residents.

THE SECOND HALF OF SEASON 1996/7

As time went on, the hopeless situation of the team worsened. The number of supporters decreased, thousands became hundreds, most of them young fans from Taibeh. A new group of fanatics began to emerge – young boys from Um El-Fahem, the town Taibeh used as its ground for home matches. But these boys found a way to enter the grounds without paying, which annoyed the team's directors. The fans' frustration grew at every game; swearing, spitting, and throwing bottles at the players, coach, referees and police occurred at most matches. At other games the supporters were apathetic, so much so that even the first goal scored after six matches did not merit acclamation.

The management replaced home players and the coach with some supposedly more skilled foreign players. Three coaches were replaced. As a consequence, supporters complained that Hapoel Taibeh was now just another team no longer representing the Arab population. Complaints were even voiced against the mayor:

It's a political game … The mayor thinks that if he'll invest in football, in a national team club, the people will love him and vote for him. (a Taibehian)

The mayor got a lot of profit out of this season … He took money from the municipality and put it in the club, and made profit from the club … It's another reason why it's better to keep away from the league. (supporter from Haifa)

There were also accusations that the political and national feelings of the supporters were exploited for the 'personal interests' of local Arab politicians.

Harsh words were used against one such individual, who used to attend matches and sit with his cellular telephone, apparently not interested in the game.

A MATTER OF LIFE AND DEATH

On 4 April 1997, half an hour into a match against Bnei Yehuda, Wahib Jebara, a 23-year-old, Taibeh-born forward, collapsed. Due to the shortage of medical equipment in Arab towns, the only ambulance that should have been waiting near the grounds was on call elsewhere. After a half-hour wait for a vehicle, Wahib Jebara died on the way to hospital. In *Panorama*, a weekly newspaper published in Taibeh, reports about Wahib's life and death dominated the news pages; poems about him were published in the literary supplements, the entire sports supplement was dedicated to him, a poster was offered to readers, and twenty-eight condolence notices were spread throughout the paper. In other Arabic papers the death was similarly headlined. The Hebrew press wrote – to a lesser degree – about the tragic death of a young and talented man. They did not read or see any possible political meaning.

By contrast, coverage in the Arab press was dominated by what became known as 'Wahib's last words'. Following the death, the team coach reported that the player had told him, shortly before he entered the field: 'Don't worry, I'll give my soul to the team.' This sentence was published in all the papers. Political newspapers used the death to question the political agenda: discrimination by the state (the fact that a town with 30,000 people had just one ambulance); unprofessionalism of the Arab leadership (for not criticising the lack of doctors and aid equipment); racism and discrimination on the part of Israeli society (the callous attitude of the IFA which did not stop the match after the player's death); the behaviour of fans in various towns, who a week later disturbed the pre-match moment of silence proclaimed by the IFA by shouting 'Death to the Arabs'.

In the popular press, Hapoel Taibeh was identified with the Arabs who fight for their place in the Jewish state. In this national struggle the football ground is a battlefield, and the dead player a warrior. '... Wahib died in the battlefield. His pure body fell on the green field he loved so much' (*Kol El-Arab*, 10 April 1997). Unlike the political press, which concentrated on interviewing doctors, sportsmen, journalists and politicians, the popular press focused on the family, friends and neighbours. While the political press spoke in the name of the elites, the popular press claimed to represent 'the people'. The dead player became a political martyr, and his last words a will of sacrifice. The headlines of two Arab papers (*Panorama* and *Kol El-Arab*) described Wahib as a Shahid of Arab football. The term Shahid means 'a witness' and is derived from Islam. Its original meaning implies a witness of God's truth. The concept was re-appropriated and used as part of the national Palestinian vocabulary to denote a man who died for the liberation of Palestine (Steinberg and Oliver 1990).

Taibehans said Wahib's was the biggest funeral in the history of Taibeh. Public figures from sport and politics, both Arab and Israeli, attended; others sent telegrams. Directors and players, the old enemy of Beitar Jerusalem, visited Wahib's parents. The Palestinian Authority sent this declaration:

> In hearts full with grief and sorrow, we accept the news about the death of the football player, Wahib Jebara, in the battlefield. He died as a hero while fulfilling his holy duty to ... the Palestinian sports movement. (*Panorama*, 10 April 1997)

The club changed its name to Hapoel Wahib Taibeh. Wahib was beloved by the masses as a saint and a hero. Poems were written in his name and men mourned him. His death brought back thousands of supporters to the matches. More than 2,000 filled the Um El-Fahem stadium a week after his death to cheer the first and only game that Taibeh won in the second half of the season. When a goal was scored (by a Jewish player), Wahib's mother fainted. The supporters chanted (in paraphrase of a well-known political slogan), 'Wahib, we will redeem you in our blood and souls!' It was too late to keep the team in the national league, but, as we write, Hapoel Wahib Taibeh seem to have overcome the crisis and are doing well in the second division.

GOING INTO EXTRA TIME

Arab fans of Taibeh attached to the club two missions which corresponded to their own predicaments: the struggle to earn respect in Israeli society, and the inner struggle regarding the character of Arab society in Israel. Among the Jews of liberal/left political persuasion, the Taibeh team was seen to provide living proof of the integration of Arabs into at least some state institutions. For others of more nationalistic and right-wing persuasion, an Arab team in the top league became an overt target for their nationalist and racist passions. From the Arabs' point of view, the first mission the Taibeh team represented ended in failure. While fans were initially proud of getting to the top division, their games provided an opportunity for a degree of political protest, a form of catharsis, and a chance (in the event of success) of writing a different end to the real story.

The team, however, was inferior to the others in terms of budget, players, and ground facilities. Hated by some rival fans, prone to biased refereeing, treated more harshly than their Jewish counterparts by police,[2] no 'different end' could be written. The picture was not that much different in terms of the second mission – the team as representing the Arabs from within. The Hapoel Taibeh story presented organisational incapacity. The management made mistakes, players did not always reach the necessary level of professionalism, coaches did not succeed in turning individual players into a coherent team. This failure can be conceived as one among many other symptoms of a wider leadership crisis in the Arab population in Israel (Beshara 1993; Ghanem 1997).

However, Hapoel Taibeh's story has other dimensions. While the team ultimately failed, the fans retained their loyalty, strengthening their own image as people who resist surrender. In interviews with members of the team's management, this image was attributed to 'the Arab mentality'. Whenever they tried to describe their resilience, their resources in coping with the situation, the fact that they were a people of honour, and the warm relationship between the management and the team, they always referred to their 'Arab mentality'. (Honour, as a resource, and as an ultimate source of significance for the season as a whole, was particularly invoked with the death of Wahib Jebarah.) Against the weakness, the poverty, and the helplessness, Wahib turned out to be a symbol of struggle and unlimited devotion – the 'Shahid'. Although the state and its Jewish sports establishment tried to co-opt and appropriate the player's death on the field through the politics of the all-human, transnational significance of sports, for the Taibeh team and fans, Wahib's death became a vehicle by which they could transcend reality both on and beyond the field of play. A sporting tragedy turned, for a moment, into a vehicle for recuperating an 'injured' identity (Ghanem 1997). With Wahib as a symbol, the team was not defeated: it simply did not yet win.

The participation of Hapoel Taibeh brought the Jewish-Arab conflict to the football stadium; the team brought discourse into a sphere in which Jewish domination had, thus far, been taken for granted. The Taibeh team, by their very participation, gained for itself a hope for a better end. They suggested the option of a wider participation, materialising the dreams that the game was about.

Notes

1. 'Galilee, the Triangle and the Nakab [Negev]' are where most of the Arab population in Israel lives. The political meaning of the expression is: All the Arabs in Israel.
2. Farbstein and Semyonov (1990) assert that more violent events were observed in matches in which Arab teams were involved. From our experience of Taibeh, we would argue that more people were hurt by policemen than by fights and confrontations between rival fans.

14 From Ends to Trenches, and Back: Football in the Former Yugoslavia
Srdjan Vrcan and Drazen Lalic

Fan behaviour in the former Yugoslavia reveals a structural nexus between football fandom and politics during times of grave social crisis. This politicisation of the fan world and political instrumentalisation of fan behaviour occurred during the massive social crisis of civil war that afflicted Yugoslavia between August 1991 to the present day and in the context of the ethnicification of politics (Offe 1994) following the death of Tito in May 1980. In turn, this has resulted in the emergence of new states which act not only as nation states but also as nationalising states (Brubaker 1996). There is no chasm between the subculture of football followers and the mainstream culture; both in regard to violence as legitimate during social and political crises. The 'tribal' activity of football following, particularly 'hooligan' actions, was transferred from the ends to the trenches. Waving banners and scarves was replaced by the brandishing of weapons, evidencing what one writer calls the 'move from dramatic and ritualistic representation or rather from symbolic behaviour to non-symbolic behaviour' (Battacchi 1988: 325). To borrow Ficoneri's (1990: 59) words, 'these absurd soccer warriors' turned almost overnight into soldiers in a cruel war. The symbolism of fan aggression was easily transformed, first into aggressive political symbolism, then into military symbolism, demonstrating that 'it is possible to die by symbolism, and that this was not purely symbolic at least for the dying ones' (Battacchi 1988: 326).

DESTINY VIA SPORT

There is no doubt that a movement from the terraces to trenches occurred in Croatia and Serbia. Arkan, the infamous leader of the Red Star fans in Belgrade, became the commander of the voluntary Serbian paramilitary unit named the 'Tigers'. Involved in fighting in Croatia and Bosnia, Arkan was subsequently wanted for war crimes. He was to declare that the civil war had been initiated not by the generals or the federal army, but by the fans at the match against Dinamo Zagreb. Brutal off-pitch clashes took place between the 'BBB' (Bad Blue Boys) of Dinamo and the *Delije* (Braves) of Red Star; the mass intervention of the police was also televised live. *The Red Star Review* in 1992 published a war report, stating that the '*Delije*' had left their paraphenalia under the ends and taken up weapons to go to war (Čolović 1996).

Some basic military organisation and training had been practised by *Delije* members well before the first shots were fired. Militant fans became hardcore volunteers, elevated to the status of national heroes. At the same time the hardcore Croatian fans, particularly the BBB and the '*Torcida*' from Split, organised their fighting mobs into political assault squads on the streets and squares of Croatian cities. They were among the first to join the military units of the emerging Croatian army. In the first phases of the war the fans' symbolism was used by soldiers on both sides of the conflict. The first armed clashes were frequently described by those participants as a direct continuation of the clashes between Croatian and Serbian fan groups. Therefore, there should be nothing surprising in the fact that monuments were later erected in Croatian football stadiums in memory of their fallen comrades.

The previous commitment of these fans to nationalist politics caused the war, making them, at least at the beginning, a war vanguard. It was not the case that the whole society was immersed in a tidal wave of organised political violence; rather, the football fans acted as the catalyst for political violence on a mass scale. These actors gave organised political violence a social and moral legitimacy. They introduced and intensified the conflict in the context of the radical ethnification of politics. They gave the existing conflict the appearance of inevitability, an 'all or nothing' and 'either/or' ethos. The fan subcultures themselves contain a strange mixture. On one hand, they are spontaneous, ad hoc, inventive, with a predilection for the eccentric and the chaotic. On the other hand, they possess an organised, rigid, disciplinary order. It was therefore an easy passage for these fans, from a chaotic spontaneity and almost unrestricted freedom, to the rigidity of military discipline and order.

It seems pertinent in this respect to remember Caillois's view that a superior intellect can foresee the destiny of some societies and civilisations if it looks first at the most dominant games. The fate of Sparta might have been predicted from the rigidity of its military games; the fall of the Roman Empire could have been foretold from the nature and expansion of gladiatorial games (Caillois 1958: 162). Considering events in Yugoslavian stadiums in the late 1980s, one may state that no great intellect was needed to predict the nation's fate. The actions, banners, slogans, chants and symbolism used on a massive scale in football stadiums, and the climate created by fans from Zagreb, Split and Belgrade, were all clear indicators of the impending collapse of the social system. They anticipated the merging of nationalist political strategies, leading to violent clashes and ultimately all-out war. Mihailovic, writing in 1990 before the first shots were fired, noted that:

> the need for sadistic exploits, for aggression and violence are a feature of disintegrating social systems, which disappeared from the historical scene. This was

demonstrated at the end of the eighties and at the start of the last decade of the twentieth century, in Yugoslav sport and first of all in football. The scale of violence in and around football signalled that the Balkan madness was arriving. (Mihailovic 1990: 10)

Čolovic similarly contends that:

> the story of dissolution of Yugoslavia, in a rage of hatred and war, and in the glory of the gods of ethnic nationalism and pre-modern militarism, may be told as a story of the evolution of violence in the Yugoslav sport and more particularly among football fan hooligans and about the gradual transfer of such a violence in the late eighties and early nineties to the field of 'grand-national' politics, and, from there, to the battlefields. (Čolovic 1996: 419)

In this case, one may invert the well-known thesis that sport is to be seen as metaphor of the society at large to argue instead that it was society at large that became an immensely amplified metaphor of sport.

A BALKAN ISSUE?

There are ways of justifying the point that the Yugoslav case is a unique one in a global sense. First, it may be claimed that the behaviour of football fans in the former Yugoslavia stands outside the European matrix of contemporary fan behaviour, representing basically an anomalous phenomenon. Second, one could state that the Yugoslav dispute should be interpreted as a strictly Balkan one without any wider relevance. However, we would argue that fan behaviour in the former Yugoslavia may be more plausibly interpreted as belonging to the European matrix. Therefore, for sociological analysis, it has the symptomatic advantage of being an extreme case that can disclose some insights for elsewhere. At the same time, we should add that the former Yugoslavia has very particular social, political and cultural circumstances. There are, of course, peculiarly Balkan components, but these specific ingredients add a manifest brutality to fan behaviour.

Some might also seek to minimise the sociological relevance of the fan behaviour by introducing two distinct interpretative frameworks: one that is applied to Croatian fans and the other Serbian fans. This presumes that there have been two radically different types of fan behaviour, in terms of origin, motivation and social structuring. Such an argument presupposes further that there are two different processes of potential ethnicification and two different types of state formation taking place which to us sounds highly dubious.

However, notwithstanding the important differences between Croatian and Serbian fans, there is evidently some common structural, political and cultural properties in their behaviour. It seems plausible to assert that there is an elective affinity, or a cognitive and normative resonance, between one specific political culture, and the dominant fan subculture. This is evidently the case when nationalism represents the most radical political expression of a contemporary trend towards the ethnicification of politics.[1]

THE WAY TO THE TRENCHES

Conflict is a permanent and defining trait of the fan subculture. It has been suggested that conflicts between football fans acquire meaning only within a totally shared culture of symbolic, gestural and musical terms. This has been the main reason for some observers to conclude that their conflicts are not based on social issues, but are instead connected to contrasting interests (such as trade unions conflicts), issues of power, or cultural differences (political or ethnic).

Conflicts between football fans are interpreted as emerging from structured and symbolic kinds of opposition. However, in analysing the conflicts between rival fan groups, it is plausible to introduce a distinction between the international language of symbolism, gestures and music, and the particular aspects of the specific groups which sometimes relate back to the wider culture. Fan conflicts frequently represent the irreconcilable conflicts of culture and identity. As Touraine (1992) explains, these are by necessity more drastic and dramatic than simple conflicts of interest; they are basically non-negotiable, involving absolutist expressions of identities, and the radical exclusion of others.

There are some fundamental aspects in contemporary football subcultures which intrinsically favour politicalisation giving rise to acute political conflicts and ultimately to war. The Italian sociologist Dal Lago (1990) points to the 'war metaphor' as a fundamental feature of football. He describes the dominant climate and the emotional tonality of football as saturated with warlike moments or at least conflictual ones. However, under some circumstances, it is not only the metaphor that is celebrated; the game may also be a prelude and an ideological preparation for war. The war metaphor is easily transferred from football playgrounds to the society at large and to the world of everday life. It functions to legitimatise the real war. Furthermore, there is only one rather small step to make from the metaphoric to the real war. There is a gradual process that begins with football as a kind of war leading to the practice of politics as war, and ending ultimately in real war (which is experienced as a continuation of football *qua* war). This process was followed by Croatian and Serbian football fans, in an easy rather than expected or accidental manner easily.

Football emboldens the very peculiar metaphor of war as a total one. The war of the fan subculture requires from its members a quasi-religious commitment without any mental reserves. This commitment frequently requires unusual and supreme sacrifices, and does not leave anyone in an untouchable position; it does not spare anyone. Therefore, the war metaphor is applied not only to players and opposing fans, but to everybody: club managers, match officials, coaches, the families of players, their fiancées and wives, their ancestors, their cities, their history. Applying current military terminology, we may say that the war metaphor in the fan subculture does not leave any neutrals or civilians. In this sense the metaphor for the subculture contains the image of total war, which seeks not only the defeat of hostile forces, but also the submission and total elimination of the enemy. In this sense, the total war waged in the former Yugoslavia may be seen as a true amplification of the fan war metaphor.

The war metaphor includes a model of behaviour that is considered necessary particularly at away matches, in the territory that belongs to the enemy. This model at least legitimises vandalism, destruction and plunder as acts that are normal and meritorious. The switch from a metaphoric ritualistic war to real warfare has a genuine impact on the behaviour of fans who become soldiers. Furthermore, the typical culture of the hardcore groups does not require a cool, detached sense of identity or a conditional kind of belonging, but an exaggerated affirmation of identity and total loyalty. The political potential of such a cultural trait is obvious, and very congenial to what was requested of soldiers.

A dominant metaphor is built into the fan subculture which exacerbates social cleavages in terms of 'friend or foe'. Without such a divisive metaphor for the 'other', fan behaviour loses much of its meaning. This peculiar ritual was transferred from the fan subculture to everyday life, bringing with it a specific and intensified notion of division. Moreover, the fan subculture also glorifies a masculinity of sexual potency, courage and loyalty, and one that is expressive of the tribe's 'will to power' and to dominate. This functions in two fundamental ways: to exalt stereotyped masculinity at individual and collective levels; and also to symbolically emasculate the others through such offensive insults as 'gay', 'pussycat' and 'cuckold'. These constructions of masculinity were easily transferred from fans to fan-soldiers.

A very peculiar dialectic of love and hatred is evidenced in fan culture and easily transferred to the world of politics. Love and hatred do not appear as feelings divided by an insurmountable abyss; instead, hatred appears as the almost essential face of love, so that it emerges as the necessary precondition to love. There is no love without hatred and no hatred without love; the intensity of love is to be measured primarily by the intensity of the respective hatred. This peculiar dialectic functions in the most drastic way when the 'others' are not total strangers, and when the narcissism of small differences become manifest. The dialectic is particularly transferrable to the politics of identity and nationalism. During incandescent conflicts this dialectic may easily produce the most pathological hatreds. There is an elective affinity therefore between fan subcultures, nationalism, and authoritarian populism.

Fan subcultures contains very particular notions of what is and is not permissible, legitimate and fair. Some of these notions can be basically different from conventional distinctions. One should admit that this difference can radically challenge or provoke the established order, or represent an expression of pure freedom. Nevertheless, it is a fact that some of the most brutal and criminal of war actions in the early stages of the civil war were committed by units full of football fans.

FROM THE TRENCHES TO THE ENDS, AGAIN

The last shells in the most cruel war on European soil since World War II were fired in the summer of 1995 in Croatia and in the spring of 1996 in Bosnia and Herzegovina. Since that time, the Pax Americana has not resulted in a mass return of refugees who had been driven by force from their homes. Nor has the peace established more tolerant relationships between the members of different ethnic groups. There has been no coherent democratisation of social life. The peace has resulted in a precarious return to normality, in which Croats, Serbs, Bosnians and others can live without the fear of war. The return of routine has seen most of the members of the fan groups return from the battlefields to the soccer stadiums. At the same time a new generation of fans has emerged who were children when the war broke out. Football was played to some extent in the early 1990s, and some fans continued to practise their traditional rituals. However, the attention of the public was focused on the battlegrounds of war rather than football's playgrounds. With the end of the war, fan behaviour has once again become a matter of public interest and sociological analysis. Unfortunately, due to an almost total break in communications, the scope of this final analysis has to be confined solely to fan behaviour in Croatia.

It is necessary to emphasise that the return to the ends occurs in a radically different political, cultural and sporting context. The new emerging states which aim at national homogeneity and purity have changed that context. Football in general and the club championship in particular has been homogenised and ethnically cleansed. There is no chance of teams with different national connotations meeting and competing in the league championship or in any friendly matches. Serbian and Croatian clubs now meet only in international competition, and their matches have so far been seen as an extension of the war. However, football in Bosnia and Herzegovina represents a paradigmatic case where there are two distinct championships in operation and no matches between clubs from the rival leagues. Additionally, the Bosnia national team is composed exclusively of Muslim players in spite of Bosnia and Herzegovina being reorganised, since the Dayton Agreement, as a single state by the international community.

Consequently, match attendances have become nationally homogeneous and ethnically 'cleansed'. The rare matches between Croatian and Serbian clubs in Europe have so far been played before totally homogeneous crowds: no Croatian following was permitted to attend a recent match between Dinamo Croatia and Partizan in Belgrade, and no Serbian followers were allowed into Zagreb. Leadership at the national and club levels in Croatia has come under the total political control of the HDZ, the Croatian national political party. Securing order at the matches has seen the new nationally homogeneous and ethnically cleansed state and military police move into action. Therefore, there are no police officers to represent an illegitimate regime or to be opposed by fans voicing political dissent at the regime. The old homogeneous and nationalist political identity of Croatian fans has been eroded.

Also finished are the old truces and friendships of different Croatian followings, in nationalist unity against Serbian fans. Violent clashes between different Croatian fan groups in the Croatian championship have lately become common. Secondly, there has been an escalation of fan violence in Croatian football, characterised by more traditional territorial – regional and urban – antagonisms and rivalries, on surrounding streets and squares. The clashes between fans seem to be less violent and perilous than before. However, the match between Croatia Zagreb and Hajduk Split saw the Croatian police register 80 incidents of fan violence; hundreds of fans were arrested and a dozen persons injured. At the same time, the aggressive behaviour of the Croatian BBB during a European soccer competition resulted in Croatia Zagreb being fined 200,000 Swiss francs by UEFA.

Croatia's President Tudmann has made a series of direct political interventions into the Croatian football world. A keen supporter of Croatia Zagreb, Tudmann does not hide his personal influence in the club's activities. He has declared on several occasion that Croatia Zagreb ought to represent both the Republic of Croatia and its government on the international football scene. He requested publicly that Zagreb's leading club change its name from 'Dinamo' to the current 'Croatia', purely for political reasons. However, the name change has been opposed by the BBB, who insist that the use of the name Croatia should be reserved only for the national team and not for any one Croatian club. They have publically expressed their opposition on several occasions, by waving their old scarves and banners with the name of Dinamo, and chanting about the 'holy name of Dinamo'. These protest actions have led to violence, and even a fire in the Zagreb stadium in 1993. Police intervention followed when they arrested and questioned more than 1,200 BBB members. In this respect, it is interesting to mention the public correspondence between President Tudman and the BBB in late 1994. Through the press, the President addressed a long letter to members of the BBB, defending the change of name. He declared that the very name 'Dinamo' would remind the Western world that 'we have not yet totally set ourselves free of the Bolshevik and Balkan heritage'. The BBB replied unemotionally stating that 'the future would give its verdict about the name of the club'.

THE POST-WAR WARRIORS

New fans have been more eager than the old returning war veterans to engage in aggressive and violent behaviour. Their aim is to experience some emotional arousal, to enjoy a new experience, to get some kind of rare self-affirmation within the respective group, and also to demonstrate their frustrations. Yet the fall of the former Yugoslavia and the establishment of the independent Croatian state, has provoked strong public optimism about the efforts of radical political change upon fan behaviour. For instance, the president of the Croatian Olympic Committee and one of the leading personalities of the governing party, declared that there would be no more fan violence and rioting in the independent Croatia, because there are no more ethnically heterogeneous crowds. Such a view was generally shared by many politicians (mostly on the political right), by sports officials and many journalists. However, this view was not shared by the fans themselves. One of them, a leader of the BBB and a war veteran, declared in the spring of 1993 that:

> when Miloševic* came to power, we felt that there would be shit coming, and that, therefore, we were not going to fight any more with Croatian boys. Now, the current clashes have been normal ones to me. I am fascinated by English soccer, and it is normal for me to quarrel and fight again, that does not mean that we are not going to make peace again. It is normal for me to clash and brawl but within the limits of normality, with no more knives and sticks.

We would argue that three crucial factors have had a decisive impact upon the reappearance of fan violence in Croatia. First, the fan subculture has not been an indigenous one. Followers of the subcultural style draw upon its features that come from England, Italy, Holland and other countries. It has been a global phenomenon for almost two decades. The subcultural style has distinctive properties in terms of dress, argot and music. It also has its own peculiar and ritualised code of violence, which is partly verbal (such as when insulting the others) and partly physical (such as fighting, pitch invasion and vandalism). The ritual which often culminates in violence, also serves to act as 'the twelfth player' on the field of play.

Second, a kind of social protest and rebellion provides the basis for recent violent behaviour. Here we may introduce Mike Brake's (1985: 8) analysis, which defines the subculture as an 'attempt to solve structural contradictions arising out of the wider societal context' and as 'meaning systems, modes of expression or life styles developed by groups in subordinate structural positions in response to dominant meaning systems'. The nature of the fan rebellion is mirrored in the properties and rituals of the style that they follow. The 'resistance through ritual' (Hall and Jefferson 1975) of football fans in Croatia, as well as in some other parts of the former Yugoslavia, indicates the subordinate and marginal social

---

*Slobodan Miloševic was a former Communist apparatchik loyal to Tito. After the death of the latter in 1980 he became President of the former republic of Yugoslavia as a Serbian Nationalist. He supported the brutal military campaign by Bosnian Serbs in the civil war which eventually led to the creation of a separate Serbian republic.

position of this young generation and the wider social groups to which it belongs. The young generation have suffered most from the consequences of the long and devastating war; they are at the sharp end of structural transition, such as the unjust privatisation of services, and the creeping social and economic crisis. In their rituals they frequently challenge both the rigidly imposed traditionalist culture and the cynicism and arrogance of the new powers-that-be. Therefore, it is no surprise that President Tudmann was whistled at and mercilessly insulted by 'Torcida' followers in Split when he appeared at the stadium. Nor is it surprising that in Zagreb, Split, Rijeka and other Croatian cities fans riot and clash with the police. Radical political changes have not diminished rebellious attitudes. Instead, these attitudes have been diverted from the political arenas of the late eighties and early nineties, and into the cultural field revealing itself mostly symbolically around football.

Rebellion was previously expressed by supporting nationalist causes and joining the war; now it is revealed symbolically, through rituals and other stylistic aspects. Football fans and their behaviour have recently been exposed to a controlling pressure from the new regime. Rather like the old regime, the new authorities aim to deprive the fans of their relative autonomy from the new official culture. Such a pressure exists on two distinct levels: football and society at large. At the football level, the very presence of fan violence in Croatia may be understood as a spontaneous reaction by some fans against official efforts to limit their influence upon clubs. The name change of the Zagreb club from 'Dinamo' to 'Croatia', for example, has resulted in BBB resistance to this ersatz-identity and to the use and abuse of their club for political goals. In a similar way, other fan groups consider themselves to be the only permanent guardians of the genuine spirit of their respective clubs. Everybody else (players, coaches, management, directors) is considered liable to self-interest, with no loyalty to the club concerned. Significantly, all the presidents of football clubs in Croatia are leading members of the governing political party.

At the wider level, the fan subculture represents an opposition – mostly a spontaneous and unreflective one – to repeated efforts to impose a kind of official 'cultural hegemony' (Gramsci 1971). The fan groups oppose the way in which the official culture presents a system of values, norms, and symbols through the mass media, as the only possible and legitimate 'project for living' (Kluckhohn 1962). Generally speaking, the fan ritual acts as 'a spectacle of identity' (Dal Lago 1990) that is motivated by a collective feeling of belonging. Any outside attempt to change this club identity is regarded by fans as a direct attack on them, and as a challenge to their own identity and subculture. Therefore, it is resisted by an escalation of fan violence. In the final analysis, this seems to confirm that there is a major conflict going on. On the one side stands an authoritarian regime with neo-totalitarian ambitions, which promotes at all costs the official culture while trying to impose itself upon all the crucial areas of social life. On the other side stand the existing fan subcultures trying to safeguard and preserve their identities and autonomy. In this way the fan subculture functions as a kind of oasis in the emerging civil society. Together with some elements of the media, the fan subculture opposes both the expansion of a neo-totalitarian wasteland and its presentation of the official culture and 'social reality' (Berger and Luckmann 1985).

The fall of the communist system brought seismic structural changes to the former Yugoslavia and then the new republics. It did not bring about a radical change in the social position of young people or to their wider social strata. Hence, the macro-social changes have not had a crucial impact upon the basic properties of the fan subcultures. In a society where almost everything has been changing on a large scale, the fan subcultures seem to remain basically unchanged and particularly resistant to changes that are imposed from above. The fan subculture has been able to motivate the fans' political engagement along a range of different and contradictory political lines. Constant themes have been politics of identity and recognition (Taylor 1994: 25). Therefore, an apparently bizarre conclusion seems to be very plausible. The members of the BBB, as well as some other followings, may be regarded as defending *and* promoting the autonomy of the emerging civil society, which had been seriously undermined by the long years of one-party rule.

Note

1. In this respect, it would be very interesting to make a detailed comparison between the political culture of nationalism as described by Lemberg (1967) and the aggressive fan subculture as elaborated upon by Salvini (1988).

Part V
New Tactics: Contemporary Players

15 Bhola Lethu: Football in Urban South Africa[1]

John Nauright

Ubani Ongathinta Thina
(Who can touch us)
Sisho Ngebhola Webafana?
(We mean as far as football is concerned boys?)
from 'Bhola Lethu' (Our Football), 1984.

The above quote from a song entitled 'Bhola Lethu' (Our Football) by the widely popular 1980s South African group Juluka encapsulates the meaning that football has had for black communities in South Africa over the past several decades. Football is played and watched by more South Africans than any other sport. Although the literature on South African football is limited, it is possible to reconstruct elements of its history and to discuss its contemporary meaning in the popular culture of South Africa. For although cricket and rugby union have been promoted as possible unifying sports for the new post-apartheid South Africa, it is football that resonates most strongly with the great majority of black South Africans and also with some whites. The game has a long history in black districts and talented exports have travelled to Britain for decades. As early as 1939, Boksburg near Johannesburg was known as a hotbed of football talent, a place of less than 20,000 inhabitants which has contributed nine players to first-class English and Scottish football.

Despite South Africa's absence from world football during much of the apartheid years of 1948 to 1990 (gaining readmission to world football in 1992), many South Africans have been known to international football audiences. These include great white footballers such as Gary Bailey, who kept goal for Manchester United in the late 1970s and early 1980s, and 1990s national team defender Mark Fish. Albert Johannsen, who was designated 'Coloured'[2] played on the wing from 1959–70 with Leeds United and for two additional years with York City. Laterally, several black South Africans currently play in Europe, the most successful of these has been Phil Masinga who played for Leeds United during the 1990s. Previously, in the 1970s, South African football legend Jomo Sono played for the New York Cosmos alongside Pelé and Franz Beckenbauer and returned to buy a professional team – the Jomo Cosmos of Soweto.

While rugby union remains popular in the townships of Cape Town, Port Elizabeth and East London and its nearby areas, football is overwhelmingly the most popular sport among black South Africans, particularly in the urban areas.

Soon after large scale black urbanisation developed, teams and competitions emerged. Johannesburg and Durban have been the historical centres of football's development, though in every city and town, football is widely popular. Soweto, the conglomeration of townships to the south-west of Johannesburg, has been the centre of South African football, supplying several leading teams and many of the top players of the past half century. The teams with the largest and most fanatical support have been Kaizer Chiefs (founded in 1970), Orlando Pirates (1937) and Moroka Swallows (1947). Orlando Pirates are so widely popular that they are also known as the 'People's Team'. Another team nearby which had much success in recent years is Mamelodi Sundowns (1962) based in Mamelodi township in Pretoria. Durban also has a long history of football and teams there have played at a high level.

There are several reasons for football's success within black communities. One is the nature of the game itself, allowing for an open expression of individual skills which can be readily viewed by spectators. Indeed, white officials attempted unsuccessfully to stamp out what they saw as an over-emphasis on individualism in football during the 1930s and 1940s. Football can be played by all shapes and sizes on any space of open ground with no special equipment needed. Among whites, football was played by working class males but the game increasingly became identified as a black sport. Thus, black success in football was no threat to white culture and interests. White officials promoted football among urban blacks in the 1920s and 1930s as an antidote to the possible ills of urban society. Black elites also viewed sport in this light and sports administration became a key area where educated black men could exercise political, economic and administrative control. The popularity of football ultimately led to national professional leagues being formed in the 1960s with elite teams slowly moving away from a local community base thereby gaining national popularity.

THE DEVELOPMENT OF FOOTBALL IN SOUTH AFRICA

The first known football club in South Africa was the white club Pietermaritzburg County begun by white settlers in the Natal colony in 1879, thirteen years after the first recorded football match played in the town. Three white Natal clubs, Natal Wasps, Durban Alphas and Umgeni Stars, formed the first football association in South Africa in 1882 called the Natal Football Association, six more clubs joining them the following year. In Cape Town teams from four military regiments formed an association in 1891 (Couzens 1983; Parker 1897). The Football Association of South Africa (FASA) was founded in 1892 with additional provincial associations appearing in Western Province in 1896 and the Transvaal in 1899 (Archer and Bouillon 1982). As with other sports developed in Britain and exported throughout the Empire, football links were cemented through contact with 'home' in the form of sporting tours. But, by the First World War, rugby was clearly the dominant sport among white men and the successes of the 1906 and 1912 Springbok tours of the British Isles and France confirmed this status through glowing British and local press reports. By 1900 both British and Afrikaner men played rugby widely and across class lines, while football remained a sport played by working class white immigrants and Indians and increasingly by Africans (Nauright 1997). Football was the one sport played by whites that did not develop an elite white following. As late as 1981, a popular history of (white) South Africa did not even mention football in the section on 'Sporting Life'.

Black football associations were formed across South Africa in the first few decades of the twentieth century. In 1898 the Orange Free State Bantu Football Club was formed followed by other clubs in Bloemfontein eventually leading to the establishment of the Orange Free State Bantu Football Association in 1930. In 1931 the Natal Bantu Football Association was formed with headquarters in Pietermaritzburg. During the early 1900s many African national political meetings were held in Bloemfontein due to its relatively central location. Football was no different and in 1928 African football officials decided to form regional Football Associations. In 1933 the South African Bantu Football Association appeared with affiliated associations from the Transvaal, Orange Free State, Natal and Northern Cape. In the Western Cape black football became organised later. Coloured leagues emerged in the 1920s, but it was only in the 1960s that African football began to develop in Langa. Langa was an old township and rugby was played there at least since the 1920s, however, the Coloured labour preference policy that operated in the Western Cape limited opportunities for black sporting competitions unless resources could be mustered for travel. From the 1960s, however, Africans began to arrive in the Western Cape in far greater numbers. Immigrant workers and those from the Orange Free State and Transvaal who came to work at the vineyards or in military camps formed football clubs during the Second World War and township football began to appear by the 1960s. The white Superintendent of Langa promoted the game as he had been a Western Province football player. Many white officials viewed football as an ideal game to market among blacks, particularly for migrant mineworkers on the Transvaal gold mines.

MINING PROFITS

Football came to Johannesburg from Natal where it gained in popularity during the 1890s. Early black clubs developed in Ladysmith and Pietermaritzburg after men there had seen British soldiers playing the game during the 1890s (Couzens 1983). In 1916 the Durban and District African Football Association (DDAFA) was founded. The first President was D. Evans (1916–23), a white man from Johannesburg who managed the Somtseu Road Men's Hostel for migrant workers.

After Evans resigned in 1923, black men ran the DDAFA opening the way for links with other African run associations in Natal and the rest of South Africa (Magubane 1963). Charles and William Dube, brothers of John Dube, first African National Congress (ANC) President and founder of the Ohlange Institute, which was modelled on Booker T. Washington's Tuskeegee, were early leaders in the organisation of football in Durban (Couzens 1983).

As with the Dubes in Durban, leaders of the African game in Johannesburg were closely linked to political elites and were members of the African edu-cated class. Dan Twala, a leading force behind the organisation of football in Johannesburg, was the nephew of R. W. Msimang, one of the four lawyers who founded the ANC in 1912. Albert Luthuli was later President of the ANC and winner of the Nobel Peace Prize in 1961. In 1932, Luthuli, then Vice-President of the DDAFA, declined the office of President due to his duties as secretary of the Natal Teachers Association. Magubane (1963) identified 31 leading DDAFA administrators for the period of 1924–32. Six DDAFA administrators were ANC members, with two serving on Joint Councils and fourteen on local Advisory Boards. At this stage, the ANC was very much an elite organisation of educated Africans who opposed segregationist practices, but it was not very radical in its approaches to white officialdom.

Many of the Johannesburg elite also took to football, but its early organisation of football on the Witwatersrand was largely undertaken by the gold mines. By the early 1920s the Witwatersrand District Native Football Association (WDNFA) had been formed mainly for mine teams. Mines and other businesses recruited good football players and offered them the better jobs available to blacks in order to attract and entertain workers at weekends. Many leisure activities were tried on the mines with the help of missionaries in attempts to 'moralise' recreation (Couzens 1982), but only football and movies proved popular. The WDNFA fell away during 1928 and 1929 and it had not been successful in organising black football in townships. As a result of football's growing popularity, but lack of organisation, the Johannesburg Municipality made Bantu Men's Social Centre (BMSC) secretary Sol Senaoane the director of 'Native Recreation' for the city. With the assistance of Graham Ballenden (Johannesburg Manager of Native Affairs), Phillips, Senaoane, R. W. Msimang (an ANC leader) and D. M. Denalane (of Robinson Deep Mine), the Johannesburg Bantu Football Association (JBFA) was formed in 1929 (Badenhorst 1992; Cobley 1994; Couzens 1983).

The JBFA claimed 153 senior clubs and 282 junior clubs as members by 1937 (Thabe 1983; Callinicos 1987), and by 1948, it had 218 affiliated clubs (Badenhorst 1992). The success of the JBFA led to the formation of the Bantu Sports Club (BSC) by the BMSC in 1931 on twelve acres of land that had been donated by accountants Howard Pim and John Hardy in 1925. The BSC had a stand which seated over 2,000 spectators with total seating for 5,000, two football fields and several tennis courts (Archer and Bouillon 1982; Couzens 1982). The BSC's grand opening demonstrated its links to an ideology of 'respectability' as a cricket match between a black and a white team took place in the presence of the Mayor of Johannesburg (Nauright 1997). The building of the BSC allowed the JBFA to collect gate-money at matches and revenue was shared between the football association and the club. In 1932 the BSC lowered entrance fees to attract more spectators without consulting the JBFA or the Municipality. The JBFA in protest moved their matches to the Wemmer Sports Grounds controlled by the Johannesburg City Council (Badenhorst 1992). In March 1933 Dan Twala led a move which took a number of teams out of the JBFA, forming the Johannesburg African Football Association (JAFA) that in effect reformed the defunct WDNFA in 1932. George Thabe, former football administrator and complier of *It's a Goal! 50 Years of Sweat, Tears and Drama in Black Soccer* argued that the 'split became the festering sore that would malign the body of Black organised football for about 40 years' (Thabe 1983: 6). White officials condemned the split which they argued was indicative of African behaviour. White officials did not like the independence shown by the JAFA, though they often paid lip-service to African initiative and progress.

PROTOCOL AND PATRONAGE

The JAFA began with Denalane as President, prominent Alexandra businessman R. G. Baloyi became the Vice-President with Twala as Secretary. Twala later became President, holding the position for twenty years. JAFA's administrators were all African and their focus centred on both townships and the mines. The division between the JAFA and JBFA fundamentally was based on whether African officials or white municipal officials would control the football's administration and organisation. The involvement of wealthy businessmen like Baloyi suggests that money could be made from a successfully run competition, however, the Non-European Affairs Department (NEAD) of the Johannesburg Municipality refused to allow the JAFA access to municipal grounds. As a result, the JAFA found itself restricted to the two fields at the BMSC. Eventually some of the mines allowed JAFA matches to be played on their vacant land.

Similar to concerns that led to the formation of the JAFA, in Natal, obstacles to the formation of a provincial association were hampered by Pietermaritzburg African football officials' objections to the DDAFA being run initially by a white man. Durban and Ladysmith joined together in 1920 to form the Natal Native Football Association (NNFA), but Pietermaritzburg only agreed to link with the rest of Natal in 1925 after Evans had resigned as DDAFA head. In 1930 the DDAFA sent a letter to all provincial associations urging the formation of the South African African Football Association (SAAFA), after the DDAFA had been offered a trophy worth £100 for such an association (Magubane 1963). Transvaal and Natal became the nucleus of the Association and they first played for the Deans Shield in 1932. Significantly, the NNFA and the SAAFA, like the JAFA, were African controlled organisations, though Magubane (1963) pointed out that they were not adverse to accepting assistance from whites interested in African recreation.

The administrative organisation of black football associations has been highly centralised with small numbers of officials holding wide powers. Sport and political organisations in black and white South African societies have historically been the positions that have occupied the greatest prestige within local and national communities. Black officials ran their organisations and meetings with strict attention to protocol with meetings nearly always held in English. The use of English also meant that only a small percentage of Africans who became involved in sport could serve on association executives as most Africans did not speak English. Although the prestige associated with sports administrative positions led to numerous political battles and sometimes to splits within associations, the relative stability in administration allowed many black sporting organisations to survive the onslaught of apartheid and its many disruptive relocation policies and social restrictions. Magubane (1963) identified 30 administrative offices within the DDAFA. The contributors to Thabe's commemorative history show that other associations experienced similar administrative stability to that of the DDAFA (Thabe 1983).

The opportunity to become a sports official provided one of the few avenues for political and administrative achievement for educated blacks denied so many opportunities in wider society. Additionally, patronage or ownership of leading local clubs provided an avenue for men to gain substantial local reputations and importance when local political opportunities were limited by the segregation and apartheid states. Football matches allowed team patrons and club and association officials to present themselves in large public forums as leading men of the community – an opportunity only matched by local and national political leaders in times of mass protest or crisis. By the 1940s, football was on a solid footing with associations throughout the country. Moves were made towards organising inter-race competitions and international tours, though black football players and teams were excluded from competing with whites. Prestige was not the only benefit football officials received from being involved in administration. Thabe, who lived in the wealthy Dube area of Soweto, for instance, was known to have made a large portion of his personal wealth through sport and sports promotion (Archer and Bouillon 1982). Businessmen such as Baloyi and James Moroka donated trophies that in essence were forms of sponsorship of competitions. Their close connections to football could not have hurt their other business enterprises in the townships around Johannesburg.

Despite splits between various associations, clubs and competitions, football 'brought together many people – migrant workers, clerks, factory workers, people of different language groups and backgrounds – to help form a new culture of the city' (Callinicos 1987: 217). By the 1940s, the JAFA attracted up to 10,000 spectators to Sunday matches drawing domestic labourers and mine workers to its matches (Badenhorst 1992). The growth of black football led to expanded competitions as well as to a strain on facilities. Black urbanisation greatly accelerated in the 1940s and major football matches became a central focus of urban black popular culture, particularly in the Transvaal and Natal. While social control of blacks and the establishment of 'proper' behaviour among urbanising Africans were important aims of white officialdom, outlets for non-political release of energy were also deemed crucial to the survival of white minority rule and an orderly society.

PROFESSIONALISM AND SPECTACLE IN THE 1940s AND 1950s

Thabe (1983: 7) argues that the 'years between 1942 and 1954 were the most eventful in the history of Black football in the Transvaal'. In this period Inter-District competitions were popular with matches attracting crowds of several thousand spectators. Club football also grew dramatically with clubs such as Transvaal Jumpers, Orlando Pirates, Moroka Swallows, Hungry Lions, Naughty Boys, the Evergreen Mighty Greens, Pimville Champions and others which became household names in the townships surrounding Johannesburg and nearby towns. Leading clubs usually played friendly matches against other top clubs while local associations ran competitions in townships such as Orlando (part of what became Soweto) and Alexandra. Often clubs would play each other in special matches for a prize with 'Ox Competitions' being most popular in the 1940s. Thousands of spectators attended these well advertised matches with the winning team taking a prize ox that they slaughtered or sold for profit (Thabe 1983: 11). Although matches between top teams began to take place across regions and between cities, players remained rooted in local communities in this period. While much initial impetus for the growth of football came from white officials and black educated elites, spontaneous football matches and competitions rapidly sprang up in urban black working class settlements. Throughout the period 1920–60, players commonly represented their own street, yard or section within a township, reflecting close links with supporters and local communities.

Even though the authorities constantly worked to limit access to playing fields, new clubs continued to appear. In 1947 Johannesburg's estimated population of 380,000 Africans had access to just 30 football pitches, only five rugby fields and 26 tennis courts (Archer and Bouillon 1982). Unofficial matches and matches between streets and yards took place on any of the rare open spaces that were available. Alexandra had three squares and Number Two square became the township's main football ground and public political meeting place. In Pretoria, Sundowns, formed in the early 1960s, had to bribe the caretaker of the bus depot to train on the lawn there (Dassie 1996). Leading Johannesburg teams developed a reputation for being the best in South Africa, leading other top clubs to seek matches there. The Transvaal Jumpers took on extra road work training when playing leading Johannesburg sides in the 1940s and once they dominated the Vereeniging competition, the Jumpers began to play at the Wemmer Football Ground against leading JBFA teams such as Orlando Pirates, Naughty Boys and Moroka Swallows (Jeffrey 1992).

By the 1950s regular competitions expanded throughout the country. The Transvaal Bantu Football Association ran several competitions including the Transvaal Challenge Cup and the Senanoane Cup. The Transvaal Jumpers dominated these competitions between 1947 and 1953 (Ramokhoase 1983: 39). As the Jumpers became too good for their Vereeniging opponents and began to play in Johannesburg on a regular basis, the club assisted in the spread of football's popularity between towns. Other teams such as the Hume Zebras from Germiston, led by Albert 'Hurry Hurry' Johannson before he went to Leeds United, and Pretoria Home Stars, also succeeded during the 1950s, demonstrating that Transvaal football talent was not limited to Johannesburg and Vereeniging. The success of non-Johannesburg clubs also ignited thoughts of establishing a professional football league. With amalgamation between the JAFA and JBFA continuing to remain unlikely as the 1950s began, Twala and others began to turn their attention towards professional football as a solution to divisions.

PROFESSIONAL FOOTBALL ARRIVES

In 1948 the first move towards non-racialism and ultimately national unity in football began. A. J. Albertyn, Vice-President of the South African Coloured Football Association travelled to Johannesburg to address the SAAFA and arranged a friendly between the two associations for Cape Town. In May 1950 in Cape Town the two organisations agreed to form the Federation of South African Football Associations and a further meeting in Durban in 1951 brought in the South African Indian Football Association, thus forming the South African Soccer Federation (SASF) (Couzens 1983). The SASF thus organised all-black football organisations into a single national union in 1952 and formally became a non-racial federation by 1963. The SASF had a membership of 46,000 players by 1962 while the whites-only FASA claimed just 20,000 (de Broglio 1970). The SASF applied for affiliation to FIFA in 1955 on the basis of being more representative of South African football players than the all-white FASA. FIFA rejected the application as the SASF did not control all football in the country. The FASA offered SASF affiliation with non-voting powers so that a unified body could then be affiliated to FIFA. Predictably, SASF officials rejected the plan.

When South Africa left the British Commonwealth in 1961 and became a Republic, FASA lost its imperial connection to the English FA. Though FIFA did not accept the SASF, it suspended FASA in 1961, soon after the English FA withdrew support, though Sir Stanley Rous, president of FIFA and a supporter of FASA, came to South Africa to investigate the situation. Rous subsequently reinstated FASA in 1963. In 1964, however, FIFA expelled South Africa at its Tokyo Congress attended by several newly independent African countries. The government responded by issuing banning orders including the house arrest of George Singh, the SASF representative who led the campaign for SASF recognition and FASA expulsion from FIFA. In 1959 some white players broke away from the amateur FASA to form a whites-only professional competition called the National Football League.

In response to the League and calls for a black competition, SASF began a professional competition the same year called the South African Soccer Federation Professional League (SASF-PL). Leading clubs such as Orlando Pirates and Moroka Swallows joined the SASF-PL from the outset. Between 1962 and 1966 three professional football teams formed in the Western Cape and affiliated to the SASF-PL. These were Cape Ramblers, Mother City and Ocean XI demonstrating the league's national appeal. The FASA with government assistance created black affiliated associations and SASF-PL teams found themselves excluded from municipal grounds. The FASA also established a professional competition for Africans called the National Professional Soccer League (NPSL). The white association had much greater access to capital and to municipally controlled grounds that put it in an advantageous position during the 1960s. As a result of being excluded from municipal grounds, Pirates and Swallows, with their huge bands of supporters, eventually left the SASF-PL and joined the NPSL, spelling the end of the SASF-PL's mass spectator appeal.

The white NSL also split with some joining the SASF-PL and others the NPSL. The NPSL with large African support for Pirates and Swallows attracted greater sponsorship and became the dominant professional league in the 1970s. In 1985 a split occurred in the NPSL which led to the formation of the National Soccer League (NSL). Kaizer Motaung, Abdul Bhamjee and Cyril Kobus led an attack on George Thabe stating that he and the NPSL frustrated the clubs. Sponsors immediately supported the NSL, forcing the NPSL to try to survive without major sponsorship. Although Bhamjee and Kobus were later accused of stealing millions of rands from the NSL, the league remained dominant in the 1990s. For the 1996–7 season, the NSL began a Premier League of eighteen teams on the model of premier leagues in England and Italy. At the next level two regional leagues operate, one along the coastal region and one inland.

Along with initiatives from administrators and players, other developments have heightened the public profile of football from the 1930s onwards. Black newspapers which covered African football clubs from the outset came under the pressures of apartheid censorship in the 1950s and lost much political content by the early 1960s. Exceptions appeared in the magazine *Drum* and the *Golden City Post* both set up by Jim Bailey, son of South African Associated Newspapers owner, Sir Abe Bailey. In 1980, the Argus Group established the *Sowetan* (Tomaselli and Tomaselli 1987). South African Associated Newspapers set up the Golden City Press in early 1982. The paper tried to reproduce the sex, violence and sensationalist format of the 1950s but had financial problems. The paper then turned into 'a Kaizer Chiefs propaganda sheet', attracting much township attention, thereby allowing it to survive (Tomaselli and Tomaselli 1987: 49). As Tomaselli et al. (1987) show in their study of the South African press, the black press in the 1970s and 1980s was very opposed to apartheid but through its ownership and ultimate white editorial control, the press did not critique the capitalist system. Black editors often avoided conflict by concentrating on crime, sport and funerals. When they challenged the capitalist system or went too far in their anti-apartheid critiques, white business interests or the government stepped in to limit or eliminate oppositional news. These practices meant that black sport, especially football and boxing, received even greater coverage and sensationalisation than might otherwise have been the case. Black sporting stars achieved celebrity status in the black print media, especially those playing for the elite Soweto teams of Kaizer Chiefs, Orlando Pirates, Moroka Swallows and Jomo Cosmos.

Elite teams have in recent years become more removed from their local communities as major sponsorship, television and full-scale professionalism has appeared since the late 1970s. As in many other countries, leading club sides have gained national followings with Orlando Pirates, for example, resembling Manchester United or Bayern Munich on a national scale. Public announcements made by Pirates are often attended by thousands. In December 1994, 12,000 attended a public Pirates meeting and party at their home base at Orlando stadium (Sowetan, 5/12/94). Kaizer Chiefs' national following is such that there are 65 official fan clubs located throughout South Africa, while Sundowns have 38 fan clubs. During the 1970s and 1980s certain teams gained reputations and nicknames based on styles of play or dress. Kaizer Chiefs supporters in the 1970s began to dress like Kaizer Motaung, the team founder. Chiefs' fans became known as 'The Hippies' as they wore Afros and bell-bottomed trousers (Mlokoti 1996).

Football's popularity has led to a number of problems in the game. Corruption charges are rife and tensions run high when leading teams play each other. In March 1996 a match between Kaizer Chiefs and Sundowns in the Cola-Cola Challenge Cup was called off with Chiefs leading 2–0. A Chiefs supporter injured a Sundowns player by throwing an apple at him. The player had to leave the field and Sundowns, with no substitutions left, were left to continue with ten players, but refused to play on. During late 1996, the Pickard Commission of Inquiry investigated allegations against Kaizer Chiefs of corruption and the use of drug money to run the club. In addition to problems surrounding administration and spectating, South Africa is rapidly following the rest of Africa in being a net exporter of top quality professional football players. The best players from the national team play in Europe. South African teams also import a number of players as well, particularly from poorer nearby southern and central African nations. In the 1995 season, Orlando Pirates signed a one million rand sponsorship deal assisting the club in signing three West African players. In 1996 players in the NSL came from three continents and 23 foreign countries.

Top international and professional club matches draw massive crowds, particularly at Soweto's First National Bank Stadium also called 'Soccer City' which has a capacity of over 80,000. A number of important matches are also played at Ellis Park Rugby Stadium which holds up to 70,000. The FNB Stadium opened in 1989 when Kaizer Chiefs and Moroka Swallows met in the Castle Challenge Cup Final. Further development of the stadium is planned that will increase its seating capacity to about 120,000. The headquarters of the National Football League and the SAAFA are located at the stadium. The entry of South Africa into international competition in 1992 has led to a devoted following for the national team *'Bafana Bafana'* (our boys). South Africa won the 1996 Africa Nations Cup that it hosted.

FOOTBALL AND POLITICS

The popularity of football in the townships provided a unique opportunity during the apartheid years for political leaders to address mass audiences without the necessity of trying to obtain a police permit, which for many anti-apartheid groups was not likely to be granted anyway. Even before apartheid, political leaders had links with football. Many ANC elites were involved in football administration and James 'Sofasonke' Mpanza, leader of the Orlando squatters movement of 1946 had played football with Rev Sivetye at Adams College. Mpanza was called 'Magebula' by Orlando residents for his work in 'turning the sods' on the ground for houses in Orlando and Moroka. 'Magebula' as a name then became synonymous with Orlando Pirates (Couzens 1983). Local elites such as R. G. Baloyi and James Moroka also used their sponsorship of football and other activities to lift their personal and political profiles. Baloyi was prominent in Alexandra Township politics in the 1930s and early 1940s, and both he and Moroka were active in national political issues through membership in the ANC and other organisations. George Thabe used his position as a football administrator to secure the chair of the Vaal Triangle Community Council in 1977. According to Jeffrey (1992: 87): 'his status and control originated from his role in football administration and it is not surprising that there was a good deal of overlap between local government and football'. Thabe's chief local political rival on the Community Council, Knox Matjila of Evaton, was also a football rival of Thabe's. The two fell out in the mid-1970s as Matjila tried to take control of the SANFA from Thabe. In 1981 Thabe resigned from the Vaal Council after being defeated twice in succession for the chair by Matjila (Jeffrey 1992).

During the 1970s and 1980s groups such as the Black Consciousness Movement led by Steve Biko and the later the United Democratic Front (UDF) often used football matches to address audiences (Lewis 1992/3). Founded in 1983, the UDF was an umbrella organisation for hundreds of groups aligned to the ANC. The loose organisation of the UDF made it impossible for the government to round up the leaders as it had done to the ANC in 1963. While mass rallies were held throughout the 1980s, the state of emergency from 1986 through 1989 made it more difficult for the UDF to hold large meetings. As a result, football matches and other public events provided the opportunity for political organisation and speech making. Significantly, the ANC held mass rallies at the FNB stadium upon the release of its political prisoners in 1989 and 1990. These initial rallies were held in front of almost 90,000 people, attracting crowds similar in size to those at Pirates and Chiefs clashes. Ironically, the South African Communist Party held its first legal rally at the Bank's stadium in May 1990. To mark his inauguration in 1994, President Mandela arranged for a football game to be played at Ellis Park, South Africa's leading rugby stadium, between South Africa and Zambia. Thus, football was the first sport to be played officially in the new democratic South Africa.

Added to the overtly political and liberatory uses of football have been discourses surrounding the game that support individual freedom, team spirit and reward for hard work, as evidenced in Castle beer advertisements of the early 1990s. Castle ads depicted the game as representative of the spirit of the 'New South Africa'. One ad showed a star young black player who has the opportunity to play in England, but who cannot go because he cannot afford it. A white teammate leads a campaign to raise the money. Desiree Lewis (1992/3: 13) argues that the ad 'is an appropriation and transferral of the liberatory meanings of football. The advert is an index of the pervasiveness of football's emancipatory meanings'. Lewis argues that the structure of the game allows football to be represented as emancipatory even though such representations can be captured by beer and other companies. Football throughout its history in South Africa has signified 'respectability', African initiative, political struggle, individual freedom, escapism and capitalism through its pervasive role in urban black communities. With the increasing success of *Bafana Bafana* in international football, the game could well become a major force in the generation of transracial national identification in the new South Africa.

Notes

1. Further discussions of soccer in South Africa appear in John Nauright (1997).
2. 'Coloured' was an official term during segregation and apartheid to refer to mixed race South Africans, it has been commonly used to refer to this group of South Africans, though the term is by no means ideal.

16 No Longer Worlds Apart? British Influences and Norwegian Football
Matti Goksøyr and Hans Hognestad

British influences have dominated the development of football in Norway in a process characterised more by admiration than antagonism. Today millions of Norwegians support one team in England and a local team in Norway. A person supporting a local team can relate the club to their own autobiographical universe as an authentically experienced reality. A Norwegian supporter of an English team is necessarily a 'long-distance supporter'. This affects the 'tribal' aspects of the game (Mangan 1996), i.e. the structuring of rivalries and enemies associated with football. Our analysis considers to what extent we can relate the development of ways of playing and ways of support in Norway to hybridisation (Archetti 1998a). With the progress Norway has made in football competition in the 1990s and the beginnings of militant forms of fandom, there is a sense of 'tradition in the making' in Norway. Current public discourses on these changes tend to take a normative platform related to a more historical attempt at the 'de-rivalisation' of the game. Analysed through historical and anthropological perspectives, this chapter aims to illustrate how the influences from and contacts with the British have fuelled the construction of football playing and supporting in Norway.

FOOTBALL: A FOREIGNER IN NORWEGIAN CULTURE?

Since the introduction of football in the 1880s, the game has held a special position in Norway's sporting scene. Until the 1930s football was played mostly by middle class students and merchants' sons. Since then it has become the largest sport in the Norwegian Sports Federation, being described as a 'folk-sport' or 'our national summer sport' (Juve 1934). It is now the largest participatory sport for males and females in Norway. Despite the fact that the female national side is well established on the world stage, female football generates little public interest compared with male football. Despite its popularity, however, the game has never threatened the status of skiing as Norway's national sport, because the game cannot provide the key symbols of Norwegian identity or manifest genuine national virtues. Norwegians have never been in a position to label football 'our game' in the same way as British or Latin peoples. Winter sports are more easily construed as 'Norwegian', due to natural conditions for practise in many parts of Norway. However, it still offers an arena for identification with 'our' representatives against others (cf. Goksøyr 1996).

A globalised game cannot be analysed only via its internal effects. The history of Norwegian football clearly shows how the international character of the game was present at an early stage. The recognition that football was a particularly British sport was prevalent in the early years. That said, British influences were not the sole or the most dominant ones. In 1907 Norway joined FIFA, an organisation in which continental Europe had a substantial input. When it came to playing the game, clubs from Denmark and the Swedish national team were the first international opponents, and implicitly teachers. Football in Norway developed despite a general lack of international success and an absence of the nation-building images generated by skiing and winter sports. Apart from a brief period between 1936 and 1938, football brought Norway no international acclaim. However, over the last decade or so, the national team has achieved previously unparalleled international success. Such performances have generated new interest in the national team and assisted the building of a Norwegian tradition in football.

Football was brought to Norway by different social groups: by sailors working on British naval and merchant ships berthed in Norwegian ports; Britons who travelled to Norway for work; by Norwegians returning home from British-related business or studies. British coaches operated in Norway from the turn of the century, primarily on an amateur 'hobby' basis, as a pastime which complemented their professional occupation. That said, some Scotsmen and Englishmen came to Norway as professional coaches, hired to prepare the Olympic teams both in 1912 and 1920 (Halvorsen 1947: 40), and SK Brann, from Bergen on Norway's North Sea coast, hired the Scotsman George Coleman as coach during the First World War. The first three clubs to cross the North Sea were Scottish: Glasgow Rangers in 1911, followed by Hearts and Celtic the following year. Dartford, the amateur side from England, appeared the next year, while professional English sides such as Newcastle and Arsenal visited Norway after 1918. Clubs from Germany and Holland (Ajax) also played summer exhibition matches in Norway.

The work of such coaches and visits of Scottish clubs paved the ground for Scotland's influence in Norwegian football (*Norsk Idrætsblad og Sport*, 1920, No. 20). The Scots encouraged a short passing game, focused on technical skills and team-work. This differed from the long passing style practised until then by most Norwegian clubs and the national team. However, after a few unconvincing years in the early 1920s, the Norwegian national team was criticised for playing too 'Scottish', to the neglect of the English idea of transient, direct and penetrative play. The remedy was to invite more English teams to play in Norway (*Sportsmanden*, 1924, No. 86). Before the 1930s this was translated into a discussion between the foremost club-team protagonists of these two playing styles: Odd of Skien and SK Brann of Bergen. When Norway in the 1930s experienced its first (and until the 1990s only) period of international success – resulting in bronze medals in the Olympic Games of 1936 and a narrow and dubious defeat to the coming champions Italy in the 1938 World Cup, the team played an 'adjusted short passing style', giving the then captain reason to warn his forwards against 'exaggerating the passes and forgetting efficiency' (Halvorsen 1947: 158).[1]

Even though Norway had beaten 'England' (the national name used by all Norwegian papers even though Britain was the correct term) at the 1920 Olympic Games in Antwerp, Britain's cultural hegemony was unshakeable. The victory was taken merely as an exception from the rule (*Norsk Idrætsblad og Sport*, 1920, No. 31). Nevertheless, victory over the English amateur side, combined with others over Denmark and Sweden a year earlier, did promote a greater Norwegian self-confidence. This confidence rarely showed itself except through occasional, all-out effort, a mentality prevailing well into the 1980s which, while resulting in the occasional win – over Scotland in 1963, France in 1969, England in 1981, was rarely capable of avoiding the traditional last place in the World Cup's qualifying groups.[2]

Debates around the national team in the 1920s was typified by discussions concerning whether the best club team, or a selected team, should represent Norway. The Scandinavian successes in 1919 was explained at the time by the well known Swedish author and journalist Torstein Tegner who believed that selected teams did not suit the Swedes for psychological reasons, but did suit Norway: 'Norway documented a playing force much stronger than any of its club teams. [The Norwegian team had played] a sufficient amount of matches each year to perform in perfect interaction without being satiated or indifferent. Each match was a real event for the players and the nation.' (Tegner in *Idrottsbladet*, Christmas edition 1919, quoted in *Sportsmanden*, 1920, No. 7). According to Tegner, the Norwegian player was characterised by an 'outstanding physique, high intelligence and first class attitudes' (ibid). This way of connecting abilities to cultural and physical traits was typical of inter-war football commentators.

Before the Second World War differences in playing style and performance were interpreted via cultural differences. The captain of Norway's successful 1936 team, Jørgen Juve also worked as sports editor for the newspaper *Tidens Tegn*. In 1934 he published a book with the modest title *Alt om fotball* (Everything about Football) in which he described the national team of the thirties as playing in a 'Norwegian' way, an opinion based upon a different understanding of a playing style similar to those witnessed in the 1990s. Advocates of the current national team describe its style in modern, almost scientific terms stressing efficiency while ignoring national symbolism (Olsen, Semb and Larsen 1994). Juve and other journalists had described their team in an almost nationalistic way: 'Norwegian football is built upon the best national qualities of our youth; the speed, the force, the simple and tough technique, and the tactical brain'. These qualities were compared to other nations: 'Football among the Germans develops forwardness and systematics, among the Latin Americans it keeps the warm-blooded temper under control, while their love of excitement can thrive freely, among the Englishmen it strengthens their stoicism, their tactical abilities and their fairness, among the Danes their speed, joy and humour, and among the Norwegians their velocity, their force, their skill and their ability to fight is growing' (Juve 1934: 19–20). Styles of play are in this perspective, conceived as nothing less than a transfer of alleged national virtues and vices.

During the inter-war years, the game continued to attract new performers and spectators. Simultaneously, as football was declared 'our national game' the game's international character became more visible. Norway played 141 international matches before the Second World War, the opponents varied from the USA to Russia with other European and especially Nordic nations as the more frequent opponents. Professional coaches were attracted to the far north. In 1939 there were 16 foreigners, seven of whom were English (Halvorsen 1947: 35). No drastic changes took place in Norwegian football after 1945 until gradual professionalisation started up in the 1970s. The everyday understanding of professional play constituted by wage and employee relationship is only one aspect among many to define professionalism (Peterson 1993).

Bill Sund (1997: 13) has stated that the early years of Scandinavian football was dominated by 'middle-class ethics and aristocratic aesthetics', and blended British sporting attitudes minus the professional players. Norwegian receptiveness to football favoured amateurism without the biases. Both the middle and working classes played the amateur game. Following the First World War football spread rapidly to become a working-class sport, but remained within an amateur framework. Although the Football Association and the press strived for sportsmanlike attitudes and fair play, the Corinthians never became a model for Norwegian footballers. Nor did the debate on the short versus long passing style have a class bias in the sense described in Britain (Mason 1980). Amateur laws meant that full-time players did not become a reality until the late 1970s, and even then such a status was often disguised. Even today, many players in the Norwegian top division are part-timers.

Notably, the incentives to this development came from Britain – but not from mainstream British coaching approaches. British trainers were imported. Hostile towards theory, these men based their work on their playing experiences, thereby reproducing traditional playing styles. More lasting influences paradoxically came from more educated trainers who lacking an ex-professional background at a high level paradoxically found it difficult to get a job 'back home'. This latter group shared a solid educational and practical background. They were professionals in the more modern sense and achieved success thereby creating a 'school' of coaching. Trainers' courses and literature created an almost identical football terminology.

Their success was enhanced by the lack of hostility in Norway towards theory compared to that found in most other European countries. A collaboration between the national associations and the state-run sports colleges had already been established. This promoted the ideology of instrumental action or goal rationality in certain milieus. The former Norwegian coach, Egil Olsen, hails from the Norwegian University of Sport, and maintains a theoretical profile. Compared to British clubs, Norwegian football has not been so tied up with ideas of traditional action, the absence of a successful footballing tradition does not function as the 'straitjacket' found in more established football cultures, where ways of playing can be considered as paradigmatic ideals (cf. Archetti 1998a). Successful results gained by clubs and the national team in the 1990s and the consequent export of Norwegian players to England has brought new dimensions into the footballing relationship between Norway and Britain: namely, a growing belief in original, self-made ways, and a reluctance simply to copy the bigger nations. Such independence has made the skiing nation a net exporter of football players in the nineties.[3]

The successes of the national side over the past decade has been interpreted as resulting from a clever choice of playing style by the present Norwegian coach, Egil Olsen. The national teams of recent years have created a tradition built on a rational, goal-oriented approach. Inspired by British influences, this style represses notions of elegance and beauty, in favour of results.[4] The direct, rational style is seen as a manifestation of smart thinking, thus reinforcing the national self image. The relative unpopularity of such a style is taken as confirmation of Norway's innovating abilities, thus reducing Norwegians' historical respect towards football's powers. Modesty no longer characterises Norwegian press reporting of Norwegian performances. The Norwegian self image has risen to previously unexperienced heights. As a consequence, education, organisation and research of and into football has been intensified.

SATELLITE TRANSMITTED PASSION?

Until the 1960s, interest in English football in Norway was generated by the Norwegian press. Columns such as 'the situation in the English league' or 'English football just now' appeared regularly from the 1920s onwards in the sports press. They included detailed match reports, enthused over the 'staggering' (*Sportsmanden*, 1924, No. 3: 6) number of spectators, and stressed the differences between the two countries. By the mid-twenties, the daily press had also started a thorough coverage of British (mainly English) football. Occasionally media interest focused around Norwegians playing abroad, the most famous being Asbjørn Halvorsen who played for Hamburger Sportverein in the 1920s. English football acquired a mythological status during the inter-war years. In 1946 the Norwegian parliament voted to introduce a state-run football pools gambling scheme. The betting in 1948 was on the outcome of English league matches. The football pools became immensely popular thereby creating even closer relations between English clubs and Norwegians who every week hoped that maybe the

Wolves would win and make them rich. Stakes were much reduced when English matches were replaced by Norwegian ones in the summer seasons.

In 1969 these ties were strengthened further when the Norwegian broadcasting corporation (NRK) introduced live coverage of English matches during the long winter break in Norway. '*Tippekampen*', the vernacular term for the Saturday afternoon match, should be seen both as an outcome of existing and latent interest, and as a reason for the later hype of English football in Norway. Norwegian authors wrote about their lifelong 'secret' passions for English football, and 'their' English teams – passions begun long before the start of televised matches (Skrede 1977; Solstad and Michelet 1982). After the Second World War almost every Norwegian newspaper, even the very local ones, printed the full English league tables and results. This fact made Stanley Matthews a hero in Norway long before televised games.

A previously unparalleled nationwide movement of what we could call a 'satellite transmitted passion' was produced by *Tippekampen*. English football now became accessible to people even in the most remote parts of Norway. English football became a cult, particularly among youngsters. Clubs like Liverpool, Leeds, Manchester United, Arsenal and Tottenham attracted the largest support, but people developed various degrees of support and interest in a wide diversity of teams. Substantial newspaper coverage of English football, the distribution of English football magazines, and radio commentary, primarily for dedicated fans in the Western parts of Norway with good BBC Radio reception, contributed to the creation of a semiotic process in which support for English teams played a key role in school yards, playing fields and work places. From the late seventies travelling to watch English games became a popular pursuit for Norwegian fans. During the 1990s this trend developed into more consumer-oriented football holidays to England.

Over the last twenty years numerous Norwegian or Scandinavian supporters clubs for English teams have been established. Manchester City was the first (1974), then clubs for Manchester United, Liverpool, Leeds and Arsenal were formed between 1977 and 1982. In 1985 *Supporterunionen for Britisk Fotball* was founded, this special union for supporters of British teams was established to provide services for supporters as well as organising meetings and social events. By 1997 it had a membership of 53,000 covering 45 teams.[5] In recent years several supporters clubs have been developed for lower division teams which have never appeared on Norwegian television. The general commodification of football in the nineties has also reduced the significance of televised Saturday games. From the 1998/9 season these games will be restricted to a pay-per-view channel, which in effect means the end of an era. In response a new trend in Norway, as in many other countries, is for fans to gather in pubs to watch games televised on giant screens on Sky Sports satellite TV.

It has often been argued that footballing success is a prerequisite to a foot-balling tradition (cf. Archetti 1997b), from which players, spectators, officials and reporters may apply as a paradigm for future sporting achievements. Thus, we can see how in the 1970s domestic football in Norway was among the weakest in Europe in terms of success, and no Norwegian team could compete with foreign clubs and national sides in terms of creating a paradigmatic basis of how the game should be played. In this void the 1966 World Cup victory, and the domination of English teams in Europe enhanced the image of English football as an ideal standard. Despite recent successes of both Norwegian clubs and national sides, Norwegian support for English football prevails. The outsider will quite correctly ask both how a phenomenon from a different, more abstract sociocultural universe can arouse so much attention and passion, and how these impulses and inspirations from English football have influenced football practices in Norway. The answer is, inevitably, multi-faceted.

The Argentine-born anthropologist Eduardo Archetti, who lives in Norway, reflected recently that 'in football it is impossible to love a possible enemy' (Archetti 1998b). This states succinctly the generally accepted notion that identity in football is linked to experiences of conflict and emotion, be it at a local or national universe. In a climate of competition and rivalry, football identity is carved out both in relation and in contrast to a series of others. For the partisan fan it is often unthinkable to support more than one club or one nation. It might be argued that this 'tribalistic' aspect of football still applies as a dominant feature in most countries where football has and continues to play a significant role in generating social and cultural identities (cf. Armstrong and Giulianotti 1997). However, in Norway, support for an English club often runs parallel to that for a Norwegian club, in ways which do not necessarily privilege the local side. Norwegian and the English teams have generally been classified as adhering to two different universes, which due to the assumed gap in sporting abilities would never clash. However, when SK Brann met Liverpool in the quarter-finals of the European Cup Winners Cup in March 1997, the two worlds collided. Several Brann supporters also members of Liverpool's Norwegian Supporters Club, admitted that this caused them a great moral dilemma. Simultaneously, the attraction of English football provides a possible creative space for hybridisation based on parallel identities rather than conflict and rivalry as is often the case in football (cf. Archetti 1998a).

NEW TIMES, NEW RIVALRIES

The late Scottish writer John Fairgrieve (1986) explains the popularity of football by pointing to the fact that teams gain support by appealing to opposing identities. As such, the dynamics of rivalry has fuelled the playful folklore of football terraces in Britian for over a century. The expressions often heard on the British football terraces take the shape of Bakhtin's definition of carnivalesque laughter: 'gay and triumphant, and at the same time mocking and deriding'

(Bakhtin 1968: 11–12). This 'sarcastic commitment' evolves parallel to, or in accordance with, a set of unwritten rules. Chants of 'part-time supporters' are often directed at fans who do not show a morally sufficient commitment (ibid.). The 'professional' fan becomes the morally correct protagonist of support, while the 'part-timer' is regarded as unloyal and lacking in morale, in ways comparable to Geertz's famous depiction of 'deep players' and 'shadow players' (Geertz 1973). In British sports, Hargreaves (1986: 67) relates the historical change in values and approach to professionalisation of the late nineteenth century onwards. The ideals of amateurism dominating the traditional middle-class sports gradually gave way to a more dominant working-class influence. The professionalisation of British football was followed by a professionalisation in support, as a kind of commitment structured around principles of rivalry and conflict.

Despite the absence of a professional league, social and geographical differences are recurrent themes in various expressions of support in the domestic Norwegian football universe. Yet the influences from British football have not produced simple imitation. Norwegian football has grown out of a vastly different geographical and social structure. It has developed within a traditionally more homogeneous social democratic landscape; out of a morally paradigmatic sports movement bent on promoting national ideals in which the rural rather than the urban, winter rather than the summer represents the idealised space for sports. In Britain high density populations and relatively short distances between static venues provide possibilities for fans to explore and frequently confront different identities. However, in Norway the distance between Oslo and Tromsø is equal to that between London and Tirana in Albania.

Away support is rare in a league which has few popular teams located near to one another. Hence, monological and invariably positive support among home fans prevails in Norway in contrast to the dynamic negativity of fandom so frequently generated between opposing supporters in Britain. An indication of the limited scope for participating fandom in Norway may lie in the fact that the Norwegian language has no equivalent word for 'fan' or 'supporter', consequently the more general term 'patriot' is sometimes applied. The most common word is the term *'tilhenger'*, (trailer), implying a more passive spectatorship. Traditionally, the morally correct participant in sports is the athlete participant and not the spectator whose 'participation' is ideally restricted to polite and positive applause.[6]

Despite the influence of, and admiration for English football, both in terms of support for English teams and in the construction of the sport in Norway, there is little to suggest such influences have led to the adoption or emulation of the various forms of militant support. Even big games attracting large crowds have, to date, produced no serious incidents of disorder and violence. Outside the stadium there is no segregation and rival fans mingle peacefully. Such a reality must be linked to the dominant ascribed role for supporters as promoting 'polite amateurism'. The World Cup qualifier in London in 1992, illustrated the disparity.

For the first time ever, thousands of Norwegians followed the national team abroad. Outside a pub famous as a pre-match rendezvous for England fans in the West End of London, English fans threw the occasional beer glass at coaches transporting Norwegian supporters, while also ridiculing Norwegian passers-by who were visible via their tiny hand-held national flags. No responses came from the visitors. Before the match contemptuous hissing noise greeted the playing of the Norwegian national anthem, while the Norwegians kept respectfully quiet during the English national anthem or even sang along. During the match at Wembley, England supporters continuously addressed chants towards the visiting supporters, but earned no reply. When Kjetil Rekdal scored a famous equaliser for Norway, there were scenes of extreme joy among the Norwegian fans, without malicious intention or gloating directed towards the home fans. Despite hoping for a good Norwegian result it would be plausible to argue that it was difficult for most visitors to treat England as an enemy, due to its paradigmatic role in the wider development of football in Norway.[7]

English hooligans are regarded with fear and fascination in Norway. Their inspiration appears to be limited to different notions of staunch audio-visual forms of support, but no legitimacy is given to the exercise of more violent pursuits. The notorious reputation of English fans turned Oslo into a city of fear on two recent occasions. The first was the World Cup qualifier in 1993 between Norway and England, the second the friendly international between the two sides in late 1995. Policing was ubiquitous throughout the city before and after these matches, particularly for the latter, which took place six months after the disorder caused by England fans in a game against Ireland in Dublin.

However, some fans have begun to adopt more militant practices. They have generated substantial public debate around issues of sportsmanship and codes of conduct. The autonomous, partisan supporter is still regarded with suspicion in Norwegian sports. This was ably demonstrated in 1994 when a premier league match between Tromsø and Rosenborg became the front-page story of a major tabloid newspaper. Tromsø supporters were reported to have chanted '*grisetryne*' (pigface) at Nils Arne Eggen, a Rosenborg coach, accompanied by behaviour described in terms of 'rowdiness' and 'drunkenness', but not physically violent. A league match again involving Rosenborg, this time away to Lillestrøm in April 1997, produced similarly sensationalist reporting. The Rosenborg goalkeeper was interviewed on national TV after the game whereupon he told how shocked he had been at the sight of a small boy standing behind his goal, chanting 'Homo!' The following week, a national newspaper published a moralising feature on 'terrace culture', including a guide to acceptable and unacceptable behaviours (*Aftenposten*, 27 April 1997).

Tradition is in the making in contemporary Norwegian football, both in terms of styles of playing and styles of support. Even if one can detect the emergence of militant Norwegian supporter groups, the conditions surrounding Norwegian supporters compared to the British are relatively idyllic. Norwegian football's historical British hang-up does not seem to have lead to a copying of everything. Instead it enables some Norwegians to play with their own identities. The styles and ideas from Britain may have been appropriated not from an absence of tradition, but from a tradition without particular success (Archetti 1997). The fact that long-distance forms of supporter are increasing in the 1990s, despite the growing success of Norwegian club teams, raises interesting questions concerning how the different football cultures of Britain and Norway will develop. With the increasing commodification of football, the two football worlds may share an increasingly disciplined and middle-class ethos in which autonomous displays of support are continuously restricted and criminalised (cf. Armstrong 1998). We might thus witness the reinforcement of a process in which constructions of football identity, that are based on antagonism and rivalry, will gradually submit to practices which are more inclusive and cosmopolitan, but less partisan. One timely question with a global significance emerges here; how can football survive as a generator of passionate identities in a pacified 'paradise' without enemies?

Notes

1. All quotations from Scandinavian sources are translated by the authors.
2. Norway came close to qualifying for the World Cups in 1982 and 1986, thereby indicating a certain degree of progress before the achievements of the nineties.
3. The English Premier League and Division One currently hold the largest contingent of Norwegian footballers numbering 26 in March 1998, Norwegian professionals play in numerous leagues outside Scandinavia: Scotland, Italy, Germany, Belgium, Spain, Greece and Austria.
4. Egil Olsen submitted a thesis at the Norwegian University of Sport and Physical Education called 'Scoringer i fotball' (Goals in Football), (Olsen 1973).
5. Statistics taken from the 1997/8 annual Year Book of *Supporterunionen for Britisk Fotball*.
6. In a documentary film about the Norwegian footballer Sander Solberg, who had transfer talks with Hearts FC in November 1997, the manager of the Scottish team, Jim Jefferies, introduced Solberg to the Scottish football cosmos. Jefferies stated before a local derby match against Hearts' city rivals Hibernian FC: 'This is not like Norway where people applaud politely. Here you will final real passion. Fans get right behind their team. This is Hibs you know, and the fans don't like them.'
7. Eleven years earlier when England and Norway met in another World Cup qualifier at Wembley, the awe inspired by England was manifested most visibly when the Norwegian players brought cameras to take pictures of themselves at Wembley!

17 The Suburban Soccer Field: Sport and America's Culture of Privilege

Detlev Zwick and David L. Andrews

No other nation, however, is likely ever to be as suburban as the United States is now, if only because their economic resources and prospects are even more limited than those of the American republic. Thus, the United States is not only the world's first suburban nation, but it will also be its last. The extensive deconcentration of the American people was the result of a set of circumstances that will not be duplicated elsewhere. (Jackson 1985: 304)

As the twentieth century draws to a close, there is compelling evidence to suggest that the suburb has assumed the mantle previously assumed by the western frontier, the arable heartland, and more recently, the industrial metropolis: the suburb has become the economic, political, and cultural epicentre of American existence. However, anyone with more than a passing acquaintance with the post-war American suburb would be well aware that they are far from a uniform or homogeneous entity. Paraphrasing Jacobs (1992), America's fractured cities are enveloped by equally fractured suburbs. Without question, there exists considerable variation in the socio-economic, racial, and ethnic composition of the centres of relatively low, and primarily residential, population density found within America's metropolitan statistical areas (MSAs) as designated by the US Bureau of the Census. Within contemporary America, the adjective 'suburban' could thus legitimately encompass anything from zones of underclass poverty, to sectors of middle/upper class affluence, and a multitude of variations in between. Despite its inherent variability and changeability, the vision of the American suburb that pervades the popular imagination continues to be that of the almost exclusively European American post-war bourgeois utopia: those privileged metropolitan peripheries and populations dominated by an aesthetic and consumer oriented possessive individualism, that underlies a more self-righteously advanced adherence to notions of family, morality and community (Duncan and Duncan 1997; Fishman 1987; Jackson 1985; Lemann 1989).

It is to such idealised suburban spaces and populations that we turn in this chapter. For, since the early 1970s, within these settings football (henceforth referred to in the American vernacular as soccer) has become the de rigueur pastime for young affluent suburbanites (cf. Gardner 1996, 1997; Soccer Industry Council of America

1997; Sugden 1994). Soccer's presence and significance within suburban culture is graphically expressed in the words of a Libertyville (a suburb of Chicago) mother, who blithely explained 'There's only so much family time, so you have to make choices about what activities are best for your child ... Sometimes that means you do soccer in front of church' (Walker 1997: 1). That soccer should be viewed as challenging the position of religion within suburban culture – after all, this quote was taken from an angst-ridden *Christian Science Monitor* article titled 'Defending the Sabbath from soccer' – illustrates the degree to which soccer has been successfully inculcated into the core values and ideals of suburban life.

As Dennis Manzardo, vice president of the Greater Libertyville Soccer Association, proselytised: 'What we feel we're providing is so family-oriented, so healthy for the growth of children, that we like to think it provides all the positives despite the fact that some people may miss church services' (Walker 1997: 1). Given this grass roots deification of suburban soccer, it is little wonder that in recent times soccer imagery has increasingly been appropriated within numerous advertising campaigns for non-sport related products (i.e. television advertisements for Motrin, Benadryl, GMC, Buick, McDonald's, Cellular One, Lender's Bagels, Dutch Boy paint). According to the representational logic underpinning these advertisements, the soccer ball has joined (and is frequently conjoined with) the cathedral ceilinged single family home, the ubiquitous sport utility vehicle, and the obligatory Gap clad offspring, as a standard signifier of the highly desirable bourgeois utopia that suburban America is perceived to be.

As a pervasive suburban cultural practice and symbol, soccer has become a mechanism for distinguishing and delineating the normalised and normalising spaces, practices, and identities associated with white, middle-class, achievement-oriented, morally up-standing, and thereby wholly deserving, suburban affluence (Dumm 1993). Thus, having already offered explanations for the suburbanisation of soccer, or should that be the soccerisation of suburbia (see Andrews et al. 1997), within this discussion we seek to critically examine soccer's appropriation into the everyday practices and ideologies of elite suburban American existence. In other words, we seek to identify the degree to which soccer has become a constituted experience, and constitutive expression, of America's suburban culture of privilege.

EXCAVATING THE SUBURBAN AMERICAN SOCCER PHENOMENON

In many parts of the world, football's 150 year or so evolution in the maelstrom of industrialisation has resulted in the game becoming constitutively intertwined with the structure, experience, and identity of the urban working class. Though somewhat anachronistic in the hypercommercial world of *new* football (cf. Coman et al. 1997; Conn 1997; Horton 1997; Redhead 1997), within many national settings football continues to be advanced and romanticised as the people's game: a component of popular culture, inextricably tied to the pleasures, desires, fears, and anxieties of the nation's populace. Nowhere is this football scenario more inapplicable than in the United States of America, where soccer is considered anything but a core component of national popular culture, linked in some organic sense to the sensibilities of the national psyche. Despite having secured a more prominent place within the highly commercialised US sporting landscape – largely due to increasing patterns of participation and presently stabilising levels of spectatorship (see Major League Soccer 1998; SICA 1997) – soccer continues to be shunned by the American popular imaginary. As one informed journalist noted, invoking an iconic advertising by-line, 'Soccer is not as American as baseball, hot dogs, apple pie and Chevrolet ... *Never was, never will be*' (Coughlin 1997: C1, emphasis added).

Soccer in America is widely construed as being both the game of the *peoples* (those urban populations of variable ethnic and national origin implicitly labelled quasi-American by the American establishment), and the game of *the* people (the statistically, culturally, and ideologically domineering suburban populace, whose mythologised existence delimits the boundaries of a virulent strain of *authentic* Americanness). At one and the same time soccer is rendered both a distinctly un-American, and an explicitly American cultural practice; an ambiguity which prohibits its accession to the status of a national popular practice. As evidence of soccer's terminal polysemia, the marketers of Major League Soccer (MLS) openly acknowledge their primary target audiences reside in America's predominantly European American suburban and Hispanic American urban communities (Delgado 1997; Langdon 1998). Yet, such are the socio-economic, racial, ethnic, and indeed spatial barriers between these primary soccer markets, that they appear to co-exist in a state of mutual disdain toward one another.

Rather than expressing a common affinity toward the game, America's starkly contrasting soccer cultures express the structural inequalities that continue to blight the American social formation. While in many impoverished urban Hispanic American communities, soccer is often fervently upheld as a symbol of hope, pride and identity, within the predominantly European American spaces of suburban affluence, the game has been conclusively appropriated into everyday regimes of privilege. In this way, MLS in particular, and American soccer culture in general, reveals the internal complexities and contradictions of the contemporary American condition; a fact which precludes its acceptance as part of the carefully policed frontiers of national popular culture (Grossberg 1992). Without question, the frequently overlooked complexities of America's multi-ethnic soccer cultures demand more searching scrutiny than they have received up to this point (see Delgado 1997; Pooley 1976; Walter et al. 1991). However, within this discussion we limit ourselves to furthering the understanding of the suburban American soccer phenomenon.

Up to this point, the status and importance of soccer within the suburban American setting has been the focus of only one preliminary study (see Andrews et al. 1997). More frequently, the suburban soccer phenomenon has warranted little more than cursory acknowledgement, within nonetheless important works focused on broader aspects of American soccer culture (see Delgado 1997; Gardner 1996; Markovits 1990; Markovits and Hellerman 1995; Sugden 1994). More significantly perhaps, many researchers within cultural studies have recently been drawn to the suburbs as a context for explicating the cultural politics of space, identity and experience (cf. Dumm 1993; McCarthy et al. 1996; Silverstone 1997; Twine 1996). Unfortunately, those within the critical wing of the sociology of sport community have yet to respond to – or even openly concede the importance of – suburban spaces, populations, and cultures, as meaningful sites for critical analysis. This is perhaps attributable to the fact that many politically oriented academics feel less inclined to explore the privileged and valorised suburban cultural settings and populations, preferring to focus on – and thereby hoping in some way to attenuate – the demonised spaces, experiences, and identities of Otherness; those predominantly urban cultural settings and populations whose open marginalisation and oppression illustrates the injustices and inequalities deriving from the workings of modern power.

Paraphrasing Foucault, the mechanisms of modern discursive power are not only agents of repression, they also act as persuasive forces of substantiation and legitimation for the spaces, experiences and identities of privilege which also inhabit the increasingly polarised American social formation. We argue that it is equally as important to problematise the fetishised utopias of American existence, as it is to deproblematise its pathologised dystopias, since both are necessarily inter-related manifestations of the same regime of power. Hence, our goal within this project is to demonstrate the manner and extent to which soccer has been appropriated as an expression of the valorised spaces, practices and identities, associated with suburban American culture. In other words, we seek to decipher the degree to which soccer has become a constitutive and reproductive agent of America's suburban culture of unconscious and self-righteous privilege. For, as Bourdieu identified, the space of sport 'is inserted into a universe of practices and consumptions themselves structured and constituted as a system' (1990b: 159).

In order to examine the position and influence of soccer within suburban American culture, we chose Reynoldsville Soccer Club (henceforth known as RSC), and more specifically their fifteen-strong Under-17 Girls squad, as the research forum for our analysis. The data collection process lasted from summer 1996 to spring 1997. During this time, our aim was for one of the investigators to become immersed in the ethnographic field as an 'observer as participant' (Adler and Adler 1987); in this case by assuming the full role and responsibilities of an assistant coach to the team at practice sessions, games and tournaments. This allowed for the investigator to become a fully integrated part of the Under-17 Girls team/RSC in particular, and suburban soccer environment in general, thereby eliminating manifold barriers that could potentially hinder the data collection process. It should be noted that the investigator's successful immersion into the field was very much facilitated by the unconditional support – and subsequent actions – of Paul, the team's head coach. In a meeting prior to the beginning of the fieldwork phase, both players and their parents were informed of the investigators' identities and the purpose of the study. They were then asked if they consented to participate in the study. Both the players and parents unanimously endorsed the research enterprise, with the proviso that the final project be written in such a way as to maintain the anonymity of the principal research subjects, and indeed the soccer club as a whole (a request with which the researcher duly concurred).

During the subsequent 10 months in the field, extensive and in-depth fieldnotes, encompassing personal observations and informal conversational recollections were taken, which were augmented by a series of open-ended and unstructured group interviews with the primary research subjects (players, parents and coaches). Taking the scope and variety of ethnographic data into account, and referring back to Bourdieu, it is our firm belief that we obtained a good 'feel for the game'. In other words, we generated a comprehensive body of empirical data from which it is possible to draw some preliminary conclusions pertaining to the cultural significance of competitive youth soccer within the elite American suburb.

SETTING THE ELITE SUBURBAN SCENE

In almost every respect, Reynoldsville represents precisely the type of thriving and energetic suburban enclave to which Americans are encouraged (by the normalising workings of the bourgeois commercial culture industries) to inhabit as concrete evidence of their apparent self-actualisation (Langdon 1995). Located on the northern periphery of a southern US metropolitan area whose population hovers around the 1 million mark, Reynoldsville itself numbers roughly 30,000 people. The community's annual per capita income of approaching $30,000 contrasts disturbingly with numerous impoverished urban zones within the wider metropolitan area (many of whose annual per capita income falls between $10,000 and $15,000), it was also significantly higher than the figure for the older eastern and western suburban communities (whose aggregate annual per capita income fluctuated between $10,000 and $15,000). Whereas the racial breakdown of the metropolitan area was roughly 55 per cent black and 45 per cent white, that for Reynoldsville was 95 per cent white, 2 per cent black, and 3 per cent other. Hence, both in terms of economic prosperity and racial composition, the demographic breakdown of Reynoldsville's populace evidences its status as an archetypal affluent, predominantly white, American suburb.

Clearly, Reynoldsville's demographic profile would strongly suggest that it was the type of suburban American community where soccer has flourished over the past two decades. This proved to be the case, as evidenced by the fact that Reynoldsville was significantly over-represented – in relation to other suburban and urban communities within the metropolitan area – in terms of its distribution of registered youth soccer players. Moreover, from the most superficial informal observations, it was evident that Reynoldsville was a more than suitable site for our research. The hoards of Umbro and Adidas clad youth enjoying their post-match McDonald's or TCBY on Saturday lunchtimes and afternoons, the very presence of 'soccer stores', a multitude of soccer related bumper stickers adoring 'family' vehicles, and even the conversations of self-confessed 'Soccer Grand-Moms' waiting in-line at the local bagel cafe, all pointed to suitability of Reynoldsville for our purpose of examining the American suburban soccer phenomenon. In many respects it is the archetypal American soccer community, inhabited by those much sought after soccer families 'with median household incomes of \$43k + ' (Sponsorquest advertisement, in *Advertising Age*, 8 December 1997: 37).

Space limitations preclude us from developing an expansive discussion of the team's experiences during the 1997 season, and indeed from delving into the revealing complexities of the history, structure and organisation of RSC (both of which we hope to engage in future studies). Instead, within this discussion, we will confine ourselves to highlighting some of the ways that soccer has become complicit in the [re]production of Reynoldsville's elite suburban culture. Following Bourdieu, we conceive the suburb to be a social space that comprises of multiple inter-related fields and sub-fields of forces: 'a network or a configuration of objective relations' (Wacquant 1989: 39) within which individual agents struggle for the various types of capital (economic, cultural, intellectual, physical) through which they seek to shape the material and symbolic aspects of their existence, in ways which enable them to distinguish themselves as fully fledged members of a suburban elite. As evidenced within Bourdieu's (1993) discussion of the French artistic and literary world, the very existence of a field of cultural production, and indeed one's occupancy (or otherwise) within it, is dependent upon a series of oppositions out of which the field and its occupants are able to be defined. With regard to this discussion, the constitution of suburban spaces and populations is defined externally in relation to the dystopian visions of inner urban America (see Giroux 1994; McCarthy et al. 1996), and internally with respect to the myriad of hierarchically ordered taste cultures, through which the gradations of socio-economic diversity within suburban populations are expressed (Bourdieu 1984; Honneth 1986).

As a sub-field of the broader suburban field, soccer in Reynoldsville represents a revealing site of struggle at which an elite suburban bourgeoisie endeavors to consolidate its elevated position, through disguised and perhaps largely unwitting – but nonetheless effective – practices of exclusion and differentiation. It is to soccer's precise role in protecting internal and external suburban boundaries, and thereby maintaining the exclusivity of this broader field of cultural production, that we now turn. In order to do so, it would be instructive to reflect upon to Bourdieu's explanation for the class distribution of sporting practices, which takes into account the positive and negative determining factors, the most important of which are spare time (a transformed form of economic capital), economic capital (more or less indispensable depending on the sport), and cultural capital (again, more or less necessary depending on the sport) (Bourdieu 1978: 834).

The variated distribution of, and thereby the ability to manipulate, these various types of capital are both determined by, and a determinant of, wider structural relations. So, the accessibility of the suburban middle class to such capital(s) allows for the establishment of numerous fields of cultural production, such as the soccer field, and the consequent erection of the material and symbolic barriers through which the dominant suburban middle class is able to differentiate itself from the subordinate masses. Hence, within the remainder of this discussion, we will focus on the ways that economic and cultural capital are mobilised within the suburban soccer field, as a mechanism for reproducing particular class relations, experiences, and identities.

EXCLUSION AND DIFFERENTIATION IN THE SUBURBAN SOCCER FIELD

Access to economic capital is probably the single most critical determinant of participation in suburban youth soccer. Not that formal barriers are erected to preclude membership of highly competitive organisations such as RSC, yet, the significant financial outlay demanded by participation effectively precludes any but the most economically secure middle class families. The basic cost structure for RSC includes an initial, one time membership fee of $125 to join the club, and then a sliding scale of annual club fees, based on age group: Under-10s annual fees are $270; Under-11s through Under-15s are $725; Under-14s through Under-20s are $850. These are the direct costs of participation. Added to this, players are also responsible for: providing soccer balls for practice sessions; purchasing at least two sets of new uniforms per season; and wearing the obligatory high-end soccer boots (or 'cleats').

Teams also participate in numerous weekend tournaments during the season. The Girls Under-17 team took part in nine such events (each a weekend trip involving return journeys of anything between 400 and 1,100 miles), primarily because Paul felt that the length and level of competition offered in the local leagues was simply not acceptable. The 10–12 game local league schedule ran from early March to early May, and comprised fixtures against teams viewed by Paul as generally sub-standard. Hence, he scoured the schedule of tournaments across a sizeable geographic area, to pinpoint those events where the team would face the stiffest competition. Participation in such 'travelling teams' represents the high end of youth soccer participation, primarily because parents are expected to pay for tournament entrance fees, travelling, accommodation, meals and entertainment expenses, on a regular basis. To illustrate this point, from an informal survey of RSC coaches, we determined that the annual soccer related expenses per child was between $3,500 and $4,000, most of which derived from tournament related expenses.

Given the economics of suburban soccer participation, the urban and suburban poor, the working class, and even many of the lower middle class, are effectively denied access to the game in its bourgeois incarnation. This class division is explicitly racialised, especially when one considers the sizeable majority of the United States' African American (34 million) and Hispanic American (29 million) populations inhabit depressed and poverty-impacted metropolitan neighborhoods (Jacobs 1992; Rusk 1995), and thereby represent the people's most economically and geographically distanced from the suburban (soccer) jamboree. America's socio-spatial apartheid has resulted in the nation's affluent suburbs – and thereby soccer as a field of suburban cultural production – continuing to be the domain of the white middle class (see Jackson 1985; McCarthy et al. 1996). Confirming this broader distribution of soccer participants, the vast majority of RSC players (76 per cent) are drawn from Reynoldsville and its neighbouring, and equally affluent, northern suburbs. The remainder (24 per cent) are drawn from across the wider metropolitan area and beyond; many living over fifty miles from the club itself. Very few (4.4 per cent) of the RSC players resided in the depressed inner urban core, or the older eastern and western suburban zones, of the greater metropolitan area. Given the aforementioned racial breakdown of the metropolitan area, and of the northern suburbs in particular, it should come as no surprise that the RSC's playing personnel are almost exclusively European American, with a minuscule number of African Americans and Asian Americans scattered randomly throughout the teams.

All fifteen members of the Girls Under-17 squad lived in either Reynoldsville or one of the neighbouring northern suburbs, and all were of European American descent. With regard to school attendance, the players were divided almost equally between attendance at one of the exclusive private girls' schools and one of the highly regarded co-educational high schools, each of which offered suburban residents reassuring alternatives to the perceived perils of the city school system. Furthermore, the girls' parents worked in an equally narrow range of upper-level profession. They were doctors, lawyers, senior managers in numerous large companies and owners of small companies, and one was a commercial pilot. Here was the social, economic and racial homogeneity, over which soccer marketers salivated, and about which cultural commentators complained, and that we had expected to encounter, but never in such an exaggerated form. From the most preliminary of observations, it was evident that Reynoldsville's soccer culture represents the sporting version of the gated residential community; an artificial space and population protected from the perils and unease created by the proximity of social undesirables and economic subordinates, by exorbitant property values. Thus, in Reynoldsville and other elite suburbs, soccer is ascribed an exclusivity, or rarified symbolic value, through which the ever-status-conscious suburban middle class is able to nonchalantly 'distinguish itself from the less fortunate' (Ehrenreich 1989: 39). Youth soccer, heretofore 'noncommodifiable phenomena' has, in terms of Bourdieu's analysis, been discursively constructed as a highly exclusive asset in the field of cultural production, whose scarcity makes it a prized activity in the cultural marketplace and puts those with access to it in a position of cultural privilege.

Evidently, a child's very membership of a suburban soccer team signifies a great deal in terms of a family's class habitus, since the 'social value accruing from the pursuit of certain sports' is dependent on the 'value of the distinctive rarity they derive from their class distribution' (Bourdieu 1978: 835). Eloquently updating Bourdieu's understanding of the link between economic and cultural capital in the establishment and legitimation of class based distinctions and differences, Clarke noted:

> The new middle classes have constructed a system of equivalences between their economic function and their cultural formation. Symbolic manipulation underpins these equivalences, along with the focus on creativity (as the production of difference), and the promotion of lifestyle as the purpose of consumption. (1991: 68)

Since a group's habitus lies at the intersection of the economic and the cultural – from which is generated a set of stable dispositions that frames the structure and experience of every facet of a class-based lifestyle – for both players and parents alike active engagement with the suburban soccer community provides a forum for embodying and expressing the particular logic of consumerist practice associated with suburban middle-class culture. Hence, more than the simple act of 'playing the game', the entire *soccer field* has been incorporated into the complex universe of 'practices and consumptions' (Bourdieu 1990b) which structure and constitute the suburban cultural system.

Certainly the players in the Under-17 team were fully attuned to the nuances of converting economic capital to cultural capital, through an ever-evolving process of consumer stylisation of the self. While such familiarity was undoubtedly a product of socialisation into/through the wider culture of the new middle class (Lury 1996), the search for distinction through the aestheticisation of existence was an important part of the soccer field. The increasingly convoluted taste cultures of middle-class youth had evidently penetrated the soccer setting (there is even evidence to suggest that 'soccer style' has informed wider aesthetic trends), and merely responding to the fleeting ascendancy of particular fashion statements (be they Adidas, Nike, Umbro, or alternative 'other'; single coloured or multi-coloured; round-necked or v-necked; cotton or nylon; 'grunge', 'retro' or 'urban') demanded considerable financial outlay. However, of appreciably more concern was that individuals were attuned, and acted according, to the ever-changing codes of what was deemed aesthetically appropriate attire, both in terms of what one wore to and for practice sessions. Wearing an outdated T-shirt, sporting an unsuitable haircut, or having a bad hair day, would be immediately criticised for being an indication of lack of care of the 'self'.

It was perfectly acceptable for the girls to dress up and wear makeup for dinners on road trips, evening team meetings, or any other social activity, unless the chosen outfit, jewellery or cosmetic arrangement was deemed too ostentatious. Nobody escaped the omnipresent and normalising gaze of the player's taste culture, as the coach, parents, and even researchers were subject to open critique for their aesthetic 'flaws'. Conversely, demonstrations of good taste, like the personalised painting of a soccer ball, the wearing of idiosyncratic green and red soccer shoes, or showing up for practice in a particular car (many of the girls had their own cars) with the 'right' music on were received with warm and open admiration. What we witnessed here was, in essence, the adolescent version of the middle-class habitus. The parents of the players were equally aware of the importance of the aesthetic project[ing] of the self. This was particularly apparent in the stunning uniformity in terms of the cosmetic appearance, dress and choice of luxury vehicle displayed by parents at games, practices and meetings. Thus, although manifest in very different cultural products and expressions, by subtly embodying the cultural codes of the consumerist habitus, both players and parents used the soccer field as a context for further demonstrating their membership of an exclusive suburban elite.

One of the most telling, but frequently overlooked, expressions of privilege associated with suburban soccer culture revolves around the ability of players to possess the substantial amount of spare time demanded by participation. For example, the Girls Under-17 squad practised for 10 months during the year. Each week the team had two 90-minute squad practice sessions, as well as individual training sessions for goalkeepers and 'strikers' on two nights per week, plus compulsory small-sided games and skills sessions on Saturdays if there was no game on that day. Not including the nine weekend tournaments in which the team competed during the season (which for the Under-17s ran from March to early May), the team played at least one game per week, with three games usually being played over a two-week period. Such are the demands of this regime (which is by no means unique in American youth soccer) that players are regularly participating in games/training sessions on five days a week during the season, and four days a week during the off season.

That individual players are able to apportion considerable amounts of their time to soccer, speaks more than their evident commitment to the game: it also illustrates the extent to which their lives encompass an 'absence of necessity' (Bourdieu 1984, 1986) that is pointedly missing from the lives of children from less privileged populations. As Bourdieu (1986: 246) maintained: 'it can immediately be seen that the link between economic and cultural capital is established through the mediation of time needed for acquisition (of cultural capital)'. This simple economic logic is an everyday reality for the vast majority of adolescents in the US, much of whose time is taken up working at the local mall,

McDonald's, etc., as a necessary means of augmenting their own or their families' economic capital. The members of the Under-17 team certainly did not face such pressures to enter the labour force. Their parents' financial stability afforded them a wholly unfettered out-of-school time, without which they simply could not have been a member of the soccer team.

As with other trappings of their existence, the privilege of 'spare time' passed unrecognised by the girls, who viewed it simply as a taken-for-granted condition of being a teenager, rather than an expression of membership of a dominant class (Shilling 1993). This was ably illustrated by the girls' vehement reaction to the suggestion of one of their teammates that she was 'considering' applying for a part-time job. Incredulity abounded as she was reprimanded for potentially compromising her performance within more important academic, social and soccer settings. The thought that she was thinking of applying for a job because she needed the money did not even enter the realm of possibility. In a true Bourdieuian sense, it was evident that the girls existed in a state characterised by an almost complete 'absence of necessity'.

There is a widely held opinion that suburban youth soccer participants involved in highly competitive teams, and especially their parents, are motivated by the desire for an athletic scholarship which would offset the increasing costs of a university education. This is thought to be especially true for females, since the long overdue enforcement of Title IX of the Education Amendments Acts originally passed in 1972 (see Andrews et al. 1997) has resulted in an explosion in the number of women's collegiate soccer programs (Schrof 1995). However, our experience did not suggest there was a desire to convert physical capital (soccer ability) into economic capital (a university scholarship) and subsequently cultural capital (a university education). Rather, the parents of the Under-17 Girls team repeatedly proclaimed the importance of a formal education, and expressed with almost obsessive zeal their desire for their daughters to go to a 'good school'. While fully supportive of their daughters' involvement in soccer, their sole criteria for choosing an institution was its academic reputation. For many, a soccer program and the possibility of a scholarship, was viewed as a welcome but by no means essential accompaniment. For others, the mere thought of a soccer scholarship was frowned upon since the time and energy expended on the soccer field was viewed as detracting from academic pursuits, and would thus be a hindrance to personal growth. These sentiments clearly influenced the attitudes of the players, who were equally fervent that they should attend the right type of school (i.e. academic and exclusive), and were largely ambivalent as to their soccer futures.

Once again the experience of an 'absence of necessity' for these affluent suburban families allowed them not to be troubled by the same fiscal realities, that undoubtedly prompt many suburban families to encourage their children's participation in soccer. More than anything, this demonstrates the extent to which the elite suburban habitus imbues the population with a sense of the *rules of the game*: an internalised disposition toward the importance of education in the process of dominant class reproduction, wherein high economic capital is converted into exclusive cultural capital, which is used to further the acquisition of elevated levels of economic capital. Within America's *democratised* higher education system, the masses labour under the illusion that attending university is the important factor, whereas the social elite are attenuated to the fact that *which* university one attends is the primary consideration. It is this recognition – graphically expressed and mobilised within the suburban soccer field – that laughs in the face of America's pseudo-meritocracy, and allows the suburban elite to benefit from education's traditional function as 'one of the foundations of domination and of the legitimation of domination' (Bourdieu 1989: 13).

ENDNOTES ON THE SUBURBAN SOCCER FIELD

Far from being 'a huge joke, part of a competition to see who can come up with the silliest research project' (Gardner 1997: 11) – as one of our more fatuous critics characterised our earlier work in this area (Andrews et al. 1997) – it is our belief that the suburban soccer phenomenon warrants more expansive critical attention than was possible in this abbreviated discussion. After all, the suburban soccer field represents a transparent window into the workings and experiences of power and privilege within contemporary America. This chapter has merely reported on the most preliminary and general findings of our ethnographic investigation, and as such represents a statement on work in progress. Nevertheless, even at this early stage, we are under no illusion that soccer in an elite suburban setting has been enthusiastically incorporated into :

> The institutionalised strategies of distinction through which 'status groups' seek to make de facto differences permanent and quasi-natural, and therefore legitimate, by symbolically enhancing the effect of distinction associated with occupying a rare position in the social structure. (Bourdieu 1990a: 138)

From our observations, it is evident that soccer plays an important part in reproducing, in a way which subtly disguises their structural derivations, the patterns and experience of white suburban privilege. While, from a personal viewpoint, we would not wish openly to condemn the practices, experiences or attitudes of our research subjects, it is virtually impossible not to feel a significant degree of contempt for the nonchalant and self-righteously affluent suburban culture, of which their *soccer lives* are such a representative part. This is particularly true when one considers the social, racial and economic polarisation which has come to characterise the post-industrial American condition (Harrison 1994; Wilson 1996). This football is definitely not the people's game: *never was, never will be.*

18 The Japanese Dream: Soccer Culture towards the New Millennium

Haruo Nogawa and Hiroko Maeda

A British major, Archfield Douglas, and the soldiers under his command introduced the game of soccer to Japan in September 1873. They were visiting the
country to give training instructions to the Japanese Navy. In between the sessions, they played soccer; the watching Japanese assumed the game was a British
version of Kemari, an ancient Japanese ballgame (Japan Football Association
1996: 42–3). Soccer was mostly played in Yokohama and Kobe, areas where the
majority of foreigners lived. Like many other sports, soccer spread and developed
mainly via college students. Through the influence of the school systems, soccer
became popular among boys who became men who in 1917 represented the
country in the third Far Eastern Games staged in Tokyo, the first international
championship to take place in Japan (JFA 1996: 35). By way of encouragement
the English Football Association in 1919 sent a silver FA Cup trophy to Japan
assuming that the Japanese Football Association (JFA) had already been established. It was not in fact organised until 1921 and affiliated to the Japanese
Amateur Sports Association in 1921 then affiliated to FIFA in 1929.

THE BERLIN TO MEXICO OLYMPICS: 1936 TO 1968

The Japanese national team entered its first Olympic Games in 1936 and enjoyed
a miraculous victory over Sweden in one of the major upsets at the Berlin
Olympiad. After World War Two, the JFA re-affiliated to FIFA in 1950. A year
later Japan participated in the first Asian Games and won third place in New
Delhi, after which the JFA became affiliated to the Asian Football Congress
(AFC) in 1954. Japan competed in the 1958 Melbourne Olympic Games but did
not win a single game. Japanese soccer was left far behind the rest of the world.
The JFA realised that a long-term development plan and more intensive international exposure would be needed. To prepare the national team for the Tokyo
Olympics, the JFA sought a highly qualified foreign coach to develop the international side. The JFA chose the German coach Dettmar Cramer, as a special advi-
sor for the national team in the 1960s and early 1970s. This was a turning point
for the modernisation of Japanese soccer. A decade of his preparation paid off at
two successive Olympic Games. Japan shocked Argentina, with a 3–2 win in the

1964 Tokyo games, and then captured the bronze medal at the 1968 Mexico Olympics. It was the first major international success not only for Japanese soccer but also Asian soccer as well. Nevertheless, Japan failed to participate at another Olympics until 1996. The biggest dream of Japanese soccer, competing at the World Cup finals, only materialised in 1998.

FROM JSL TO J-LEAGUE: 1960s TO 1992

Following the Tokyo Olympics, the Japan Soccer League (JSL) was inaugurated with eight corporate teams in 1965. Major industries such as Mitsubishi, Hitachi and Furukawa fielded their varsity teams in the new league. Prior to the JSL, college athletic teams had been the powerhouse of Japanese sport. This was a turning point as a number of Japanese corporate giants began to involve themselves with sport organisations and to sponsor athletic teams to both back sport and to upgrade their company's public image. The era of the so-called 'corporate amateur' started to emerge. A home-and-away league format was adapted for this new league. Up until the JSL was organised, a single knock-out tournament had been conventional in most sports; no round robin league format had existed except in professional baseball.

The JSL was the first nationwide amateur sport league. Other sports such as volleyball, basketball and ice hockey followed JSL's model as soon as they saw its instant success. The JSL attracted quite a few spectators at each game for the first several years and the league was expanded from 8 to 10 teams in 1973, and to 12 teams in 1985. The second division league was added in 1972. However, spectator attendances declined and never recovered until the league was renovated as a professional league, becoming the so-called J-League in 1993.

Foreign players were allowed to play in the JSL from 1967 onwards, but had to be amateurs. A Brazilian Japanese, Nelson Yoshimura, was the first foreign player to join the Yanmer FC and became naturalised later on. His play-making abilities and ball control skills convinced other JSL clubs that recruiting Brazilian talent would upgrade their team performance. All teams in the JSL were corporate sponsored so that players had to become employees of a given company. Transferring between teams and from one company to another was prohibited unless the company terminated the team. This prohibition seemed to be rooted in the deeper unwritten code that employees had to be loyal to one company throughout their life. Switching jobs was strongly discouraged as it was seen as disloyal conduct.

That said, some Japanese players changed clubs and continents. FC Cologne of West Germany bought Yasuhiko Okudera from Furukawa FC in 1977. Okudera was transferred to FC Cologne and became the first Japanese professional player in European soccer. A few other players followed Okudera and played in the *Bundesliga*; Bun-Kon Cha of Korea became a star striker for Eintracht Frankfurt FC. This was a turning point in Asian soccer history, Asian players realised they were able to make it to the European professional league. The Japanese Football Association finally changed its regulations on the amateur code and introduced professionalism in 1985. Two players registered as full time professionals while one hundred others registered as 'non-amateurs'.

Of the original eight teams of the JSL five were from heavy industry and all were corporate giants: Mitsubishi Heavy Industry, Furukawa Heavy Industry, Hitachi Heavy Industry, Toyo Industry (now Mazda), Yanmer Heavy Industry, Toyota Textile, Yahata Iron Manufacture (now New Japan Iron Manufacture) and Nagoya Sogo Bank. In 1971, the Yomiuri club began to build a European-type club. Yomiuri is one of the major newspaper companies and is the owner of Yomiuri Giants, the professional baseball team. Yomiuri provided a large budget to cover team costs including facilities, equipment, coaches' salaries, travelling expenses, league registration fees and players' salaries. The club consisted of a top team, second team, youth team, and junior team; while other teams had to rely on players from college and high school teams Yomiuri was able to develop talented players from their 'farm system'. The Yomiuri club hired well-known professional coaches from overseas and recruited young semi-professional foreign players from Brazil. The occupations of the players varied, none of them was a company employee, and this fact was instrumental in the club's insistence upon forming a professional league upon entering the JSL. This movement had benefits and drawbacks for the establishment of the professional league. Yomiuri Club was promoted to the first division in 1978 and has been one of the major forces in Japanese soccer since then. Three other club teams followed Yomiuri's approach during the 1980s.

In 1989, facing a steady decline in attendance and continuous failure at international competitions, the JSL invited four major advertising companies to organise a special committee whose tasks were to envision the future of Japanese soccer and to finalise a specific plan for a new professional league, which was disclosed to the mass media in February, 1991. The 1991–2 season was the final one for the JSL. The last round of six games was played on 29 March, 1992; approximately 43,000 fans watched these games. During 27 seasons of the JSL, 2,452 games were played with a total of 9.7 million fans in attendance (Ohsumi 1996: 236–44).

WORLD CUP FEVER: 1993 TO THE PRESENT DAY

After its tremendous success at the Mexico Olympics, Japanese soccer went downhill and struggled in international competitions such as the World Cup and Olympic qualification matches. After an absence of twenty-eight years, a young Japanese team qualified for the 1994 Atlanta Olympic Games and enjoyed another miraculous 1–0 victory over the mighty Brazil. It was Japan's second victory against Brazil and the biggest upset in the tournament. Although, the Japanese lost to Nigeria (the eventual champions), they enjoyed a victory over Hungary. Japan completed their first round, winning two games and losing one. However, due to an inferior goal difference, Japan failed to advance to the quarter-final.

With the phenomenal J-league success in 1993, Japan had high hopes for the national team in the USA World Cup. Under the first foreign team manager, Hans Offt of the Netherlands, the Japanese team went through the first preliminary round and advanced to the final qualification round in Dohha, Qatar. It was a league format tournament; the first two teams out of six would qualify. Japan was riding high and led by one goal against Iraq in the final minute of the final match. However, Iraq scored an equaliser from a free kick after 92 minutes and shattered the Japanese dream. This game was broadcast live to Japan after midnight, with an audience rating of 49 per cent! It was a nightmare. The nation was shocked at what was for Japan the most devastating and humiliating defeat since the Second World War. Only an inferior goal difference kept Japan from qualifying. Instead, the Republic of Korea, Japan's arch rival, progressed to the finals.

Four years later, Japan won the preliminary round again and advanced to the final round. Japan had to beat the Republic of Korea, but they struggled and failed to take first place in their group. Japan was somewhat fortunate to advance to a play-off against Iran for the third representative country from the Asian region. The play-off was staged in Johorbale, Malaysia. The stadium had a capacity of 20,000 seats. Nearly 15,000 Japanese residents flew to Malaysia and 4,500 Japanese living in Singapore and southeast Asian countries travelled to support the national team. The game was drawn over 90 minutes and went into extra time, when the Japanese substitute, Okano, scored from close range in the final moments. A capacity crowd of 20,000 spectators, 97 per cent of whom were Japanese, became jubilant and started a fiesta which lasted throughout the night. The television audience rating in Japan for this game reached nearly 48 per cent at midnight. The whole nation were elated by this victory. The socio-economic impact of the World Cup, even the preliminary rounds, has been very significant.

WOMEN'S SOCCER IN JAPAN

Soccer in Japan has long been considered to be a male sport. This has led to the idea that soccer is not suitable for females. Thus, there has been very little opportunity for women to learn how to play the game in the school system. In Japan, the extent to which sport prevails and becomes competitive, depends a great deal on the school system, in particular, extracurricular activities for secondary school children. Soccer is one of the most popular extracurricular sport activities, but it is still mainly male dominated.

The first female team was formed in a girls' secondary school in 1966 (*The Asahi Journal*, 1996). The first league for women began in the Kansai region, which included the cities of Osaka and Kobe, in 1975. In the same year, the

Kanto women's soccer league was established in the Tokyo metropolitan area. The first national championship was decided between the winners of the two leagues at the end of the 1975 season. The women's soccer league spread out in other regions and eventually from 1979 the winners of nine regional leagues earned the right to participate in the national championship.

Female players were allowed to register with the JFA in 1979. Initially there were only 52 teams and 919 female players, by 1997 there were 1,179 teams and 23,764 players (Japan Football Association 1997). A significant change took place when the first women's national championship was organised in 1980. Until 1980, women played an eight-a-side game rather than a full eleven-a-side game. Since 1980, the number of teams and players has dramatically increased and women's soccer has gained popularity. The Japanese women's team took part in its first international competition in 1981. In contrast to the men's national team, the women's team has significantly improved its status and has been a runner-up twice in consecutive Asian Games in 1990 and 1994 behind the Chinese. Japan has qualified for the first two Women's World Championships. Moreover, the women's team qualified for the Atlanta Olympics but failed to advance to the quarter finals.

Some well-known corporations began to support women's soccer financially and eventually the Japan Ladies' Soccer League was started in 1989. The majority of the players in the L-League while so-called 'corporate amateurs' were de facto soccer professionals. A number of decent elite foreign players have joined this league. No other countries have been able to provide this kind of financial opportunities to elite female players. With an increase of decent foreign players, the quality of the league has risen dramatically. However, the Japan Ladies' Soccer League has not been accepted as a spectator sport. The average attendance at league games is below one thousand and those paying to enter would lower this figure. As long as the Japanese economy is in a slump, sponsoring companies will not make the financial sacrifice of carrying their teams for the sake of women's soccer development. Thus, the L-League may face either restructuring or demotion to a regional league.

In 1996, a total of 6,955 male high school teams were registered; but only 21 female high school teams. At schools where there are male teams, girls tend to be given the so-called 'assistant team managers' role. The main duties of the assistant manager in athletic teams (regardless of sport) are geared towards gender stereotypes such as preparing drinks for the players, doing laundry, looking after the equipment and keeping the score .

MARKETING STRATEGIES AND THE J-LEAGUE

Facing the steady decline in attendance and continuous failure at international competitions, the JSL invited four major advertising companies to organise a committee to plan a new professional league in 1989. In order to come up with a model for the new league, the committee carefully scrutinised the structures and marketing strategies of other professional leagues such as the Japan Professional Baseball Leagues, National Basketball Association (NBA), National Football League (NFL), and German Soccer League (Mamiya 1995: 178).

The following principles for the J-League were disclosed on 1 November 1991:

(1) Every participating team was required to form a company independent from a parent company;
(2) A franchise system, a so-called Hometown system, was to be established,
(3) Every participating team was required to have a stadium with a capacity of 15,000 or more;
(4) Every participating team had to organise a youth team (Under-18), junior team (Under-15) in addition to a varsity team and junior varsity team;
(5) Every participating team had to hire qualified coaches with specific coaching licenses;
(6) Every participating team had to share the financial cost of establishing the league, advertising costs, and the operational costs of the league administration office; and
(7) The league was to have the rights to league matches, sponsorship money, TV broadcasting and merchandising. (Mamaiya 1995: 178–9)

The opening games were played before near capacity crowds on 15 May 1993. The TV audience was recorded at 32.4 per cent. The league expected only two million spectators for the first year; however, a total of 4,118,837 paying spectators attended. Average match attendance in 1993 was 17,976. It was a phenomenal success. The following year was even better. The average attendance in 1994 rose to 19,598 which alarmed the professional baseball league. Nevertheless, the average attendance dramatically declined from 17,976 in 1994 to 10,131 in 1997, as the league expanded from ten to 17 teams. One of the most distinctive features in the Japanese soccer scene is the large proportion of female spectators since the J-League started. Gross sales of J-League paraphernalia such as mascots and badges exceeded 130,000 million yen (US$100,000 million) in the 1993 season alone (Mamiya 1996). Research conducted to determine the market scale of various spectator sports reported that the estimated market value (economic impact and marketability) of the J-League to be 305,600 million yen (US$2, 350 million), two-thirds of the value of the professional baseball league (Mamiya 1997).

The secrets of the J-League success from a marketing perspective were that the J-League had very positive and strong cooperation with the mass media (Mamiya 1995). The Japanese had also become rather bored with pro baseball and Sumo wrestling in the late 1980s and were looking for something fresh and exciting. The emergence of the J-League stimulated public interests not only in soccer but spectator sports in general. It helped to revitalise the value of the sport market. Another important factor was the J-League's pursuit of the younger generations as the main consumers, particularly younger females. Young females tend to be front-runners of fashions and fads and are very conspicuous consumers. Thus, the marketing strategy was to cultivate the interests of young female spectators and make a new and more fashionable image for the league.

Part of the popularity of the J-League was that soccer matches became festivals for young spectators. The slogan 'Be the Twelfth Player in the Stadium' encouraged spectators to become actively involved with the game and change their spectating behavior from the traditional passive style to a much more pro-active European style (Nogawa and Maeda 1997). The stadium became a live theater rather than merely the venue for a sports game as spectators learned a new way to participate in a sports spectacle (Sugimoto 1997). Regardless of gender, enthusiastic fans would display team colours or masquerade in carnival style (e.g., paint faces, wear thematic costumes); cheer and boo; wave banners and display signs in the stadiums; and travel to other cities to follow their home team. Female spectators use 'patriarchal language' at these matches much more freely than socially permitted in their daily settings. The majority of female spectators never exceeded the bounds of carnival behaviour, female spectators whilst vocal and active remained in the stands and did not fight or invade the field (Nogawa and Maeda 1997).

TOWARDS 2002: RELATIONS WITH THE REPUBLIC OF KOREA

The executive committee of FIFA in Zurich, Switzerland, decided the site of the 2002 World Cup on 31 May 1996. There were only two candidates, Japan and the Republic of Korea. Unexpectedly but rather fortunately, FIFA ruled that the tournament was to be held jointly by the two nations. This was the first occasion in which two countries would host the tournament. Regardless of the soccer world, quite a few Japanese people were overwhelmed by this unbelievable decision and wondered if and how these two countries would ever be able to co-operate to stage this huge event. They have never previously conducted any joint project be it in sport or other social domains.

In fact strong animosity has existed since 1910 between the two nations, particularly from the Korean side. The reason for this hatred stems from Japan's invasion and annexation of Korea that same year. The Japanese forced Koreans to speak Japanese, and made the use of Japanese surnames mandatory (Oka 1991). Approximately two million Koreans were forced to migrate to Japan between 1910 and 1945. These involuntary migrants worked in the mines and mills as virtual slave labourers (Lee and De Vos, 1984). While the majority of Koreans returned to their homeland after the Second World War, nearly 600,000 remained because of the unstable economic conditions in Korea (Fukuoka 1993). However, the Koreans found themselves stateless; the Japanese government established alien registration and immigration laws which reclassified Koreans as 'alien residents' in 1947 and stripped them of most of their previous rights in 1952 (Nakai 1989; Min 1992).

Alien residents were permitted no citizenship, no voting rights, and no protection against occupational and educational discrimination for the next thirty years (Kan and Kim 1989). The alien registration and immigration laws were designed to exclude the Koreans and Chinese from Japan, yet these same people had been brought to Japan for forced labour during the colonial era (Kan and Kim 1989; Fukuoka 1993; Lee and De Vos 1984). The Japanese government employed a harsh policy of forced assimilation against minority groups (Min 1992). The assimilation policy forced members of minority groups to lose their language and ethnic identity. The alien status of Koreans, the largest ethnic minority group, did not stop with first-generation immigrants. It has included their Japanese-born children and grandchildren, the second and third generations. Unlike the US government, the Japanese government has not granted automatic citizenship to Japanese born children of alien residents.

For over four decades the government of Japan not only denied the accreditation of Korean ethnic schools, but forced many of them to close down in 1949 (Kan and Kim 1989). As we write, there are a total of 159 Korean schools in Japan, 155 of which have no financial support or accreditation from the Japanese government (Fukuoka 1993). The area of athletics is no exception. Students of non-Japanese high schools until 1993 were totally excluded from interscholastic athletics. Japanese-born Koreans were able to take part in all official athletic tournaments with one condition: the student must have attended a Japanese high school. This institutionalised inequality on the basis of citizenship ceased in 1981. Nevertheless, discrimination on the basis of school affiliation still endured against Japanese-born Koreans in ethnic schools for the next thirteen years. This institutionalised exclusion has become a controversial social issue since the 1970s and the Ministry of Education, Science, Sport and Culture was finally forced to modify its policy slightly at the beginning of the 1994 academic year (Nogawa 1994).

In November of 1993, the Japan High School Sports Association (JHSSA), the governing body of inter-scholastic athletics, decided from 1994 onward to grant students of non-Japanese institutions and non-accredited schools permission to take part in the All-Japan Inter-High School Athletic Meeting, one of the three biggest athletic events for high school students (*The Yomiuri*: 29 July 1994). This was the first major breakthrough for Korean schools within the mainstream culture, although their membership status with the JHSSA is still withheld (*The Yomiuri*: 30 July 1994). Their participation in two other major tournaments (the National Sports Festival and the All-Japan High School Championships) has been allowed recently. Despite their isolation Korean ethnic secondary schools became soccer powerhouses during the 1970s and 1980s. Their first appearance in high school tournaments proved that they are one of the top national teams. Nevertheless, the membership status of Korean schools has not yet been finalised. If the membership status of Korean schools remains the same as now – as special members – this will lead to another inequality. Without a full-membership status, Korean schools have no voting right, no right to become board members, and no way to obtain a powerful position in sports organisations. Moreover, institutionalised inequality against Japanese-born Koreans has been perpetuated beyond high school athletics (Nogawa 1994).

THE BEHAVIOUR OF SOCCER SPECTATORS

Collective demonstrative behaviour appears to be almost unique to sport crowds in Japan compared with other types of leisure crowds. Sport spectating as a form of leisure behaviour did not attract large numbers of Japanese until the late 1960s. Like Europe and North America, this pattern was influenced by shorter working hours, the growth in urban settings, an increased standard of living, the availability of public and private transport, and the increasing attention given by the mass media to sport events.

Enthusiastic and committed soccer supporters are generally young and new to the game; they attend matches at the amateur, professional, and international levels. Soccer spectators have learned how to harass referees and opposing players from watching European and South American matches on TV. These supporters pay both to consume sport and have an emotional investment in the event. Since 1995, this normative behaviour has occasionally been the impetus for soccer spectators to invade the field and attack the referee or opposing team. Such incidents never happened before in the twenty-seven year history of the Japanese Soccer League. Nor has it happened in professional baseball although fans occasionally throw small objects on to the field. Lately, soccer disorder has escalated to the physical harassment of visiting teams and supporters in and outside the stadium (see below).

The worst occasion occurred when Japan played against the United Arab Emirates (UAE) on 26 October 1997. 'The road to France' was a long and winding one for both the national team and Japanese people. After the first game against Uzbekistan, Japan struggled in four consecutive games including the heartbreaking defeat by Korea. The frustration of Japanese fans and the mass media was at a peak when Japan hosted the UAE. Approximately 60,000 Japanese fans attended this crucial game. A newly naturalized Brasilian striker, Lopes Wagner, scored a fine goal early in the first half but the UAE equalised. Japan desperately attacked the UAE goal, but failed to score a winner. The referee played no injury time and blew the whistle. Most spectators as well as the players could not believe their ears and started berating the referee. The draw left Japan with little hope of qualification. A thousand angered fans rioted for more than one hour. At first, they verbally harassed the officials, and then the players and team manager. The team bus and players' cars were attacked as fans threw cans, bottles, small objects, raw eggs, and even chairs at the players and their cars.

26 April 1995 Ohmiya, Saitama

After a match between the Urawa Reds and the Shimizu S-Pulse, angered Reds supporters invaded the pitch and forced the Brazilian goalkeeper of S-Pulse to kneel down and apologise to them.

26 April 1995 Hiratsuka, Kanagawa

Following a league game, Hiratsuka supporters who felt neglected by their team players invaded the pitch and demanded that the players pay respect to the supporters.

12 July 1995 Kashima, Ibaragi

Kashima Antlers supporters upset about the transfer of their Brazilian player remained at the stadium and demanded an explanation from team officials. Some supporters threw fireworks at the team officials.

23 September 1995 Urawa, Saitama

One of the Reds' star players engaged in a fist fight with a Reds supporter after the game. The player injured the supporter, but not too seriously. Subsequently, the player was suspended from the game for three months.

27 September 1995 Kobe, Hyogo

A group of Gamba Osaka fans frustrated about their team's poor performances stopped the team bus after a game. The team captain had to come out of the bus to apologise for the team.

30 September 1995 Hiratsuka, Kanagawa

Visiting Antlers supporters dissatisfied with some controversial decisions during the game invaded the pitch and caused physical damage to the stadium. The game was interrupted for four minutes.

4 October 1995 Kashiwa, Chiba

A game between the Kashiwa Reysol and the Gamba Osaka: losing by several goals, frustrated Gamba supporters angry about the referee's decisions threw bottles on the pitch and started fights with Reysol supporters in the stand. Fighting between the two supporter groups continued outside the stadium.

4 October 1995 Todoroki, Kanagawa

Visiting Yokohama Marinos supporters invaded the pitch angry over the standard of refereeing. Several hundred remained on the pitch after the match protesting.

7 May 1997 Ohmiya, Saitama

After four consecutive home defeats, the Reds supporters threw coins and raw eggs at their players after the game.

10 May 1997 Nagoya, Aichi

Fights broke out between the Urawa Reds and Nagoya Grampus supporters in the stadium.

28 May 1997 Todoroki, Kanagawa

Following poor performances by Verdi, the home team, fireworks and bottles were thrown from the stand by Verdi supporters.

26 October 1997 National Stadium, Tokyo

Following Japan's draw against the United Arab Emirates in a World Cup qualifying game, a thousand angered Japanese fans rioted for more than one hour. They stopped the team bus and insulted the players and manager. Some fans threw bottles, raw eggs, cans, and chairs at the team bus and cars of officials.

13 February 1998 Kashiwa, Ibaragi

Following Kashima Antlers' defeat to Jubilo Iwata in the J-League championship play-off, more than 40 Antlers supporters invaded the pitch and chased the Jubilo players. They then damaged tables and advertising boards set up for the award ceremony.

Some obstructed the street to prevent the team bus from coming out of the stadium. Police had to come to clear the fans but did not make any arrests. Although nobody was injured, this was probably the most serious crowd disturbance in Japanese sporting history. But as seen above the game provokes a wide variety of disorders, some of which have a unique Japanese element.

The game of soccer is now established in Japan albeit in an ersatz style to some Western eyes and its popularity is being sustained if attendances are the indicator. The Japanese dream of world recognition in sport is being recognised at a time of economic distress and the hosting of the next World Cup will allow the world to see the relatively unknown Japanese culture at first hand. Whether this will be done on an equal level with the co-hosting Koreans will be of interest and what multi-nationals will sponsor the occasion in a time of recession are details that observers will watch carefully.

References

Abela, A. M. (1991). *Transmitting Values in European Malta. A Study in the Contemporary Values of Modern Society*. Valletta: Jesuit Publications.

Abela, A. M. (1992). *Changing Youth Culture in Malta*. Valletta: Jesuit Publications.

Adler, P. A., and P. Adler (1987). *Membership Roles in Field Research*. Newbury Park, CA: Sage.

Alabarces, P. (1998). 'Fútbol y televisión en la Argentina: del juego al género dramatico', in *Contratexto*, No. 12. Lima: Universidad de Lima.

Alabarces, P., and M. Rodríguez (1996). *Cuestión de pelotas: Fútbol, deporte, sociedad, cultura*. Buenos Aires: Atuel.

Alabarces, P., and M. Rodríguez (1998). 'Football and fatherland: the crisis of national representation in Argentine football', in *Culture, Sport, Society: an interdisciplinary journal*. London: Frank Cass (forthcoming).

Ambjörnsson, R. (1988). *Den skötsamma arbetaren: idéer och ideal i ett norrlännskt sågverkssamhälle 1880–1930*. Stockholm: Carlssons förlag.

Anderson, B. (1983). *Imagined Communities: Reflections on the Origins and Spread of Nationalism*. London: Verso.

Anderson, J., and I. Shuttleworth (1998). 'Sectarian demography, territoriality and policy in Northern Ireland', in *Political Geography*, 21 (2), forthcoming.

Andrews, D. L., R. Pitter; D. Zwick, and D. Ambrose (1997). 'Soccer's Racial Frontier: Sport and the Segregated Suburbanization of Contemporary America', in G. Armstrong and R. Giulianotti (eds), *Entering the Field: Studies in World Football* (part of series on *Explorations in Anthropology*) (261–81). Oxford: Berg.

Archer, R., and A. Bouillon (1982). *The South African Game: Sport and Racism*. London: Zed Press.

Archetti, E., and A. Romero (1994). 'Death and Violence in Argentinian Football', in R. Giulianotti, N. Bonney and M. Hepworth (eds) (1994).

Archetti, E. (1985). *Fútbol y ethos*. Buenos Aires: FLACSO.

Archetti, E. (1992). 'Calcio: un rituale di violenza?', in P. Lanfranchi (ed), *Il calcio e il suo pubblico*. Naples: Edizione Scentifiche Italiane.

Archetti, E. (1994). 'Argentina and the World Cup: In Search of National Identity', in J. Sugden and A. Tomlinson (eds) (1994).

Archetti, E. (1995). 'Estilo y virtudes masculinas en *El Grafico*: la creación del imaginario del fútbol Argentino', in *Desarrollo Económico. Revista de Ceincias Sociales*, No. 139, Vol 35, October–December. Buenos Aires: IDES.

Archetti, E. (1996). 'The *Potrero* and the *Pibe*: Territory and Belonging in the Mythical Account of Argentinian Football', mimeo. Dept. of Anthropology, University of Oslo.

Archetti, E. (1997a). '"And Give Joy to my Heart": Ideology and Emotions in the Argentine Cult of Maradona', in G. Armstrong and R. Giulianotti (eds) (1997).

Archetti, E. (1997b). 'The Moralities of Argentinian Football', in D. Howell (ed), *The Ethnography of Morality*. London: Routledge.

Archetti, E. (1998a). *'Masculinities: Football, Polo and the Tango in Argentina*. Oxford: Berg.

Archetti, E. (1998b). 'Opprinnelser og tradisjoner: Forestillinger om fotball', in P. Sanberg (ed) *Vinnerglede Gjennom so à*. Gjøvik: Norsk Tipping As.

Armstrong, G. (1998). *Football Hooligans: Knowing the Score*, Oxford: Berg.

Armstrong, G., and R. Giulianotti (eds) (1997). *Entering the Field: New Perspectives on World Football*. Oxford: Berg.

Asahi Journal (1996). 'Kicking the ball refreshes me'. Vol 2232.

Augustin, J.-P. (1990). 'La percée du football en terre de rugby', in *Vingtième siècle*, April–June. 97–109.

Avizur, M. (1978). 'The Village of Taibeh: Transformations and Change Process', in *Society and Welfare*, (1). Jerusalem: Department of Work and Welfare.

Badenhorst, C. (1992). 'Mines, Missionaries and Sport in Black Johannesburg 1920–1950'. Unpublished PhD thesis, Queen's University, Kingston, Ontario.

Bairner, A. (1994). 'Sweden and the World Cup: Soccer and Swedishness', in J. Sugden and A. Tomlinson (eds) (1994). 195–217.

Bairner, A. (1996). 'Sportive Nationalism and Nationalist Politics: a Comparative Analysis of Scotland, the Republic of Ireland and Sweden', *Journal of Sport and Social Issues*, 20 (3), August. 314–34.

Bairner, A. (1997). ' "Up to their knees"? Football, Sectarianism, Masculinity and Protestant Working-Class Identity', in P. Shirlow and M. McGovern (eds), *Who Are 'The People'? Unionism, Protestantism and Loyalism in Northern Ireland*. 95–113. London: Pluto Press.

Bairner, A., and J. Sugden (1986). 'Observe the Sons of Ulster: Football and Politics in Northern Ireland', in A. Tomlinson and G. Whannel (eds), *Off the Ball. The Football World Cup*. 146–57. London: Pluto Press.

Bajtin, M. (1987). *La cultura popular en la Edad Media y en el Renacimiento*. Madrid: Alianza.

Baker, D. G. (1983). *Race, Ethnicity and Power: A Comparative Study*. London: Routledge.

Bahktin, M. (1968). *Rabelais and his World*. Cambridge, MA: MIT Press.

Baldacchino, C. (1989). 'The Golden Age of Maltese Football', in *Goals, Cups and Tears 1886–1919*, Vol 1.

Baldacchino, C. (1990). 'The Great Amateur Era', in *Goals, Cups and Tears 1918–1934*, Vol 2.

Baldacchino, C. (1991). 'Glory and Upheaval', in *Goals, Cups and Tears 1934–1944*, Vol 3.

Baldacchino, C. (1993). 'The Post-War Period', in *Goals, Cups and Tears 1944–1956*, Vol 4.

Baldacchino, C. (1994). 'The Coming of Age in Maltese Football', in *Goals, Cups and Tears 1957–68*, Vol 5.

Baldacchino, C. (1997). 'The Last Days of the Empire Stadium', in *Goals, Cups and Tears 1968–1978*, Vol 6.

Bale, J. (1993). *Sport, Space and the City*. London: Routledge.

Barcilon, R., and S. Breuil (1997). *Sport et télévision 1991–1996. Bilan de six années de régulation*. Paris: CSA (Les Etudes du CSA).

Barker, C. (1997). *Global Television. An Introduction*. Oxford: Blackwell.

Battacchi, M. (1988). 'Fino a che punto i tifosi violenti sono violenti e fino a che punto sono tifosi?', in A. Salvini, *Il tifo aggressivo*. Florence: Giunti.

Baumgarten, G. C. J. H.; D. Pesch; F. J. Pesch et al. (1949). *VUVSI/ISNIS 1914–1919*. Kolff.

Bausinger, H. (1990) (1st German edn 1961). *Folk Culture in a World of Technology*. Trans Elke Dettmer. Bloomington and Indianapolis: Indiana University Press.

Bayeux, P. (1996). *Le sport et les collectivités territoriales*. Paris: PUF (Que sais-je? 3198).

Beaud, S., and G. Noiriel (1990). 'L'immigration dans le football', in *Vingtième siècle*, April–June. 83–96.

Beck, P. (1982). 'England v Germany, 1938', in *History Today*, June.

Beck, U.; A. Giddens; and S. Lash (1994). *Reflective Modernisation: Politics, Tradition and Aesthetics in the Modern Social Order*. Cambridge: Polity Press.

Becker, P. (1982). 'Haut'se, Haut'se in'ne Schnauze – Das Fußballstadium als Ort der Reproduktion sozialer Strukturen', in G. A. Pilz (ed), *Sport und Körperliche Gewalt*. 72–84. Reinbek: Rowohlt Verlag.

Bell, D. (1990). *Acts of Union: Youth Culture and Sectarianism in Northern Ireland.* London: Macmillan.

Bengtsson, E. (1975). *Heja röda vita laget.* Uddevalla: Författarförlaget.

Berger, P., and T. Luckmann (1985). *The Social Construction of Reality.* Harmondsworth: Penguin.

Berretty, W. (1934). *40 jaar voetbal in Nederlandsch-Indië 1894–1934.* Soekaboemi: Berretty.

Beshara, A. (1993). 'The Crisis of the Arab Leadership – Where is the Next Generation?', in *Notebook for Critique and Theory.* Tel Aviv: Israel.

Beshara, A. (1997). 'Put the Points on the Ies', in *Fasl Elmakal.* Nazareth: Israel.

Billing, P.; P. Peterson; and M. Stigendal (1994). 'Malmö FF mellan folkrörelse och proffesionalism', in *Arkiv*, No. 61–2. Lunds: Studentlitteratur.

Blouet, B. (1993). *The Story of Malta.* Valletta: Progress Press.

Bonello, G. (ed) (1996). *Marsa Sports Club.* Marsa: Marsa Sports Club Publications.

Bonnot, D.; R. Denis; and C. Capitaine (1997). 'Qui a peur du numérique?', in *L'Équipe*, 27 February. 9.

Bora, T., and N. Erdogan (1993). 'Dur Tarih, Vur Türkiye!' (History Stop, Turkey, Strike!), in R. Horak, W. Reiter and T. Bora (eds), *Futbol ve Kültürü.* Istanbul: Iletisim Publications.

Boratav, K. (1991). *80 'lerde Turkiye 'de Sosyal Siniflar ve Bolusum* (Social Classes and Repatriation in Turkey during the 1980s). Istanbul: Gercek Publishing.

Bouchard, J.-P., and A. Constant (1996). *Un Siècle de football.* Paris: Calmann-Lévy.

Bourdieu, P. (1978). 'Sport and Social Class', in *Social Science Information*, 17 (6). 819–40.

Bourdieu, P. (1984). *Distinction: A Social Critique of the Judgement of Taste.* Cambridge MA: Harvard University Press.

Bourdieu, P. (1986a). *Kultursociologiska texter.* Stockholm: Förlaget Salamander.

Bourdieu, P. (1986b). 'The Forms of Capital', in J. G. Richardson (ed), *Handbook of Theory and Research for the Sociology of Education.* 241–58. Westport: Greenwood Press.

Bourdieu, P. (1988). 'Program for a Sociology of Sport', in *Sociology of Sport Journal*, 5 (2). 153–61.

Bourdieu, P. (1989). 'Social Space and Symbolic Power', in *Sociological Theory*, 7 (1). 14–25.

Bourdieu, P. (1990a). *The Logic of Practice.* Cambridge: Polity Press.

Bourdieu, P. (1990b). 'Programme for a Sociology of Sport', in *In Other Words: Essays toward a Reflexive Sociology.* 156–67. Stanford: Stanford University Press.

Bourdieu, P. (1991a). 'Sport and Social Class', in C. Mukerji and M. Schudson (eds), *Rethinking Popular Culture.* Oxford: University of California Press.

Bourdieu, P. (1991b). *Kultur och kritik.* Gothenburg: Daidalos.

Bourdieu, P. (1993). *The Field of Cultural Production.* New York: Columbia University Press.

Bourg, J.-F. (1986). *Football Business.* Paris: Olivier Orban.

Bourg, J.-F. (1991). 'Aspects économiques des relations entre le sport et la télévision', *Médiaspouvoirs*, July–September.

Bradford, E. (1972). *The Shield and the Sword.* London: Fontana.

Brake, M. (1980). *The Sociology of Youth Culture and Youth Subcultures.* London: Routledge & Kegan Paul.

Brake, M. (1989). *Comparative Youth Culture.* London: Routledge & Kegan Paul.

Broady, D. (1990). *Sociologi och Epistemologi. Om Pierre Bourdieus författarskap och den historiska epistemologien.* Stockholm: HLS Förlag.

Brohm, J.-M. (1982 [1976]). *Sociología política del deporte.* México: FCE.

Bromberger, C. (1993a). 'Fireworks and the Ass', in S. Redhead (ed) (1993).

Bromberger, C.; A. Hayot; and J.-M. Mariottini (1993b). ' "Allez l'OM, forza Juve": The Passion for Football in Marseille and Turin', in S. Redhead (ed) (1993).

Broussard, P. (1990). *Génération supporter, enquête sur les ultras du football*. Paris: Laffont.

Brubaker, R. (1996). *Nationalism Reframed: Nationhood and the National Question in the New Europe*. Cambridge: Cambridge University Press.

Bruner, E. M. (1974). 'The Expression of Ethnicity in Indonesia', in A. Cohen (ed), *Urban Ethnicity*. London: Tavistock.

Bureau, J. (ed) (1986). 'L'amour foot. Une passion planétaire', in *Autrement*, 80 (May).

Caillois, R. (1958). *Les jeux et les hommes*. Paris: Gallimard.

Cakir, R. (1994). *Ne Seriat Ne Demokrasi: refah partisi 'ni anlamak* (Neither Shariat nor Democracy: Understanding the Prosperity Party). Istanbul: Metis Publications.

Caldas, W. (1990). *O Pontapé Inicial; Memória do Futebol Brasileiro (1894–1933)*. São Paulo: Ibrasa.

Callinicos, L. (1987). *Working Life: Factories, Townships, and Popular Culture on the Rand, 1886–1940*. Johannesburg: Ravan Press.

Casubolo, A. (1994). *L'Affaire OM-Valenciennes, histoire d'une corruption présumée*. Paris: Olivier Orban.

Cengiz, A. (1993). *Turkiye 'nin Batililastirilmasi* (Turkey's Westernisation). Istanbul: Ayrinti Publications.

Clarke, J., and C. Critcher (1986). 'England's World Cup victory and all that', in A. Tomlinson and G. Whannel (eds), *Off the Ball*. London: Pluto.

Clarke, J. (1991). *New Times and Old Enemies: Essays on Cultural Studies and America*. London: HarperCollins.

Clayton, P. (1996). *Enemies and Passing Friends*. London: Pluto Press.

'Clubs professionnels de football: une comparaison européenne' (1996) in *Profession Football*, 22, October–November, reprinted in 'Economic du sport', *Problèmes économiques*, 2503 (15 January 1997). 31–2.

Cobley, A. (1994). 'A Political History of Playing Fields: The Provision of Sporting Facilities for Africans in the Johannesburg Area to 1948'. *International Journal of the History of Sport*, 11 (2). 212–30.

Coddington, A. (1997). *One of the Lads*. London: HarperCollins.

Colombijn, F. (1996). 'Voetbal in Nederlands-Indië; rumoer op de Padangse velden', in *Spiegel historiael*, 31. 36–40.

Colovic, I. (1995). 'Od Delija do Tigrova', in *Erasmus*, 10. 60–2.

Colovic, I. (1996). 'Fudbal, Hulijani i Rat', in N. Poper (ed), *Srpsvia Scrana Rata*. Belgrade: Republika Press. ('Soccer Hooligans in the War', in N. Popov (ed), *The Serbian Side of the War*. Belgrade: Republika Press.)

Coman, J.; D. O'Reilly; and N. Moss (1997). 'The game that turned to gold', in *The European*, 21 August. 8.

Conference, November 1994. Savannah, Georgia.

Conn, D. (1997). *The Football Business: English Football in the 90s*. London: Mainstream.

Coughlin, S. (1997). 'Soccer: America's new, big kick the world's sport comes of age in the United States', in *Asheville Citizen-Times*, 25 July. C1.

Couzens, T. (1982). ' "Moralizing Leisure Time": The Transatlantic Connection and Black Johannesburg, 1918–1936', in S. Marks and R. Rathbone (eds), *Industrialisation and Social Change in South Africa: African Class Formation, Culture and Consciousness 1870–1930*. London: Longman.

Couzens, T. (1983). 'An Introduction to the History of Football in South Africa', in B. Bozzoli (ed), *Town and Countryside in the Transvaal*. Johannesburg: Ravan Press.

Cresswell, P., and S. Evans (1997). *European Football: A Fans' Handbook*. London: Rough Guides.

Cribb, R., and C. Brown (1995). *Modern Indonesia: A History since 1945*. London: Longman.

Critcher, C. (1979). 'Football since the War', in J. Clarke, C. Critcher and P. Johnson (eds), *Working Class Culture. Studies in History and Theory*. London: Hutchinson.

Critcher, C. (1991). 'Putting on the Style: Aspects of recent English Football', in J. Williams and S. Wagg (eds), *British Football and Social Change – Getting into Europe*. Leicester: Leicester University Press.

Critcher, C. (1994). 'England and the World Cup: World Cup willies, English football and the myth of 1966', in J. Sugden and A. Tomlinson (eds) (1994).

Cronin, M. (1994). 'Sport and a Sense of Irishness', *Irish Studies Review*, 9, Winter 13–17.

Cronin, M. (1996). 'Defenders of the Nation? The Gaelic Athletic Association and Irish National Identity', *Irish Political Studies*, 11. 1–19.

Curtis, M. Y., and R. Sarro (1997). 'The Nimba Headdress. Art, Ritual and History of the Baga and Nalu Peoples of Guinea', in *African Art at the Art Institute of Chicago*, Special Issue of *Museum Studies*, 23 (2). 121–33.

Dal Lago, A. (1990). *Descrizione di una battaglia: i rituali del calcio*. Bologna: Il Mulino.

Dal Lago, A., and R. Moscati (1992). *Regalateci un sogno. Mito e realtá del tifo calcistico in Italia*. Milano: Bompiani.

Damo, A. S. (1998). *Para o que der e vier: o pertencimento clubístico no futebol brasileiro a partir do Gremio Football Portoalegrense e seus torcedores*. Unpublished Masters thesis, Dept. of Social Anthropology, Federal University of Rio Grande do Sul.

Dassie, E. (1996). 'Moulded in the Fire of History', in *Brazilians: The Official Magazine of Sundowns FC*, 1. 6–7.

De Biase, P. (1997). 'Hinchada no hay una sola', in *Mística*, Buenos Aires, 13 December. 17–26.

de Broglio, C. (1970). *South Africa: Racism in Sport*. London: International Defence and Aid Fund.

De Gasquet, P. et al. (1997). 'La percée du foot à la Bourse', in *Les Echos*, 10–11, October. 58–9.

de Jong, F. (1997). 'The Power of a Mask: a Contextual Analysis of the Senegalese *Kumpo* Mask Performance', in *Focaal*, 29. 37–56.

DeCesare, M. (1960). 'Sliema Fans! Let's be Sportsmen!', in *Blue Review* (the official magazine of Sliema Wanderers), No. 4, January.

Delgado, F. (1997). 'Major League Soccer: The Return of the Foreign Sport', *Journal of Sport and Social Issues*, 21 (3). 285–97.

Démerin, P. (1986). 'Séville', in *Bureau*, 120–25.

Dick, H. W. (1996). 'The emergence of a national economy, 1808–1990s', in J. Th. Lindblad (ed), *Historical foundations of a national economy in Indonesia, 1890s–1990s*. 21–51. Amsterdam: North-Holland.

Dodd, P., and R. Colls (eds) (1986). *Englishness. Politics and Culture 1880–1920*. London: Croom Helm.

Dower, J. (1996). *Japan in War and Peace*. London: HarperCollins.

Duhamel, A. (1985). *Le Complexe d'Astérix. Essai sur le caractère politique des Français*. Paris: Gallimard.

Duke, V., and L. Crolley (1996). *Football, Nationality and the State*. Harlow: Longman.

Dumm, T. L. (1993). 'The new enclosures: Racism in the normalized community' in R. Gooding-Williams (ed), *Reading Rodney King: Reading Urban Uprising*. 178–95. New York: Routledge.

Dumont, L. (1970). 'Nationalism and Communalism', in L. Dumont (ed), *Religion, Politics and History in India*. Paris: Mouton.

Duncan, N. G., and J. S. Duncan (1997). 'Deep suburban irony: The perils of democracy in Westchester County, New York', in R. Silverstone (ed) (1997). 161–79.

Dutheil, G. (1996). 'Trois bouquets dans un jardin français', *Le Monde Supplément Radio et Télévision*, 15–16 December. 2–3.

Eagleton, T. (1981). *Walter Benjamin, or towards a Revolutionary Criticism*. London: New Left Books.

Echegut, A. et al. (1997). 'Mondial 98: un enjeu de 8,5 milliards', in *Les Echos*, 11 June. 54–5.

Edworthy, N. (1997). *England. The Official FA History*. London: Virgin.

Ehrenreich, B. (1989). *Fear of Falling: The Inner Life of the Middle Class*. New York: HarperCollins.

Eichberg, H. (1992). 'Crisis and Grace: Soccer in Denmark', in *Scandinavian Journal of Medicine and Science in Sport*, 2 (3). 119–28.

Eisenberg, C. (1990). 'The Middle Class and Competition: Some Considerations of the beginnings of Modern Sport in England and Germany', *International Journal of the History of Sport*, Vol 7, No. 2 (September). 265–82.

Elbaum, J. (1998). 'Apuntes para el "aguante". La construcción simbólica del cuerpo popular', in P. Alabarces et al. (eds), *Deporte y sociedad*. Buenos Aires: CBC-UBA (forthcoming).

Fairgrieve, J. (1986). *The Boys in Maroon, Heart of Midlothian: The Authorized Inside Story of an Unforgettable Season*. Edinburgh: Mainstream/Heart of Midlothian FC.

Fanthorpe, R. (1998). 'Limba "Deep Rural" Strategies', in *Journal of African History*, 39 (1). 15–38.

Farbstein, M., and M. Semyonov (1990). 'Ecology of violence in sport. The case of Israeli football', in *Megamot*, 32 (Jerusalem).

Fasseur, C. (1992). 'Hoeksteen en struikelblok; rasonderscheid en overheidsbeleid in Nederlands-Indië', *Tijdschrift voor Geschiedenis*, 105. 218–42.

Ficoneri, P. (1990). 'Cori ingrati', in *L'Espresso*, 14 October. 59–67.

Filho, M. (1964). *O Negro no Futebol Brasileiro*. Rio de Janeiro: Civilização Brasileira.

Finn, G. P. T. and R. Giulianotti (eds) (1999). *Football Culture: local contests and global visions*. London: Frank Cass.

Finn, G. P. T. (1991a). 'Racism, Religion and Social Prejudice: Irish Catholic Clubs, Soccer and Scottish Society – I. The historical roots of prejudice', in *International Journal of the History of Sport*, 8. 70–93.

Finn, G. P. T. (1991b). 'Racism, Religion and Social Prejudice: Irish Catholic Clubs, Soccer and Scottish Society – II. Social identities and conspiracy theories', in *International Journal of the History of Sport*, 8. 370–97.

Finn, G. P. T. (1994). 'Faith, Hope and Bigotry: Case-Studies of Anti-Catholic Prejudice in Scottish Soccer and Society', in G. Jarvie and G. Walker (eds), *Ninety Minute Patriots: Scottish Sport in the Making of a Nation*. Leicester: Leicester University Press.

Finn, G. P. T., and R. Giulianotti (1998). 'Scottish Fans, Not English Hooligans! Scots, Scottishness and Scottish Football', in A. Brown (ed), *Fanatics! Power, Race, Nationality and Fandom in European Football*. London: Routledge.

Fishman, R. (1987). *Bourgeois Utopias: The Rise and Fall of Suburbia*. New York: Basic Books.

Fishwick, N. (1989). *English Football and Society, 1910–1950*. Manchester: Manchester University Press.

'Football, sport du siècle' (1990). Special number, *Vingtième siècle*, 26, April–June.

Frendo, M. (1979). *Party Politics in a Fortress Colony: The Maltese Experience*. Valletta: Midsea Books.

Frydenberg, J. (1977). 'Practicas y valores en el proceso de popularizción de fútbol, Buenos Aires, 1900–1910', in *Entrepasados. Revista de Historia*, VI, 12 (Buenos Aires). 7–30.

Fukuoka, A. (1993). *Koreans in Japan* (in Japanese). Tokyo: Chuko Shinsho.

Furnivall, J. S. (1944). *Netherlands India: A Study of Plural Economy*. Cambridge: Cambridge University Press.

Ganong, T. W. (1998). *Features of Baga Morphology, Syntax and Narrative Discourse*. MA dissertation, University of Texas at Arlington.

Gardner, P. (1996). *The Simplest Game: The Intelligent Fan's Guide to the World of Soccer*. New York: Macmillan.

Gardner, P. (1997). 'Soccer's place in the suburbs: next up – soccer in the life of the Inuit in Greenland', in *Soccer America*, 11, October 13.

Geertz, C. (1961). *The Javanese Family: A Study of Kinship and Socialization*. New York: The Free Press of Glencoe.

Geertz, C. (1973). 'Deep Play: Notes on the Balinese Cockfight', in *The Interpretation of Cultures*. New York: Basic Books.

Gehrmann, S. (1988). *Fußball-Vereine-Politik. Zur Sportgeschichte des Reviers*. Essen: Reimar Hobbing Verlag.

Ghanem, A. (1997). An interview, in *Ru'ia Ukhra*, 7 (1). 32–4.

Giddens, A. (1985). *The Nation-State and Violence*. Cambridge: Polity Press.

Gillespie, N.; T. Lovett; and W. Garner (1992). *Youth Work and Working Class Youth Culture. Rules and Resistance in West Belfast*. Buckingham: Open University Press.

Giroux, H. A. (1994). *Disturbing Pleasures: Learning Popular Culture*. New York: Routledge.

Giulianotti, R. (1991). 'Scotland's Tartan Army in Italy: the case for the carnivalesque', in *Sociological Review*, 39 (3). 503–27.

Giulianotti, R. (1993a). 'Soccer Casuals as Cultural Intermediaries: the politics of Scottish style', in S. Redhead (ed), *The Passion and the Fashion*. Aldershot: Arena.

Giulianotti, R. (1993b). 'A Model of the Carnivalesque? Scottish football fans at the 1992 European Championships in Sweden and beyond', *Working Papers in Popular Cultural Studies No. 6*, Institute for Popular Culture, Manchester Metropolitan University.

Giulianotti, R. (1994a). 'Social Identity and Public Order: political and academic discourses on football violence', in R. Giulianotti, N. Bonney and M. Hepworth (eds) (1994).

Giulianotti, R. (1994b). 'Scoring Away from Home: a statistical study of Scotland football fans at international matches in Romania and Sweden', in *International Review for the Sociology of Sport*, 29 (2). 171–200.

Giulianotti, R. (1994c). 'Taking liberties: Hibs Casuals and Scottish Law', in R. Giulianotti, N. Bonney and M. Hepworth (eds) (1994).

Giulianotti, R. (1995a). 'Participant Observation and Research into Football Hooliganism: reflections on the problems of entrée and everyday risks', in *Sociology of Sport Journal*, 12 (1). 1–20.

Giulianotti, R. (1995b). 'Football and the Politics of Carnival: an ethnographic study of Scottish fans in Sweden', in *International Review for the Sociology of Sport*, 30 (2). 191–224.

Giulianotti, R. (1996a). *A Sociology of Scottish Football Fan Culture*. Unpublished PhD thesis, Dept. of Sociology, University of Aberdeen.

Giulianotti, R. (1996b). 'Back to the Future: an ethnography of Ireland's football fans at the 1994 World Cup Finals in the USA', in *International Review for the Sociology of Sport*, 31 (3). 323–48.

Giulianotti, R. (1996c). ' "All the Olympians: A Thing Never Known Again?" Reflections on Irish football culture and the 1994 World Cup finals', in *Irish Journal of Sociology*, 6. 101–26.

Giulianotti, R. (1999). *More than a Game: The Social and Historical Aspects of World Football*. Cambridge: Polity Press.

Giulianotti, R., and G. Armstrong (1997). 'Reclaiming the game – an introduction to the anthropology of football', in G. Armstrong and R. Giulianotti (eds) (1997).

Giulianotti, R.; N. Bonney; and M. Hepworth (eds) (1994). *Football, Violence and Social Identity*, London: Routledge.

Giulianotti, R., and J. Williams (eds) (1994). *Game Without Frontiers: Football, Identity and Modernity*. Aldershot: Arena.

Gogus, Z. (1991). *Bir Avrupa Ruyasi* (A European Dream). Istanbul: Afa Publishing.

Goksøyr, M. (1996). 'Our games – our virtues? National sports as symbols: a discussion of ideal types', in F. van d. Merwe (ed), *Sport as Symbol, Symbols in Sport*. Sankt Augustin, Oslo.

Goksøyr, M.; Ø. Larsen; and T. Peterson (1997). 'The Development of Playing Styles in Soccer. From Diffusion to Contraction?'. Paper for the ISSA Symposium, Oslo.

Goto, T. (1998). *World Cup* (in Japanese). Tokyo: Chuoh Kohronsha.

Graham, B. (1994). 'No Place of the Mind: Contested Protestant Representations of Ulster', in *Ecumene*, 1. 257–81.

Graham, B. (1997). 'Ulster: a representation of place yet to be imagined', in P. Shirlow and M. McGovern (eds), *Who are 'the People'? Unionism, Protestantism and Loyalism in Northern Ireland*. 34–54. London: Pluto Press.

Gramsci, A. (1971). *Selection from Prison Notebooks*. London: New Left Books.

Griffiths, J. (1985). *A Football Saga. Fifty Years of Football in Malta*. Valletta: Malta Imprint.

Grimson, A., and M. Varela (1998). *Audiencias, comunicación y poder. Estudios sobre televsión*. Buenos Aires: Biblos (forthcoming).

Grossberg, L. (1992). *We Gotta Get Out of This Place: Popular Conservatism and Postmodern Culture*. London: Routledge.

Guedes, S. (1998). *O Brasil no campo de futebol: estudoes antropológicos sobre o significado do futebol brasileiro*. Niterói: EDUFF.

Hair, P. E. H. (1997). 'The History of the Baga in Early Written Sources', in *History in Africa*, 24. 381–91.

Hall, S. (1992). 'The question of cultural identity', in S. Hall, D. Held and T. McGrew, *Modernity and its Futures*. Cambridge: Polity Press.

Hall, S., and T. Jefferson (1976). *Resistance through Rituals: Youth Cultures in Post-War Britain*. London: Hutchinson.

Halvorsen, A. (1947). *Norsk fotball-leksikon*, Vol 1. Oslo: Prent Forlag.

Hargreaves, J. (1986). *Sport, Power and Culture*. Cambridge: Polity Press.

Hargreaves, J. (1992). 'Olympism and nationalism: some preliminary considerations', in *International Review for the Sociology of Sport*, 27. 119–37.

Harrison, B. (1994). 'The dark side of flexible production', in *National Productivity Review*, 13 (4). 479–89.

Hasselt, van A. L. (1882). *Midden-Sumatra; reizen en onderzoekingen der Sumatra expeditie, uitgerust door het Aardrijkskundig Genootschap, 1877–1879*, Vol 1-III *Volksbeschrijving van Midden-Sumatra*, Leiden: Brill.

Hebdige, D. (1988). *Subculture-The Meaning of Style*. London: Routledge.

Heitmeyer, W., and J. I. Peter (1988). *Jugendliche Fußballfans*. Munich: Juventa Verlag.

Henley, D. E .F. (1996). *Nationalism and Regionalism in a Colonial Context: Minahasa in the Dutch East Indies*. Leiden: KITLV.

Hicketier, K. (1980). 'Der synthetische Fan', in R. Lindner (ed), *Der Fußballfan – Ansichten vom Zuschauer*. Frankfurt: Syndicat.

Hill, J. (1996). 'Rite of Spring: Cup finals and community in the North of England', in J. Hill and J. Williams, *Sport and Identity in the North of England*. Keele: Keele University Press.

Hoberman, J. (1986). *Sport and Political Ideology*. London: Heinemann.

Hoejbjerg, C. (1991). 'Beyond the Sacred and the Profane: The Poro Initiation Ritual', in *Folk* 32. 161–76.

Hognestad, H. (1995). 'Meaning and Identity in Dramas of Sport: Comparative Notes on Norwegian and Scottish Practices', in R. Puijk (ed), *OL-94 og forskningen*, V, ØF-rapport 07/95, Lillehammer.

Hognestad, H. (1997). 'The Jambo Experience: An Anthropological Study of Hearts-fans', in G. Armstrong and R. Giulianotti (eds) (1997).

Holmes, M. (1994). 'Symbols of national identity and sport: the case of the Irish football team', *Irish Political Studies*, 9: 81–98.

Holt, R. (1989). *Sport and the British*. Oxford: Oxford University Press.

Holt, R. (1996). 'Cricket and Englishness', in *International Journal of the History of Sport*, 13, 1.

Home Affairs Committee (1990). *Policing Football Hooliganism: Memoranda of Evidence*. HMSO, London.

Honneth, A. (1986). 'The fragmented world of symbolic forms: Reflections on Pierre Bourdieu's sociology of culture', in *Theory, Culture and Society*, 3 (3). 55–66.

Horton, E. (1997). *Moving the Goalposts: Football's Exploitation*. Edinburgh: Mainstream.

Houlihan, B. (1997). 'Sport, national identity and public policy', in *Nation and Nationalism*, 3. 113–37.

Hull, G. (1993). *The Malta Language Question: A Case Study in Cultural Imperialism*. Malta: Said International.

Humphrey, J. (1986). 'Brazil: football, nationalism and politics', in A. Tomlinson and G. Whannel (eds), *Off the Ball*. London: Pluto Press.

Idrottsbladet, Stockholm, 1920–49.

Jackson, K. T. (1985). *Crabgrass Frontier: The Suburbanization of the United States*. New York: Oxford University Press.

Jacobs, B. D. (1992). *Fractured Cities: Capitalism, Community and Empowerment in Britain and America*. London: Routledge.

Japan Football Association (1996). *The 75-Year History of the Japan Football Association* (in Japanese). Tokyo: Baseball Magazine Publishing.

Japan Football Association (1997). *Annual Leaflet* (in Japanese). Tokyo.

Japan Football League Newsletter (1993). 'Membership registration rule' (in Japanese). February, No. 104. 33.

Jarvie, G. (1993). 'Sport, nationalism and cultural identity', in L. Allison (ed), *The Changing Politics of Sport*. Manchester: Manchester University Press. 58–83.

Jary, D.; J. Horne; and T. Bucke (1991). 'Football "fanzines" and football culture: a case of successful "cultural contestation"', in *Sociological Review*, 39. 3.

Jawad, S. (1979). *The Palestinian Patriotic Resistance in Gaza, West Bank and Galilee*. Beirut: Dar Ibn-Khaldon.

Jeffrey, I. (1992). 'Street Rivalry and Patron-Managers: Football in Sharpeville, 1943–1985', in *African Studies*, 51 (1). 69–94.

Jenkins, R. (1994). 'Rethinking Ethnicity: Identity, Categorisation and Power', in *Ethnic and Racial Studies*, 17. 199–231.

Johansson, H. (1953). 'Idrotten och samhället', in *Svensk Idrott 1903–1953*. Malmö.

Jones, R., and P. Moore (1994). ' "He only has eyes for Poms": Soccer, ethnicity and locality in Perth', in J. O'Hara (ed), *Ethnicity and Soccer in Australia, ASSH Studies in Sports History*, 10. Campbelltown, NSW: Australian Society for Sports History.

Jones, S. G. (1986). *Sport, Politics and the Working Class*. Manchester: Manchester University Press.

Juve, J. (1934). *Alt om fotball*. Oslo: Johan Grundt Tanum.

Kan, J., and D. Kim (1989). *Koreans in Japan: Their History and Future Implications* (in Japanese). Tokyo: Rodo Keizaisha.

Kana'anna, S. (1984). 'The Social Change and the Mental Health within the Arab Population of Israel', in B. Zeith, M. El-Wathaiek wal-Abhath.

Kellas, J. G. (1991). *The Politics of Nationalism and Ethnicity*. Basingstoke: Macmillan.

Kellner, D. (1995). 'Theory wars and cultural studies', in *Media Culture*. London: Routledge.

Kelly, S. (1993). *The Kop*. London: Mandarin.

Kelly, S. (1998). 'Football fans 1, Fleet Street 0. An examination of the tabloid press during the European Football Championships, June 1996', paper given to Institute of Football Studies, University of Central Lancashire, Preston, March 1998.

Kemal, C., and R. Cakir (1995). 'MHP Gercegi' (The MHP Reality), *Milliyet*, 3–14, October.

King, V. (1994). 'The sociology of South-East Asia; a critical review of some concepts and issues', in *Bijdragen tot de taal-, land- en volkenkunde*, 150. 171–206.

Kluckhohn, C. (1962). 'Value and Value-Orientation: The Theory of Action' in T. Parsons and E. Shils (eds), *Towards a General Theory of Action*. New York: Harper & Row.

Kopa, R., and B. Meunier (1996). *Planète football*. Paris: La Sirène.

Kozanoglu, C. (1995). *The Pop Age Fever*. Istanbul: Illetisim.

Kozanoglu, C. (1997). *Internet, Full Moon, Community*. Istanbul: Illetisim.

Kuper, S. (1994). *Football Against the Enemy*. London: Orion.

Laciner, O. (1994). 'DEP Davasi: Milli Birlik ve Beraberlik Ruhu' (DEP Trial: The Spirit of National Unity), in *Birikim*, December.

Lalic, D. (1993). *Torcida: pogled iznutra* (Torcida: Inside Zagreb: AGM).

Lamp, F. (1996a). Dancing the Hare: Appropriation of the Imagery of Mande Power among the Baga', in J. Jansen and C. Zobel (eds), *The Younger Brother in Mande: Kinship and Politics in West Africa*. 105–16. Research School, Centre for Non-Western Studies, Leiden University.

Lamp, F. (1996b). *Art of the Baga. A Drama of Cultural Reinvention*. New York and Munich: The Museum for African Art and Prestel.

Lanfranchi, P. (ed) (1992). *Il calcio e il suo pubblico*. Naples: ESI.

Langdon, J. (1998). 'MLS ad campaign to target Hispanics', in *USA Today*, 23 January. 15C.

Langdon, P. (1995). *A Better Place to Live: Reshaping the American Suburb*. New York: HarperPerennial.

Larsson, J. (1994). *Hemmet vi ärvde: Om folkhemmet, identiteten och den gemensamma framtiden*. Stockholm: Arena Förlag.

Leclair, J.-P. (1997). Interview with Gianni Agnelli, *L'Equipe*, 815 (15 November). 74–8.

Leclerc, J. (1993). 'Mirrors and the lighthouse; a search for meaning in the monuments and great works of Sukarno's Jakarta, 1960–1966', in P. J. M. Nas (ed), *Urban Symbolism*, 38–58. Leiden: Brill.

Lecoq, G. (1997). Interview with Georges de Caune, 'Le couronnement de la télé, ce fut le sacre de Reims', in *Les Ecrits de l'Image*, 16. 129–33.

Lee, C., and De Vos, G. (1984). *Koreans in Japan: Ethnic Conflict and Accommodation*. Berkeley: University of California Press.

Leite Lopes, J. S., and J. P. Faguer (1994). 'L'invention du style brésilien: sport, journalisme et politique au Brésil', in *Actes de la Recherche en Sciences Sociales*, 103.

Leite Lopes, J. S., and S. Maresca (1987). 'La disparition de la joie du peuple: notes sur la mort d'un joueur de football', in *Actes de la Recherche en Sciences Sociales*, 79.

Leite Lopes, J. S. (1994). 'A vitória do futebol que incorporou a *pelada*; a invenção do jornalismo esportivo e a entrada dos negros no futebol brasileiro', São Paulo, *Revista USP*, 22 (3).

Leite Lopes, J. S. (1997). 'Successes and Contradictions in "Multiracial" Brazilian football', in G. Armstrong and R. Giulianotti (eds) (1997).

Lemann, N. (1989). 'Stressed out in Suburbia: A generation after the postwar boom, life in the suburbs has changed, even if our picture of it hasn't', in *The Atlantic*, November, 34.

Lemberg, E. (1967). *Nationalismus I. Psychologie und Geschichte*. Reinbek: Rowohlt.

Lever, J. (1983). *Soccer Madness*. Chicago and London: Chicago University Press.

Lewis, D. (1992/3). 'Soccer and Rugby: Popular Production of Pleasure in South African Culture', in *Southern African Political and Economic Monthly*, 6 (3–4), 13–17.

Lewis, R. (1997). 'The genesis of professional football: Bolton-Blackpool-Darwen, the centre of innovation, 1878–1885', in *International Journal of the History of Sport*, 12, 2.

Linde-Laursen, A., and J. O. Nilsson (eds) (1991). *Nationella identiteter i Norden – ett fullbordat projekt?* Copenhagen: Nordiska Rådet.

Lindner, R. (ed) (1983). *Der Satz 'Der Ball ist rund' hat eine gewisse philosophische Tiefe.* Berlin: Transit.

Lindroth, J. (1974). *Idrottens väg till folkrörelse: studier i svensk idrottsrörelse till 1915.* Uppsala: Acta Universitatis Upsaliensis.

Lindroth, J. (1987). *Idrott mellan krigen: Organisationer, ledare och idéer i den svenska idrottsrörelsen 1919–1939.* Stockholm: HLS Förlag.

Lipovetsky, G. (1987). *L'Empire de l'ephemere: la Mode et son destin dans les socites modernes.* Paris: Gallimard.

Lopez, S. (1997). *Women on the Ball.* London: Scarlet Press.

Lundkvist, S. (1977). *Folkrörelserna i det svenska samhället 1850–1920.* Uppsala: Acta Universitatis Upsaliensis.

Lury, C. (1996). *Consumer Culture.* Cambridge: Polity Press.

Lyra Filho, J. (1954). *Taça do Mundo, 1954.* Rio de Janeiro: Irmãos Pongetti.

MacClancy, J. (1996). 'Sport, Identity and Ethnicity', in J. MacClancy (ed), *Sport, Identity and Ethnicity.* 1–20. Oxford: Berg.

Maeda, H. (1994). 'Socio-historical Study of Women's Soccer in Japan: In terms of school activities' (in Japanese), in *Medicine and Science in Soccer*, 14. 73–6.

Maffesoli, M. (1990 [1988]). *El tiempo de las tribus.* Barcelona: Icaria.

Magnis-Suseno, F. (1997). *Javanese Ethics and World-View: The Javanese Idea of the Good Life.* Jakarta: Gramedia.

Magubane, B. (1963). 'Sports and Politics in an Urban African Community: A Case Study of African Voluntary Organizations'. Unpublished BA thesis, University of Natal.

Major League Soccer (1998). *Executive summary of MLS demographic profile.* New York: MLS.

Mallia-Milanes, V. (ed) (1988). *The British Colonial Experience 1800–1964: The Impact on Maltese Society.* Amsterdam: Mireva.

Mamiya, T. (1995). *Strategies and Ideas about Sport Business: How to Support Sports Programmes* (in Japanese). Tokyo: Baseball Magazine Publishing.

Mamiya, T. (1996). *Foundation of Sports Events: Planning and Operation of Sports Events* (in Japanese). Chiba: Juntendo University Press.

Mamiya, T. (1997). *Sports Event Market in Japan* (in Japanese). A survey report. Chiba: Juntendo University Press.

Mandle, W. F. (1987). *The Gaelic Athletic Association and Irish Nationalist Politics 1884–1924.* London: Christopher Helm.

Mangan, J. A. (ed) (1996). *Tribal Identities, Nationalism, Europe, Sport.* London/Portland: Frank Cass.

Mark, P. (1994). 'Art, Ritual, and Folklore. Dance and Cultural Identity among the Peoples of the Casamance', in *Cahiers d'Études africaines*, 136 (4). 563–84.

Markovits, A. S. (1990). 'The other "American exceptionalism": Why is there no soccer in the United States?', in *International Journal of the History of Sport*, 7. 231–64.

Markovits, A. S., and S. L. Hellerman (1995). 'Soccer in America: A story of marginalization', in *Entertainment and Sports Law Review*, 13 (1/2). 225–55.

Mason, T. (1980). *Association Football and English Society, 1863–1915.* Brighton: Harvester.

Mason, T. (1986). 'Some Englishmen and Scotsmen Abroad: The Spread of World Football', in A. Tomlinson and G. Whannel (eds), *Off the Ball.* London: Pluto Press.

Mason, T. (1995). *Passion of the People? Football in South America.* London: Verso.

Máximo, J. (1954). *João Saldanha*. Rio de Janeiro: Relume Dumará.
McCarthy, C.; A. Rodriguez; S. Meacham; S. David; C. Wilson-Brown; H. Godina; K. E. Supryia; and E. Buendia (1996). 'Race, suburban resentment and the representation of the inner city in contemporary film and television', in N. K. Denzin (ed), *Cultural Studies: A Research Volume*, Vol 1. 121–40. Greenwich, CT: JAI Press.
McCrone, D. (1992). *Understanding Scotland: The Sociology of a Stateless Nation*. London: Routledge.
McCrone, K. (1988). *Playing the Game: Sport and the Physical Emancipation of English Women, 1870–1914*. Lexington: University of Kentucky Press.
McIlvanney, W. (1991). *Surviving the Shipwreck*. Edinburgh: Mainstream.
Merkel, U. (1994). 'Germany and the World Cup: solid, reliable, often undramatic – but successful', in J. Sugden and A. Tomlinson (eds), *Hosts and Champions*. Aldershot: Arena.
Merkel, U. (1998). 'Sport in Divided Nations – The Case of the old, new and "re-united" Germany', in A. Bairner and J. Sugden (eds), *Sport in Divided Societies*. Aachen: Meyer and Meyer.
Merkel, U.; K. Sombert; and W. Tokarski (1996). 'Football, Racism and Xenophobia in Germany: 50 Years Later – Here We Go Again?', in U. Merkel and W. Tokarski (eds), *Racism and Xenophobia in European Football*. Aachen: Meyer and Meyer.
Metcalfe, A. (1996). 'Sport and community: a case study of the mining villages of East Northumberland, 1800–1914', in J. Hill and J. Williams, *Sport and Identity in the North of England*. Keele: Keele University Press.
Miège, C. (1993). *Les Institutions sportives*. Paris: PUF.
Miège, C. (1996). *Le Sport européen*. Paris: PUF.
Miert, van H. (1995). *Een koel hoofd en een warm hart; nationalisme, Javanisme en jeugdbeweging in Nederlands-Indië, 1918–1930*. Amsterdam: De Bataafsche Leeuw.
Mignon, P. (1990). 'Supporters et hooligans en Grande-Bretagne depuis 1871', in *Vingtième siècle*, April–June. 37–47.
Mignon, P. (1992). 'La societe francese e il calcio', in P. Lanfranchi (ed) (1992).
Mignon, P. (1996). 'Football Fan Culture in Paris: from one club to two', paper to the international conference *Fanatics! Football and Popular Culture in Europe*, Institute for Popular Culture, Manchester Metropolitan University, 11–13 June.
Mihailovic, S. (1990). 'Sport, nasilje, publika', in *Kultura*, 88–90. 9–24.
Min, P. G. (1992). 'A Comparison of the Korean Minorities in China and Japan', in *International Migration Review*, 12 (1). 4–21.
Mlokoti, C. (1996). 'Remembering the Glory Days', in *Amakhosi*, official fan magazine of Iwisa Kaizer Chiefs, 4. 16–17.
Montserrat, N. (1973). *The Kapillan of Malta*. London: Cassell.
Moore, K. (1997). *Museums and Popular Culture*. London: Cassell.
Moorhouse, H. F. (1987). 'England against Scotland: Football and Popular Culture', in *International Journal of the History of Sport*, 4, 2.
Moorhouse, H. F. (1995). 'One state, several countries: soccer and nationality in a "United Kingdom"', in *International Journal of the History of Sport*, 12, 2.
Morisaki, D. (1997). An Empirical Study of the J-League Supporters (in Japanese).
Moura, G. (1998). *O Rio corre para o Maracanã*. Unpublished Masters thesis, Dept. of History, IFCS, Federal University of Rio de Janeiro.
Mulder, N. (1989). *Individual and Society in Java: a cultural analysis*. Yogyakarta: Gadjah Mada University Press.
Murat, B. (1993). *Turkiye Dunyanin Neresinde?* (Where is Turkey in the World?). Istanbul.
Murray, B. (1994). *Football: A History of the World Game*. Aldershot: Scolar Press.
Murray, W. (1984). *The Old Firm: sectarianism, sport and society in Scotland*. Edinburgh: John Donald.

Nairn, T. (1981). *The Break-Up of Britain*. 2nd edn. London: New Left Books.
Nakai, K. (1989). *Permanent Alien Residents and Their Rights to Become Public Servants* (in Japanese). Tokyo: Tsuge Publishing Co.
Nakhle Kh. (1977). 'Anthropological and Sociological Studies on the Arabs in Israel: A Critique', in *Journal of Palestinian Studies*. 41–70.
Nauright, J. (1997). *Sport, Cultures and Identities in South Africa*. Leicester: Leicester University Press.
Negreiros, P. (1998). *A naçao entra em campo: futebol nos anos 30 e 40*. Unpublished PhD, Dept. of History, PUC/SP.
Nilsson, E. (ed) (1978). *En bok om föreningen Svensk Elitfotboll 1928–1978*. Helsingborg.
Nogawa, H. (1986). 'A Study of Sport and Ethnicity', in *Annals of Seitoku Junior College of Women*. 19. 65–71.
Nogawa, H. (1994). 'Overcoming Inequalities in Japanese Sport Scenes: Institutionalized Discrimination against Japan-born Korean Athletes'. Unpublished paper presented at the 15th North American Sociology of Sport Conference, Toronto, November.
Nogawa, H., and H. Maeda (1997). 'Internationalization of Female Soccer Spectators in Japan'. Unpublished paper presented at the 18th North American Sociology of Sport Conference, Toronto, November.
Nordisk Familjeboks Sportlexicon, 1938–49, Vols 1–7. Stockholm: Nordisk Familjeboks Förlags AB.
Nussle, P. (1986). 'Jouons "à la française"', in *Bureau*. 24–5.
O'Connor, J. (1993). Translator's Introduction to C. Bromberger, et al (1993b).
Offe, C. (1994). *Der Tunnel am Ende des Lichtes: Erkundungen der politischen Transformation in neuen Osten*. Frankfurt am Main: Campus Verlag.
Ohsumi, Y. (1995). *The 75-Year History of the Japan Football Association* (in Japanese). 236–67. Tokyo: Baseball Magazine Publishing.
Oka, T. (1993). 'Japan's Korean minority', in *The Christian Science Monitor*, 8 January. 18.
Olsen, E. (1973). *Scoringer i fotball*. Unpublished thesis, University of Sport and Physical Education, Oslo.
Olsen, E.; Ø. Larsen; and N. J. Semb (1994) *Effektiv fotball*. Oslo: Gyldendal Norsk Forlag.
Ortiz, R. (1991). 'Lo actual y la modernidad', in *Nueva Sociedad*, Caracus, November–December.
Parker, A. (1995). 'Great Expectations. Grimness or Glamour? The Football Apprentice in the 1990s', in *Sports Historian*, 15.
Parker, G. A. (1897). *South African Sports: An Official Handbook*. London.
Pedrosa, M. (ed) (1968). *Na Bôca do Túnel*. Rio de Janeiro: Livraria Editôra Gol.
Pereira, L. (1998). *Football Mania: uma história social do futebol no Rio de Janeiro (1902–1938)*. Unpublished PhD, University of Campinas.
Persson, G. (ed) (1988). *Allsvenskan genom tiderna*. Stockholm: Strömbergs/Brunnhages Förlag.
Persson, L. K. (1990). *Kamrat eller förrädare?*, in *Folkets Historia*, 3.
Persson, L. K. (1992). 'De stora läromästerna: Den brittiska fotbollen och Sverige före första världskriget', in *Idrottsarvet*. Göteborg: Årsbok for idrottsmuseet i Göteborg.
Peterson, T. (1993). *Den svengelska modellen. Svensk fotball i omvandling under efterkrigstiden*. Lund: Arkiv Forlag.
Pile, S., and M. Keith (eds) (1997). *Geographies of Resistance*. London: Routledge.
Poiseul, B. (1996). 'Sport: la télévision a-t-elle tous les droits?', in *Les Ecrits de l'Image*, 13 (December). 150–2.
Pooley, J. C. (1976). 'Ethnic soccer clubs in Milwaukee: A study in assimilation', in M. Hart (ed), *Sport in the Socio-Cultural Process*. 475–92. Dubuque, IA: W. C. Brown.
Pope, N., and H. Pope (1998). *Turkey Unveiled: Ataturk and After*. London: Murray.

Portelli, A. (1993). 'The Rich and the Poor in the Culture of Football', in S. Redhead (ed) (1993).

Portelli, L. (1960). *Malta was There Too*. Hamrun: Lux Press.

Portelli, L. (1993). 'The Hadjuk Visit and the Innu Malti', in *The Times of Malta*, 25 March.

Pramann, U. (1983). *Fußballfans – Betrachtungen einer Subkultur*. Hamburg: Stern Bücher.

PSSI (1955). *PSSI 25 tahun 1930–1955*. Jakarta: Visser.

PSSI (1960). *PSSI 30 tahun 1930–1960*.

PSSI (1974). *Pembangunan P.S.S.I. berdasarkan prasaran Bardosono dalam kongres P.S.S.I. ke-25 tgl. 14–16 desember 1974 di Yogyakarta*. Jakarta: PSSI.

PSSI (1980). *Kenang-kenangan P.S.S.I. 50th, 19 april 1930–19 april 1980*, chief editor U. R. Mohamad. Yahya. Jakarta: PSSI.

PSSI (1991). *Laporan pelaksanaan program kerja 1990/1991 dan rancangan program kerja 1991/1992*. Yahya. Jakarta: PSSI.

Ramokhoase, P. (1983). 'Transvaal Jumpers', in G. A. L. Thabe (1983).

Read, D. (1964). *The English Provinces, c. 1760–1960*. London: Edward Arnold.

Redhead, S. (1991). 'An Era of the End, or the End of an Era: Football and Youth Culture', in J. Williams and S. Wagg (eds), *British Football and Social Change – Getting into Europe*. Leicester: Leicester University Press.

Redhead, S. (1997). *Post-fandom and the Millennial Blues: The Transformation of Soccer Culture*. London: Routledge.

Redhead, S. (ed) (1993). *The Passion and the Fashion. Football Fandom in the New Europe*. Aldershot: Ashgate.

Redhead, S., and E. McLaughlin (1985). 'Soccer's Style Wars', in *New Society*, 16 August.

Rekhess, E. (1976). *The Israeli Arabs after 1967*. Tel Aviv: Tel Aviv University.

Ricklefs, M. C. (1981). *A History of Modern Indonesia c. 1300 to the Present*. London: Macmillan.

Rocheteau, D., and D. Chaumier (1997). *Le Guide du football 98*. Paris: Editions de la Lucarne.

Rosenhak, Z. (1995). 'New Developments in the Sociology of Palestinians with Israeli Citizenship: An Analytical View', in *Megamot*, 37, Jerusalem.

Rusk, D. (1995). *Cities without Suburbs*. Baltimore, MD: Woodrow Wilson Center Press.

Russell, D. (1997). *Football and the English*. Preston: Carnegie Publishing.

Salvini, A. (1988). *Il rito aggressivo. Dall'aggressivitá simbolica al comportamento violento: il caso dei tifosi ultras*. Florence: Giunti.

Sarro, R. (forthcoming). *Baga Identity: Religious Movements and Political Transformation in the Republic of Guinea*. PhD thesis, University College London.

Schefold, R. (1988). 'Hearthless house and painted concrete: aspects of ethnicity among Sa'dan Toraja and Toba Batak (Indonesia)', in P. Q. van Ufford and M. Schoffeleers (eds), *Religion and Development Towards an Integrated Approach*. Amsterdam: Free University Press.

Scher, A. (1996). *La Patria Deportista*. Buenos Aires: Planeta.

Schlesinger, P. (1991). *Media, State, Nation*. London: Sage.

Schrof, J. M. (1995). 'American Women: Getting their Kicks', in *Science and Society*, 19 June, 118, 59.

Schulze-Marmeling, D., and W. Steffen (1994). *Borussia Dortmund – Der Ruhm, der Traum und das Geld*. Göttingen: Verlag Die Werkstatt.

Sebreli, J. J. (1981). *Fútbol y masas*. Buenos Aires: Galerna.

Seyferth, G. (1989). 'As Ciências Sociais no Brasil e a questão racial', in *Cativeiro e Liberdade*. Rio de Janeiro: UERJ.

Seyferth, G. (1991). 'Os paradoxos da miscigenação: observações sobre o tema imigração e raça no Brasil', in *Estudos Afro-Asiáticos*, 20 (junho).

Seyferth, G. (1995). 'A invenção da raça e o poder discricionário dos estereótipos', in *Anuário Antropológico 93*, Rio de Janeiro: Ed. Tempo Brasileiro.

Shilling, C. (1993). *The Body and Social Theory*. London: Sage.

Shirlow, P., and M. McGovern (1996). 'Sectarianism, Socio-Economic Competition and the Political Economy of Ulster Loyalism', *Antipode*, 21. 399–432.

Silverstone, R. (ed) (1997). *Visions of Suburbia*. London: Routledge.

Skrede, I. (1977). *Fotball! Plymouth!* Oslo: Gyldendal Norsk Forlag.

Smooha, S. (1976). 'Arabs and Jews in Israel – Minority and Majority Relations', *Megamot*, 22 (Jerusalem). 397–423.

Smooha, S. (1992). *Arabs and Jews in Israel*. Bolder, Colorado: Westview Press.

Soccer Industry Council of America (1997). *Soccer in the U.S.A.: Statistical abstract on soccer participation*. Spring. North Palm Beach, FL: SICA.

Solstad, D., and J. Michelet (1982). *VM i fotball 1982*. Oslo: October A/S.

Sowden, P. (1997). 'Stade Auxerrois, la maison d'en face', in *France Football*, 19 December. 10–11.

Spradley, P., and D. W. McCurdy (1987). *Conformity and Conflict: Readings in Cultural Anthropology*. Boston: Little, Brown.

Steinberg, P., and A. M. Oliver (1990). *The Graffiti of the Intifada*. Jerusalem: Palestinian Academic Society for the Study of International Affairs.

Stokes, M. (1995). ' "Strong as a Turk": power, performance and representation in Turkish wrestling', in J. MacClancy (ed), *Sport, Identity and Ethnicity*. Oxford: Berg.

Stokvis, R. (1994). 'Supporters', *Fakta*, 2–4. 2–4.

Sugden, J. (1994). 'USA and the World Cup: American nativism and the rejection of the people's game', in J. Sugden and A. Tomlinson (eds) (1994). 219–52.

Sugden, J., and A. Bairner (1993). *Sport, Sectarianism and Society in a Divided Ireland*. Leicester: Leicester University Press.

Sugden, J., and A. Bairner (1994). 'Ireland and the World Cup: "Two teams in Ireland, there's only two teams in Ireland" ' in J. Sugden and A. Tomlinson (eds) (1994) 119–39.

Sugden, J., and S. Harvie (1995). *Sport and Community Relations in Northern Ireland*. Coleraine: Centre for the Study of Conflict, University of Ulster.

Sugden, J., and A. Tomlinson (eds) (1994). *Hosts and Champions: Soccer cultures, national identities and the USA World Cup*. Aldershot: Arena.

Sugimoto, A. (1997). *Sociology of Sport Fans* (in Japanese). Kyoto: Sekaishisohsha.

Sund, B. (1997). *Fotballens maktfält*. Uppsala: Svenska Fotball Forgalet AB.

Syariffudin, A. (1985). *Kamus istilah olah raga populer di Indonesia*. Jakarta: CV Baru.

Takahashi, Y. (1994). *Sociology of Soccer* (in Japanese). Tokyo: NHK Books.

Tanaka, H. (1991). *Alien Residents in Japan* (in Japanese). Tokyo: Iwanami Shinsho.

Tanil, B. (1995). *Milliyetciligin Kara Bahari* (The Black Spring of Nationalism). Istanbul: Birikim Publishing.

Taylor, C. (1994). 'The Politics of Recognition', in A. Gutmann (ed), *Multiculturalism*. Princeton: Princeton University Press.

Taylor, C. (1998). *The Beautiful Game: A Journey through Latin American Football*. London: Victor Gollancz.

Taylor, I. (1982). 'Class, Violence and Sport: the Case of Soccer Hooliganism in Britain', in H. Contelon and R. Gruneau (eds), *Sport, Culture and the Modern State*. Toronto: University of Toronto Press.

Teske, H. J. (1977). *FC-Gelsenkirchen Schalke 04. Zur Sozialgeschichte eines Fußballvereins in einer Industrieregion*. Essen, unpublished manuscript.

Thabe, G. A. L. (compiler) (1983). *It's a Goal!: 50 Years of Sweat, Tears and Drama in Black Soccer*. Johannesburg: Skotaville.

Thibert, J., and J.-P. Rethacker (1991). *La Fabuleuse Histoire du football*. Editions de la Martinière.

Thomas, R. (1996). *Sociologie du sport*. 2nd edn. Paris: PUF.

Thomas, R.; J.-L. Chesneau; and G. Duret (1991). *Le Football*. Paris: PUF.

Thrift, N., and D. Forbes (1983). 'A Landscape with Figures: political geography with human conflict', in *Political Geography Quarterly*, 2. 247–63.

Tischler, S. (1981). *Footballers and Businessmen. The Origins of Professional Soccer in England*. New York: Holmes & Meier.

Tomaselli, K., and R. Tomaselli (1987). 'The Political Economy of the South African Press', in K. Tomaselli et al. (1987).

Tomaselli, K.; R. Tomaselli; and J. Muller (1987). *Narrating the Crisis: Hegemony and the South African Press*. Johannesburg: Richard Lyon.

Touraine, A. (1992). *Critique de la modernité*. Paris: Fayard.

Tranter, N. (1995). 'The Cappielow Riot and the Composition and Behaviour of Soccer Crowds in Late Victorian Scotland', in *The International Journal of the History of Sport*. 12 (3). 125–40.

Tranter, N. (1998). *Sport, Economy and Society in Britain 1750–1914*. Cambridge: Cambridge University Press.

Tuastad, D. (1997). 'The political role of football for Palestinians in Jordan', in G. Armstrong and R. Giulianotti (eds) (1997).

Turner, A. (1998). '25 Millones de Argentinos: Fútbol y Discurso en el Mundial '78', in P. Alabarces et al. (eds) (1998).

Twine, F. W. (1996). 'Brown skinned white girls: Class, culture, and the construction of white identity in suburban communities', in *Gender, Place, and Culture*, 3 (2). 205–24.

Urbini, P. (1986). 'Traquenards', in *Bureau*. 99–100.

Van Langenberg, M. (1990). 'The New Order State: language, ideology, hegemony', in A. Budiman (ed), *State and Civil Society in Indonesia*. Clayton: Monash University.

Varela, M. (1998). 'Fútbol y espacio público en los comienzos de la televisión Argentina', in *Contratexto*, 12, op cit. supra.

Vella, P. (1985). *Malta: Blitzed but not Beaten*. Valletta: Progress Press.

Vinnai, G. (1974 [1971]). *El fútbol como ideología*. Buenos Aires: Siglo XXI.

Voeltz, E. A.; T. Camara; and M. Ganong (1997). 'Baga (syllabaire en langue baga)', in *Cahiers d'Étude des Langues Guinéenes*, (Conakry), 3.

Vrcan, S. (1990). *Sport i nasilje danas u nas*. Zagreb: Naprijed.

Wacquant, L. (1989). 'Towards a reflexive sociology: A workshop with Pierre Bourdieu', in *Sociological Theory*, 7. 26–63.

Wagg, S. (1984). *The Football World: a Contemporary Social History*. Brighton: Harvester Press.

Wagg, S. (1991). 'Playing the past: the media and the English football team', in J. Williams and S. Wagg, *British Football and Social Change*. Leicester: Leicester University Press.

Wagg, S. (1995). *Giving the Game Away – Football, Poltics and Culture on Five Continents*. Leicester: Leicester University Press.

Wahl, A. (1989). *Les Archives du football*. Paris, Gallimard.

Wahl, A. (1990a). *La Balle au pied. Histoire du football*. Paris: Gallimard.

Wahl, A. (1990b). 'Le mai 68 des footballeurs français', in *Vingtième siècle*, April–June. 73–82.

Walker, S. (1997). 'Defending the sabbath from soccer', in *The Christian Science Monitor*, 16 October. 1.

Wall, F. (1935). *Fifty Years of Football*. London: Football Association.

Walter, T. O.; B. Brown; and E. Grabb (1991). 'Ethnic identity and sports participation: A comparative analysis of West Indian and Italian soccer clubs in metropolitan Toronto', in *Canadian Ethnic Studies*, XXIII (1). 85–96.

Walvin, J. (1994). *The People's Game*. Edinburgh: Mainstream.

Watson, D. (1994). *Dancing in the Streets: Tales from World Cup City*. London: Victor Gollancz.

Werbner, P. (1996). ' "Our Blood is Green": Cricket, Identity and Social Empowerment among British Pakistanis', in J. MacClancy (ed), *Sport, Identity and Ethnicity*. 87–111. Oxford: Berg.

Williams, J.; E. Dunning; and P. Murphy (1989). *Hooligans Abroad*. 2nd edn. London: Routledge.

Williamson, D. (1991). *Belles on the Ball*. Exeter: R & D Associates.

Wilson, W. J. (1996). *When Work Disappears: The World of the New Urban Poor*. New York: Random House.

Yomiuri, The (1994). 'New era of inter-high school athletic championships, part 1' (in Japanese). July 29. 13. 'New era of inter-high school athletic championships, part 2' (in Japanese). July 30. 14.

Zureik, E. T. (1979). *The Palestinians in Israel: A Study in Internal Colonialism*. London: Routledge & Kegan Paul.

Index